J. Frank Torres
Crusader and Judge

J. FRANK TORRES
CRUSADER AND JUDGE

AN ORAL HISTORY
BY
LOIS GERBER FRANKE

FORWARD BY
MARC SIMMONS

SANTA FE

Book design and type composition by Vicki Ahl

© 2007 by Lois Gerber Franke. All rights reserved.

No part of this book may be reproduced in any form or by any electronic or mechanical means including information storage and retrieval systems without permission in writing from the publisher, except by a reviewer who may quote brief passages in a review.

Sunstone books may be purchased for educational, business, or sales promotional use. For information please write: Special Markets Department, Sunstone Press, P.O. Box 2321, Santa Fe, New Mexico 87504-2321.

Library of Congress Cataloging-in-Publication Data

Franke, Lois Gerber, 1921-
  J. Frank Torres : crusader and judge : an oral history / by Lois Gerber Franke ; Forward by Marc Simmons.
       p. cm.
   ISBN 978-0-86534-589-8 (hardcover : alk. paper) -- ISBN 978-0-86534-590-4 (softcover : alk. paper)
  1. Torres, J. Frank (Jose Frank), 1897- 2. Judges--United States--Biography. I. Title.

KF373.T67F73 2007
347.73'14--dc22
[B]
                                                                         2007018540

WWW.SUNSTONEPRESS.COM
SUNSTONE PRESS / POST OFFICE BOX 2321 / SANTA FE, NM 87504-2321 /USA
(505) 988-4418 / ORDERS ONLY (800) 243-5644 / FAX (505) 988-1025

This book is dedicated to Eva Torres de Aschenbrener the best daughter any father could have
and to my parents, Pauline and Henry

Also special recognition and appreciation is given to Marc Simmons for his generous encouragement and support and to Jose Esquibel for his invaluable assistance in correct Spanish usage and clarity

And my heartfelt thanks for their interest in this book to the many wonderful people of Trinidad who shared their perceptions of Judge Torres and confirmed the character and influence of this man.

Foreword

By Marc Simmons

"Ultimately, everything depends upon the quality of the individual." So wrote the psychologist Carl Jung. That unassailable truism, almost lost in today's world, finds reaffirmation in the gripping story of the life of Judge Jóse Francisco, "Frank," Torres. For here was a man of humble origins, born into a working class family, who faced Mount Everest size obstacles and by force of character and the exercise of unyielding moral values achieved his heart's desire.

In the Torres personal history, one encounters a superb example of what is noble and inspiring in the American tradition. The lessons this book imparts are no less valuable because they come from a corner of the nation--the Hispanic Southwest--that too often has been regarded as a cultural, economic, and political backwater.

Viewing the life long struggles of Frank Torres, we are reminded that courage and talent, combined with effort, truly can make a difference, proving Jung's dictum, that individual character is what counts. As his story unfolds, the reader increasingly gains respect and liking for the idealistic young man with an iron will who obtains his law degree against all odds, battles back from a near-fatal illness, and faces down the Ku Klux Klan, just for starters.

In 1973, after a successful career as an activist lawyer and then a municipal judge in Trinidad, Colorado, Frank Torres retired and with his wife Crusita moved to New Mexico's capital at Santa Fe. That same year, my biography, *The Little Lion of the Southwest, A Life of Manuel Antonio Chaves* was published by Chicago's Swallow Press. Soon after that, Judge Torres read the book, appreciated what he called "my fair treatment of the Hispanic experience in the Southwest," and wrote a letter inviting me to drop by his home on Santa Fe's East Lupita Road, so he could meet me.

I did and that first visit marked the beginning of our friendship, which lasted until his death. My chief regret now is that I did not know the full scope of Judge Torres's extraordinary career, as faithfully detailed in this book by his friend and neighbor Lois Franke. Our conversations chiefly revolved around history and philosophical ideas, and while the judge occasionally referred to some personal experience of his to make a point, the fascinating parameters of his life remained unknown to me. Not until years later, when I read Franke's biography in manuscript did I fully grasp the magnitude of Judge Torres's achievement.

Lois Franke, after gallantly laboring for more than a decade on this book, has produced a highly readable narrative. I consider it a significant contribution to the social and political history of the twentieth century Southwest.

It was Judge Torres's great wish that the chronicle of his life be published, not out of vanity, but rather because he thought that what he had suffered and accomplished in his pursuit of high ideals might prove instructive to others. It was that honest motive that led him to spend countless hours dictating his recollections to Lois Franke. I heartily approve of her book and hope he would, too.

Introduction

When first I met this unique man, the farthest thing from my mind was that I would write a book about him. Our driveway in Santa Fe runs down the side of the property and, in the early 1970s, this provided the avenue to my acquaintance with the neighbors who just had moved in next door.

Frank Torres introduced himself to me one sunny morning over the fence that separated our lots. The tall, silver haired gentleman projected a courtly manner and smiled at me with open, friendly, intelligent interest. A few minutes spent chatting and exchanging basic information established a tentative neighborliness. As the months passed, we visited frequently over the side fence, sometimes spending half a leisurely afternoon just talking, gradually becoming friends. We spoke about where we came from, what we thought. The judge was pleased to find that I was from Colorado, and searched his mind for common acquaintances we might have had.

His story, which carried the sweep of history, fascinated me. Retired from the bench for health reasons, he was forced by his family to, as he put it, "behave himself," although nothing of the problem that had imposed this family fiat was apparent in either his speech or movement. Since I taught high school, our contracts periodically required taking a few hours of college credit "professional growth" classes. A year or so after I became acquainted with this wonderful old judge, I enrolled in a Southwestern History class for the purpose of raising my education consciousness another notch. This one chanced to be taught by a new Ph.D. in Southwest Studies fresh out of an upper Midwest university.

During the first class session, the fledgling professor stood before us and, with self-assured authority, intoned: "We all know that Hispanics historically have been under motivated, under educated and under achievers." After some thirty years of living in Santa Fe, this fell on my ear as absolute graceless misinformation. The instructor then assigned a ten-page term paper to be done on anything in Southwest History that interested us.

The temptation to set him straight was overwhelming. In the next visit over the side fence, I asked the judge if he would object to my doing the paper on him. As I explained the preconceived notions of the professor, there was an amused twinkle in his unusual gold colored eyes when he replied he would be happy to help me.

Pulling together a broad sketch of what Judge Torres told me about himself, I handed in a twenty page overview of hardship, discrimination, ability, determination, education, hard work and significant achievement. I also gave the judge a copy. Driving in from an errand a week or so later, he came over to the fence to hail me as I parked the car. We exchanged generalities for a bit and then he gave me a conspiratorial, boyish grin and announced, "People have told me for years I should do a book of my memoirs, and I like the way you write. You and I are going to do the story of my life!"

My first astonished reaction was that it couldn't be done. I already had more to do than I could keep up with. But somehow he caught me with the idea. His story needed to be told.

In receiving Judge Torres' oral history, I gained not only what happened but how he assessed the persons and situations he talked of and what he felt about the society he lived in. The reminiscing and recollections proceeded as our free times coincided. Sometimes he came to my house, sometimes I went to his. The judge's wife and their son Lawrence, who lived with them, graciously accepted my being around as giving the judge a project he entered into enthusiastically.

An unshakable idealist from his first breath of life, the years had given Frank Torres a perspective from which he judged events and people with dispassionate honesty. That he and his forebears lived with blighting injustice and discrimination is evident in the chronicle of their lives. From this negative experience, he revealed no personal rancor, but rather demonstrated a life spent in total commitment to the concepts of equality and justice, come what may.

Torres had lived his life in a hurry, occupied at all times with concurrent, immediate objectives and long term goals involving a wide variety of causes. Focused on the rightness of what he was doing and indifferent to his image in the middle of it, he had saved little personal correspondence, news stories about himself, or the texts of his speeches. However, even a cursory examination of the man and his life shows him to have lived and worked with unswerving commitment to causes and courses which helped shape the American Southwest where he lived.

1
Beginnings

Nothing unusual marked José Francisco Torres' birth in a pioneer home up the Purgatoire River above Trinidad, Colorado, where he spent his childhood and growing years in an orderly and ordinary family and community, long on Spanish tradition and conventional in situation. He developed from the same ingredients as others around him, was fed, taught, worked and lived no differently. As he matured, he held firmly to this heritage while living in non-conformity to its norm and frequently cross-purposed with the life around him. No single label pinned on José Francisco Torres during ninety years of living totally defined this complex man. Yet the key to it all was basically simple. First, he believed he and all Americans were equal under the law, and second, he acted on that belief against the prevailing attitudes of his time and society.

The genesis of José Francisco, who would become Judge J. Frank Torres, began some three hundred years earlier when courageous and determined Spaniards, arriving with Don Juan de Oñate's colonists, planted the Torres family tree in the dangerous Rio Arriba northern frontier of New Spain. Many died young, but always a few held on to go forward. From the late 1700s, legal documents form a continuous public record of the Torres people as farmers, religious, soldiers, and public officials in the mountainous north country of present day New Mexico.

The modern Torres family's lineage comes into focus with Judge Torres' great grandfather, José Antonio Torres, born in the Taos-Mora area in March, 1795, the son of Manuel Torres and his wife, María Neves Valdés. He was raised by relatives after his parents were killed in an Indian raid when he was a small child. Once grown, José Antonio became a farmer in the Taos area and married María de la Luz Maestas on June 13, 1817, in the Picuris church. Hard work and child bearing wore out the lives of frontier women before their time, prompting men to take second, third, and even fourth wives to care for home and family, necessity overruling sentiment in the struggle to survive and succeed. María died in 1852 at the age of 32.

With children and a household needing care, José Antonio arranged a second marriage with sixteen year old María Gracía Lobato of Taos late in 1835 or early 1836. Typical of the times, he sired a large family. He and María Gracía's first son, Antonio Domingo Torres, grandfather to J. Frank Torres, was born November 12, 1836, in Picuris. Illiterate himself, but recognizing the importance of education, José Antonio sent Antonio Domingo to a Catholic priest's school in Santa Fe and his other sons followed as they became old enough. After María Gracía died sometime around 1870, José Antonio married once more.

During this time, change already roiled the Spanish frontier as adventurers and opportunists from the East slipped through its borders. Manifest Destiny moved west across the continent, producing clashes as national ambitions prevailed over legitimate but weak opposition from the established residents. Mountain men trapped beaver in Spanish Territory in the early 1800s, followed shortly by Anglo traders coming up the Santa Fe Trail. Texas stirred Spanish animosity with a futile claim to Spanish lands east of the Rio Grande, and Mexico successfully rebelled against Spain, briefly bringing New Mexico Territory under Mexican control.

Anglo encroachment increasingly challenged Mexican sovereignty, and American General Stephen Watts Kearney marched his troops into Santa Fe in 1846 to claim the territory for the United States. The 1848 Treaty of Guadalupe Hidalgo with Mexico, followed by the Gadsden Purchase of the disputed land, established United States sovereignty. Unfortunately, the new rulers failed to understand or respect the language and culture of the Spanish residents, beginning a period of bigotry and discrimination marked by land grabs and open, widespread injustice. Finding the government in Santa Fe unresponsive to their problems, many Spanish settlers looked to opportunities elsewhere.

Ongoing disruption to their way of life prompted the Torres families to join the movers. The Homestead Act was bringing a flood of immigrants to the west and broke up the open range into a checkerboard of barbed-wire fenced, small farms amid large scale ranches. Colorado became a state in 1876, and gained the railroad in 1878, which two factors indicated greater progress and opportunity than in New Mexico. By then, Antonio Domingo, José Antonio's first-born son, already had married María Emanuelita (Manuelita) Casias who bore him six sons, José Cayetano in 1858, Romulo in 1861, Serafin in 1864, Maximiliano in 1868, José de Jesús in 1869 and Juan Bautista in 1872, with finally a daughter named María Gracia for her grandmother. Antonio Domingo had served in the Union Army at the Battle of Glorieta and been elected from the Taos District to the Territorial Legislature in Santa Fe. There he found legislative remedy thwarted by military and government indifference to the on-going violation of Spanish rights.

Accordingly, in 1882, when the abandoned Vigil and St. Vrain grants opened to homesteading in the Trinidad, Colorado area, José Antonio Torres, together with his sons and their families, sold out and moved northeast across the mountains into Colorado, settling above Trinidad in the pristine mountain valley of the Purgatoire River, joining a small colony of fellow New Mexico Spanish homesteaders already there.

As they proved up on homesteads on the Purgatoire River at "La Junta," west of Trinidad, by living on the land for five years, the families quietly reestablished a traditional pastoral life, built adobe homes, farmed and lived close to the land and each other. Disappointingly, problems showed up there, too, but the homesteaders felt secure in the land they owned. The big cattle era had brought in Eastern and British investment and management of large ranches. Texas cowboys, who harbored a poisonous hatred for the Spanish, came north to ride the range for them. Despite the prejudice, Antonio Domingo's fifth son, José Jesús, known as "Sus," hired on in his late teens as a rider at one of the sprawling ranches where he did his work, kept out of trouble and saved his wages toward getting married.

In an arranged match between fathers Antonio Domingo Torres and Ignacio Bustos, another homesteader in the valley, cowboy José Jesús Torres, age twenty-five, and Eva Marie Bustos, age sixteen, married at Holy Trinity Catholic Church in Trinidad on December 24, 1894. A little over two years later, on March 31, 1897, the couple's first child made his way into the world as a spring "green grass baby," which, as with animals, gave the best start in life for the baby, supplying a summer of fresh air, light and warmth for growth and strength before winter brought lessened sun, confinement, and disease. Tall, lean, grey eyed Grandfather Antonio Domingo came over to approve the long baby, with his cap of thick black hair, and the "Torres light eyes" displayed in a pale, charcoal hued gaze which later would turn to gold. With parents and padrinos on hand, a priest baptized the infant José Francisco Torres in honor of his great grandfather, Southern Colorado pioneer, José Francisco Bustos. Fate had decreed the background, place and circumstances, but from these givens nothing signaled the arrival of a rebel, although the child of the early years remained integral in the adult he became.

The boy's growing up was quite ordinary for the time. The family farm home on the South Fork of the Purgatoire was located five miles west of Weston village where Sus earlier had earned extra cash by working as town constable. He later quit in response to Eva's vocal worry about the risks involved in the job, as Weston's wide open gambling produced a heyday of rowdiness. Where a man's money rested on the draw of a card and his senses were clouded with whiskey, danger always hung in the air. Short and muscular Sus carried a gun but usually relied on his fists to deal with troublemakers. Leaving that job he signed on at a better wage to break horses just over the state line in New Mexico at the sprawling Bartlett Ranch, now Vermejo Park.

Growing rapidly, young José Francisco early showed himself to be bright, curious, independent, and persistent in his need to know. At home, simple farm chores shaped in him life- long attitudes and values that were formed through equal doses of freedom and responsibility. Early on he learned to think for himself, and early on he also learned to contribute his share of the work expected from all able-bodied family members.

As a child, the young Torres had no conscious recognition of the prejudice that tainted valley life. Gradually, however, he came to see that in Trinidad stores and at public occasions, the people of the valley received less courtesy and respect than those who were not Spanish. But, too young to comprehend the scope of the problem, he had no inkling that his richly satisfying life and culture would, in time, bring him scorn and rejection. The judge remembered his early years as filled with interest, security, and joy of living.

A life-long love of nature developed as he lived intimately with it. He saw beauty and order as he watched dawn creep up the valley, breaking through blue-black cloud bands over Fisher's Peak to the east, illuminating mesas and the mountains to the west in radiant red and purple glow, as the day began. Young José Francisco milked goats, turned out the chickens and helped his father round up the horses at daybreak, listening in the dawning light for the bell of the lead horse. With his little red wagon, he trundled wood or coal from outside in to the kitchen stove, and through simple chores, learned that duty could not be shirked without someone else being left with the work.

The ever-changing world claimed the young boy's senses. He heard birdsong, the sigh of wind through evergreens, the yap of coyotes, lowing of cows, bleat of sheep, rain splattering on the roof, drew in lungsfull of fresh, new day air, felt the heat of August sun on his back, the tingle of a snowflake on his out-thrust tongue. He pondered the mystery of the mass, was comforted by his mother's work worn hand on his fevered head. He caught the perfume of renewal as rain fell on dry earth, the aromatic edge of simmering chiles, the pungency of sweaty horse and leather, the cool muskiness of newly turned soil behind the plow, and the fresh essence of coming snow in the air.

Spring brought new calves standing on awkward legs, greening pastures, and dainty white flowers in the grass. On a June day farmers guided plodding teams back and forth across the fields, sending silent prayers to San Isidro for abundant crops. Near the house laundry dried, hung on lines strung between trees or spread across fragrant bushes.

Summer meant tending of growing crops under high blue skies and dazzling sunlight. Young José Francisco, who was old enough to handle a team, brought them to the barn as summer storms gathered in rumbling black clouds on the peaks, to cross the valley in a powerful sweep of lightning, wind, rain and, sometimes, hail. The retreating storm sent slanting sun rays breaking through the dark edge of cloud, leaving a chill breeze drenched with the scent of evergreens and sagebrush. He puzzled over what made weather. If God created everything, as he had been told by his mother, how did He do it, and why was it always changing?

In the twilight of summer evening doves cooed plaintive repetitive notes into the gentle air, now redolent of growing plants, and alive with the buzz of insects. The day's work done, families sat on doorsteps, men companionably smoking a twist of punche, the tobacco-like weed the settlers cultivated, talked the weather, the herds, and the important minutiae of daily happenings, while the children played and wives finished up in the house. As darkness settled in, all went inside, the lights went out one by one, and in the black of night, searching coyotes, bears and cougars roamed while owls flew overhead. But snuggled in their beds under homemade quilts and blankets, the householders slept secure.

In autumn came harvest, branding cattle and selling off the excess animals, shocking and bringing in corn, stacking hay, picking apples, stripping the garden of its' bounty for canning, pickling and drying, and storing all against the coming winter. By late fall, the vee of migrating cranes cut the sky in perfect symmetry, their high and lonely cries coming faintly back to earth, and an almost tangible yellow moon later hung in the night sky.

Last in the eternal circle of the year, the deepening snows of winter arrived. Storms came down the mountains, draping trees in white, blanketing the fields. Young José Francisco watched wind-blasted ground blizzards send straying, sweeping streams of icy snow along the valley floor, suddenly engulfing all in a fog of swirling, directionless white, piling drifts around buildings and blocking trails. Livestock huddled in the lea of barns, eating hay forked down from a nearby stack. A diminished sun came up late and set early as freezing nights lowered the woodpile. It was a time to be indoors. The women cooked, cared for children's ills, carded wool, patched garments. The men, after tending the animals, sharpened tools, mended and oiled harness, repaired equipment and planned for the next year. The children helped their parents, listened to the adult conversations and played games. One season moved to the other in a seamless whole which went always forward.

This rich and satisfying life, lodged in the mind and spirit of José Francisco, grew into an ineradicable love of his native land and all of nature. His days, disciplined but unregimented, allowed his mind to roam free as he explored the boundaries of his world. Sustained by loving family, a devout and secure home, and a code of honor and discipline, young José Francisco learned to be attentive, to benefit from his mistakes, not to complain, not to bear grudges, and always to do his best as a matter of self respect.

Sus and Eva's family expanded with Manuel, Juanita and Pete in turn, providing José Francisco with playmates and helpers. His duties included bending over a hoe or pulling weeds in the family garden on seemingly endless hot afternoons. This cultivated plot furnished fresh vegetables for the summer table and preserved foods for winter meals. Later, as his brothers and sister each grew old enough to inherit garden duty, José Francisco worked with his father. Producing family necessities brought an element of satisfaction into what, otherwise, was only dull, hard labor.

Torres fondly remembered the foods of his childhood: whole grain cereals, venison, goat, beef and mutton, home made cheese, tortillas, chile con carne, tamales, frijoles, adobo pork, crusty bread and savory stews, empanaditas, chicos, tasajos, pinon nuts, and panocha. Later in his life, he was amused to note that these simple dishes of his growing up years had evolved into gourmet restaurant fare.

José Francisco escaped most childhood diseases except for catching smallpox during a local epidemic and becoming acutely ill. Colorful pioneer doctor, Michael Beshoar, who had set up practice in Trinidad in 1867, patched up cowboys and gunslingers alike after shoot-outs, and attended victims of coal mine accidents, also saw to the medical needs of area families; whoever, wherever and whenever. During this smallpox siege, Beshoar rattled up to the Torres home in his horse drawn buggy to examine the critically ill child, leaving instructions and medication for his care before going on up canyon to see other cases. Within two days, the pox broke out and the fever came down, leaving the child free of disfiguring scars. And so, in memory, José Francisco's early childhood passed in unfettered joy, with freedom from pressure to make him into anything other than true to himself.

Although life progressed with a dependable serenity, little disharmonies livened up valley life at times. Young José Francisco's first inkling of law as a part of society came from the obvious amusement of family around him over the outcome of a grudge quarrel between José Francisco's Uncle Francisco Griego, husband to Aunt Marilia, sister to Tío Juan Torres, and Bernardino Zamora the landholder next to them. It erupted on a summer day when the two men crossed paths and exchanged a round of slurs. Later in the afternoon Bernardino stalked out to settle the score with Francisco who worked his cornfield nearby. Francisco obliged and punches flew.

Aunt Marilia saw the fight from her kitchen window and, grabbing a club from the woodpile, dashed out to aid Uncle Griego who was then flat on the ground being choked by Bernardino. Swinging her weapon with splendid accuracy, she knocked Zamora out cold.

When Bernardino came to, he headed straight for the Justice of the Peace to file assault charges. At the hearing, both plaintiff and defendant, in self justifying accounts, substantially agreed on the facts, with Aunt Marilia admitting knocking Zamora senseless in defense of her husband, and Zamora testifying that he had suffered an attack from behind by Francisco's wife. The Justice of the Peace found the lady guilty and fined her one dollar. Aunt Marilia, slapping down the money, announced she would render Bernardino senseless all over again for that price. Bernardino prudently made for safety out the back door. The community enjoyed a good laugh, and the combatants rather sheepishly dropped the feud. Such events served as counterpoint to serious conflicts involving property, principle or overheated tempers, which frequently were settled with guns instead of fists. Seventy-five years later, the Judge still laughed over the incident.

2
LEARNING AND GROWING

Antonio Domingo Torres, José Francisco's grandfather, and a dominant formative influence in his grandson's young life, exerted strong leadership in the Purgatiore valley. Described as a tall, lean man, Antonio Domingo habitually wore black except for a wide brimmed white hat, and he perpetually smoked a pipe. He had been educated but none of his sons had the inclination or good fortune to receive the same. He ranked as a superlative horseman, unerring judge of men, and a resolute fighter against wrong. From family recollection and a scant few documents, Antonio Domingo emerges as independent and self-reliant, impatient with boundaries, able to move on without regret for what he left behind. These same traits showed up in his grandson.

Compulsory religious observance, enforced by Antonio Domingo, was an integral part of José Francisco's childhood and he was the one who assumed responsibility for his grandson's religious education. As with the men in the family before him, Antonio Domingo reportedly was a *penitente hermano*, "brother of light," entrusted with maintaining the faith of the church where there were no priests. He saw to it that his grandson was baptized and confirmed at the small San Isidro Church in the valley which the Torres families had helped build and where they worshiped. To add reward to his religious discipline, the family patriarch planned surprises, including waking the family for midnight rosaries, followed by early morning feasts of roast spare ribs or leg of lamb, an appealing tactic among growing boys. Although unexamined, this practice of faith became a necessary element of José Francisco's life. Dry spells and questionings would come, but in later years, this deeply implanted faith and its tenets anchored his life.

Christmas in the upper Purgatoire valley, as fondly recollected by the Judge, created an interlude of relaxation and festivity amid the hard work and sameness of life. All in the community came to the midnight *"Misa del Gallo,"* service at San Ysidro church. Afterward, once the families were back home, the children raced out again to take part in *"Mis Crismas,"* which, the Judge explained, resembled modern "trick or treating," as they collected goodies from homes around the neighborhood. At each house they shouted an old chant, *"Oremos, oremos, angelitos semos del cielo venemos a pedir, oremos y si no dan puertan y ventanas quebraremos,"* translated as "we are angels come from heaven to your doors and windows." However, José Francisco's interest centered on the sweets more than the lofty symbolism of the excursion. At Christmas, wind, cold and snow came but homes were snug, stomachs full, dreams happy and hearts warm. It was a special glowing time as peace and goodwill claimed the valley

In his growing up years, José Francisco, the future model of rectitude, displayed a healthy sense of mischief, his inventive pranks sometimes landing the golden-eyed boy in hot water. Quiet grandfather Bustos had his evening rosary interrupted by a firecracker tossed under his chair. Next, the culprit turned to Ramoncita Velásquez, a foundling Indian child taken in and raised by Antonio Domingo. José Francisco noted that, when she came in from the cold, teenaged Ramoncita habitually warmed herself at the fireplace, backing up and lifting her skirts to let the open flames toast her chilled rear. Once, as she made her usual beeline to the fireplace, José Francisco, standing by, tossed a pinch of pilfered gunpowder onto the burning logs. the flash, flame, and yowls of Ramoncita followed as he made his escape dash outside. This earned him a switching from Eva, Sus finding the prank too funny to censor.

Seldom caught and totally unrepentant, José Francisco included even the formidable Antonio Domingo in his mischief. His grandfather's spacious house, where gala community dances were held, was built around an interior open patio where Antonio Domingo's old-timer friends and relations, a crowd of ancients to the boy, regularly hung out. After supper, a smoke and prayers, they would roll up in their blankets and sleep outside on warm summer nights. Enlisting a couple of cousins, José Francisco silently constructed a rough plank bridge, connecting the house's dirt roof with the nearby hillside behind it. Across this the youngsters tugged the haltered family burros, pinching their noses to keep them quiet, leaving them stranded as the boys faded back into the darkness to observe. The animals milled around uneasily, then, looking down from the roof top toward the slumberers below, one gave a lusty bray, shattering the night silence, and startling the old timers awake. What had happened? they wondered, still half asleep. Gazing upward, their shocked eyes beheld in the dim starlight a gallery of unearthly faces looking down at them. Terrified that it was a supernatural visitation, they scrambled to their knees, making the sign of the cross and muttering hasty prayers of penance and petition. The pranksters took to their heels, but the next day Antonio Domingo fixed his grandson with an icy grey gaze and predicted ominous consequences should such be repeated.

Not many miles downstream from the little Purgatoire River farming community, the sleepy village of Trinidad stirred with new growth. The first commercial coal mine opened in the hills to the southwest of town in 1867, but other than furnishing fuel for home heating, made little impact. Before long, however, this was followed by big mining and coke production interests moving in from the East and buying up lands. By 1884, coal mining operations began to expand and management exercised its political clout in a deal where the politically powerful Maxwell Land Grant persuaded a friendly Congress to expand its holdings from the original ninety-six thousand to some two million acres. This allowed Maxwell to claim a vast chunk of land north over the Colorado state line, including all homesteader's properties south of the Purgatoire River. Repeatedly hearing of this conflict gave young José Francisco a first real understanding of the injustice his people of the valley endured.

A showdown brewed when the settlers refused to comply with a court decree to give up lands for which they held legal, recorded Homestead Act deeds, and the coal industry, located on Maxwell lands, elected to oust them by force. The resulting shoot-out in 1888 between the settlers and the mining company's hired fighters came after the Purgatoire farmers received a sheriff's order giving them only twenty-four hours to vacate their holdings. Unable to reach the Denver court two hundred miles away in the single day allowed for a formal protest hearing, the settlers brought out their guns to confront the tough, newly deputized gun slingers who were sent against them. The local sheriff, unwilling to face the settlers himself, had offered these bogus deputies easy money and the prospect of a good fight to go up river and enforce the order.

The drama played out against the backdrop of the great pinkish-tan rock dike named Stonewall which cuts across the upper Purgatoire River valley. Here the settlers shot it out with the deputies who had barricaded themselves in a small hotel there. At the first volley, the deputies deliberately picked off the leaders of the settlers, hitting ex-Union soldier and rancher Richard Russell, who died a lingering death five days later, and dropping the horse from under Otto Mains, a dismissed Methodist clergyman turned firebrand and settler's advocate against the Maxwell Grant. Antonio Domingo Torres took a shot in the hip. At the end of a three day, indecisive exchange of gunfire with several settlers killed, the farmers torched the hotel, which, instead of forcing the deputies out in the open as they had hoped, a changed wind direction allowed them to escape by a back door under the cover of smoke and night. In an aftermath legal appeal, the courts ruled against the settlers, instituting change that effectively destroyed the Spanish pastoral way of life in the valley and altered the Torres families' futures. Antonio Domingo's wound healed, but the scar on his spirit remained.

Colorado increasingly attracted industrial investment and development, mostly run by Anglo opportunists maneuvering for land, opening dubious smelting or mining operations, and offering financial schemes designed to line their own pockets. Large corporations absorbed smaller business operations. The John D. Rockefeller family made heavy investment in southern Colorado coal and smelting and by the turn of the century the Guggenheims had opened interests there, operating until they sold out after World War I. Most of these profitable ventures came at the cost of Spanish labor and lands.

On the Torres family farm west of Weston, cowboy Sus and housewife Eva gave little thought to their oldest son's future, assuming he would make a life in the valley. Sus taught José Francisco the essentials, putting him on a horse when he was five, and instructing him in handling guns by age ten. Eva instilled manners and proper decorum. Each year

Trinidad in about 1900.

brought new responsibility for the boy that was not then seen as child exploitation or abuse, but the necessary process of gaining needed life skills. No one worried about self-esteem. It was earned and brought accompanying self-reliance.

José Francisco early displayed the instincts of a loner, roaming the countryside with his dog. He craved time on his own to observe, think and dream. Although mostly sheltered from the prejudice and bigotry that insidiously scarred the lives of his people, he already possessed a strong sense of right and wrong, as his mother discovered one warm summer day when he was twelve years old.

From Santa Fe Trail days onward, the Purgatoire had been used as a hideout by outlaws who still frequented the area. On this particular day, as José Francisco and his black and white dog wandered across a field near the road that wound along the edge of the valley, he spotted two men, heavy pistols hung on their hips, riding westward toward him.

He somehow knew these were men to stay away from. Trotting along on their high stepping horses, with gleaming silver fitted saddles and bridles sparking reflections in the sun, the gunmen seemed in no particular hurry. Young Torres shrank back into the bushes along the fence while his dog remained out in the open, barking but making no move toward the horses. Even as the boy softly called to his pet, the near rider spotted it, tossed a laughing remark to the other rider and drawing his revolver, neatly shot the dog and rode on up canyon without a backward look.

José Francisco looked after them in sick disbelief, followed by burning anger, then ran for home to spill out his story to Eva who attempted to console him, saying that bad men did bad things for no reason, and it was wrong. She then sent him back out to bury his pet. As he steeled himself to do the task, he considered what he could do. The outlaw's horses had carried no saddlebags so they were not leaving, but would circle back later. Slipping into the house, José Francisco eased one of his father's loaded rifles out of the gun rack, and went back to position himself in the bushes, concentrating on the up river road. Perhaps an hour later, when the outlaws reappeared around the curve of the hill, he steadied the rifle.

A mother's sixth sense must have alerted Eva, for she dashed out. José Francisco, sighting in the 30-30, missed her approach until Eva grasped his arm, pulling him toward safety. They scarcely gained the back door before the men cantered by, unaware that, with every intention of putting period to one man's existence, a child had gotten them in his gun sights, ready to pull the trigger.

As Eva lectured on his foolhardiness, José Francisco protested that the men had no reason to kill his dog, and he had a right to pay them back. Eva explained that those men were dangerous killers, and ordinary people had to wait for the law to bring such to justice. Amid a frustrated urge for revenge, José Francisco took in her message. When he grew up, he resolved that he would, somehow, learn about this thing called the law and use it to make bad men pay for their actions. In the years to come, he never quite forgot this vow.

José Francisco's unhappy brush with the gunmen reflected the facts of the day. Settlement often came ahead of organized law, attracting outlaws, adventurers, and fugitives who saw the wide open territory as a place they could live without fear of answering for their crimes. Although there were justices of the peace and local people formed posses, without formal law enforcement the alternative of a rope and cottonwood tree provided only stopgap relief. As official justice came in undesirables diminished, many already dead from shoot-outs among themselves, others drifted out to try their luck elsewhere, and a few even went straight, to become respected members of their communities.

Black Jack Ketcham, who headed a gang of outlaws hanging out in the Purgatoire country, made an enduring contribution to local folklore there before his luck ran out and he met his end when, wounded in a train robbery shootout in New Mexico, he was captured and hanged. Still, legend has it that somewhere up the Purgatoire earlier, Black Jack, fleeing from a posse, had stashed a fortune in gold he had just taken in a stagecoach robbery. Torres reported that though many had searched for it in vain, belief in the hidden loot still remained, a nostalgic relic of rowdy frontier days.

3
Coal Mining

By 1900, coal mining dominated the Purgatoire valley and was the chief employer in the area. This development impacted the whole valley where the Torres families lived. Displaced by the Maxwell claim, its aftermath forced settlers to find new ways to earn a living. The American Smelting and Refining Company, ASARCO, which had taken their lands, provided a ready answer; come and work in its mines. Of necessity, most accepted. Only the old timers refused to work for those who had robbed them of their lands and self-sufficiency, although their sons found it expedient to give up self-direction for regular money and benefits. Quietly but surely, the independent farmers of the valley became employees who worked for someone else. Daily needs were met but lost was the proud and resourceful Spanish quality of hand, heart, and head working together, where love of the land and independence disappeared as head and hand toiled under the ruthless profit system of the coal industry that placed no value on the human heart. This change was inevitable since industrial employers required followers not leaders, and conformity rather than individuality. Under the management of ASARCO, money ruled all else on the land it gained after Stonewall. The valley men swallowed a bitter pill of lost freedom as they labored in digging out coal, furnishing timbers to the sawmill for use in mine tunnels, or sweating over hot and fumy ovens, loading in the raw coal and extracting finished coke. The large Morley Mine, just below Raton Pass in Colorado, was opened in 1906, although smaller coal operations had been in place there as early as 1885. Attracted by the vast amounts of high grade coking coal in the Purgatoire basin, the Guggenheim family organized a paper Carbon Coal and Coke Company to avoid anti-trust laws, buying up land north of the Purgatoire along upper Reilly Creek which extended coal operations to swallow the whole valley.

The period from the late 1880s to early 1900s ushered in company controlled mining towns wherever large-scale mineral extraction occurred. In them, worker's families usually lived a squalid existence on wages paid in company scrip. These dismal camps generally lacked sanitary conditions, safety, and community pride. At Reilly Creek in the Purgatoire valley, however, conditions were different. The Carbon and Coke Company spent over a million dollars reworking the pastoral valley into a modern village, building a widely hailed, model company town. Utilitarian but up-to-date homes rented for two dollars a month per room with water, electricity and outhouse thrown in. By 1907, a schoolhouse, saloon, bath house and washery, hotel, offices, Catholic Church and a general store were added. Extensive coke ovens down the road toward Trinidad neared completion, offering still more jobs, and the new community changed its name from Reilly Canyon to the blunt "Cokedale" of product identification.

In 1910, Cokedale's population topped fifteen hundred people, a doctor was available, and the town was connected to Trinidad by telephone, a trolley car clanked up and down the rails between Cokedale and Trinidad, and also to the transcontinental railroad. Henry Ford's first practical automobile also hastened opening of the valley from rural isolation to contact with the world.

Sus and Eva still lived on the family farm near Weston when young José Francisco Torres finally realized the first step in his dream of a formal education. There were few schools to serve the rural Spanish children but that had not discouraged his determination to learn to read and write. Already, he knew his dichos, the Spanish proverbs, and Grandfather Antonio Domingo had taught him to read and write in Spanish since Eva and Sus, while well educated in the wisdom of rural life, were functionally illiterate and unable to give him instruction. Belatedly yielding to their son's desire to learn, his parents consented for José Francisco to begin public school in the fall of 1908. He was eleven years old as he entered first grade, riding his horse or walking the five miles from home to the one room school in Weston. As the oldest in class, he saw the rest as mere babies, but no embarrassment inhibited his need to know. Schoolmaster Eligh E. Duling quickly recognized his new student as intellectually curious and exceedingly bright.

A first priority for José Francisco was to master English, to understand, read, write and speak it, which he perceived as essential to holding his own in the changing world of the Spanish. Although he knew a smattering of words enabling him usually to make out the gist of what was said, it was not enough and seemed to leave him behind a wall of non-communication. Taking hoarded money from gifts, he bought a Spanish-English dictionary that he studied intently. Page by page, he familiarized himself with spelling and nuances of meaning until, one day, he caught himself thinking in English without the mental step of first translating into Spanish. This allowed him to understand fully the speech of the Anglos and be able to talk to them. But it failed to produce any significant change in his life and he continued to be generally ignored or pushed to the side in the Anglo dominated Trinidad where he was labeled a "Mex Kid." Not that he wished to become less Spanish, he simply wanted to be a part of what went on around him while remaining uniquely and proudly who he was.

Of the school subjects, he liked history best. Reading the Declaration of Independence, the Constitution and the Bill of Rights opened a clear and compelling vision of what society should be, and life around him clearly was not. The more he studied, the more reading became his passion. It was the key to all the other things "out there" which tantalized his mind.

In the make-shift school library, José Francisco came across the magazine *The Grit* and immersed himself in its moral stories of good people winning over all obstacles and injustice. The publication invited readers to earn money as salesmen for the magazine, and he took up the offer, hopefully trudging through the Weston community selling it house to house. From the five cents a copy it sold for, he could keep a penny. He held onto his tiny income for future use, fired by a desire to emulate *The Grit*'s high minded characters who accomplished great deeds against all odds while holding to highest standards of moral behavior. He found these same real life heroes in his Grandfather Antonio Domingo, and his Grandfather's friends, Army Major Rafael Chacón, and Colorado State Senator Casimiro Barela, men who lived by principle. Not for José

Francisco were the flamboyant, swaggering cowboys, even though his father was one of them. Neither did he find anything heroic among the sooty and sweaty miners, although his father became one of them. Consciously, a life far different from the one into which he was born, became a fixed objective. What it would be, he did not know, but it would come. If the doing took "grit," so be it.

José Francisco finished eighth grade in 1912, just three years after entering school. At that time, the world was, in a sense, both widening and coming together. The first transcontinental airplane flight had been made and New Mexico, the land of his forebears, was admitted to the Union. Although still centered in home and family, the youth's imagination freely speculated on what life might be beyond the valley.

He watched as immigrants, Italians, Germans, Poles, and Slavs arrived to work the Purgatoire mines, bringing their own traditions, and customs. Newly opened to the outside world, China provided a flood of immigrants, and a work gang of Chinese once appeared briefly in the valley. José Francisco's first glimpse of the Far Easterners came at San Acacio cemetery on a Good Friday where the faithful gathered to pay respects to those buried there, and to clean the grounds. By happenstance, on that same day the Orientals picked and shoveled a water diversion ditch past the cemetery. In the grip of mutual curiosity, both sides openly gawked at each other in the clear April sunlight. All the Spanish could see peeping over the trenches were the coolie hatted, exotically different faces, with hair held back in queues. Their own actions and appearance doubtless seemed equally curious to the Chinese, but a cultural gap yawned too wide for either side to communicate across it. When a hard faced construction foreman roughly ordered the diggers to keep working, they jumped to obey. José Francisco instinctively resented the man's lack of respect, his demeaning manner toward his workers. Afterward, he would have liked to ask the Chinese workers questions about their lives, but the next time he came by, they were gone. That incident added to his growing recognition that certain groups were treated less well than others for no other reason except racial differentness. Although continually made aware of prejudice, young Torres remained an idealist, bent on transforming his experience with discrimination into working for a just and equal society. He had no clear notion of how he would do this, but the idea was there along with the promise of life, liberty and the pursuit of happiness.

José Francisco moved beyond impish boy pranks, through gangling adolescence of too large hands and feet, and emerged a tall and lanky teenager, with thick black hair and arresting golden eyes. Although Sus had taught him all he needed to know for a life in the valley, and the boy faithfully did his daily work, it offered no challenges. Sus Torres, a simple, respected, kindly, and gentle man, very likely never really understood his scholarly and idealistic son.

José Francisco in grade school.

In his teens, José Francisco began to reveal a deeply serious side. He recognized that change from outside the valley was being forced on the people he knew, and against which its residents had few defenses. The bigotry and discrimination they faced became clearer in his mind as he listened to Antonio Domingo's tales of earlier days, as he saw family and friends snubbed or served last in the shops in Trinidad, and personally felt it in the attitude of ASARCO supervisors where his father now worked. This disrespect for the people he held dearest rubbed abrasively against his idealism, and he rejected the assumption of Spanish inferiority for all-time as neither truth nor unchangeable in the workplace. A passionate belief took hold that if his people were to gain their rights and respect, someone had to challenge those negative forces and demand justice. He recognized the Anglo world's attitude toward "Mexicans," but he also had studied the principles upon which his country was founded and formed a passionate belief that the former needed to come closer to the latter.

It was well to be guided by ideals, yet how to implement them remained vague. His youthful hero models from "The Grit" magazine fought against wrong, stood for right and triumphed in the end. While he moved on in his reading choices, the idea remained fixed in his mind. A determined and resourceful person could make a difference. With so much wrong in the world, education was the key, but high school was not an option. There was no money for it and Sus, who had been thrown and badly injured by a spooked horse, needed José Francisco as the oldest, to take charge of the on-going work of the farm. Months later, when Sus' broken bones healed, one arm was permanently crippled, and his cowboy days ended. Of necessity to support his family, he looked for a job in the coal mining operations, the enemy his father had battled against at Stonewall, was the only ready employment available. Antonio Domingo raised no objection, recognizing that Sus' other options had been eliminated.

José Jesús Torres hired out to cut and deliver "props," the reinforcing timbers used to shore up mine tunnels to prevent cave-ins which could interfere with the operation's profitable outflow of coal. Sus needed the help of his son in doing this heavy work, and in the process, José Francisco discovered that no law forced mine ownership into compliance with the verbal contracts it offered. Unconscionable as it was, however, Sus had no alternative way of making a living.

Judge Torres described the process: "My father, Jesús or 'Sus,' cut props for coal mines for a couple of years and I helped my dad getting these props ready and delivered from the nearby mountains. We would cut down the right sized tree with a long saw, then hack off the branches. I would take our team of horses, tie a chain to the tree, and hitch the horses onto the chain. Then I would lead the team down the slope of the hill, pulling the tree to the wagon waiting at the road side below. This would mean several trips up and down the hillside until we had a wagon load. With my father lifting the heavy end and me the lighter, we then piled them in the wagon and drove the team down to the company railroad yard to be inspected by the superintendent. That fellow usually had a background as a gunman from the battles of the Maxwell Land Grant or had hired out in fights against the miners of the CF&I coal camps in Colfax County, New Mexico or southern Colorado."

Torres recalled always having to wait after cutting the load and driving down to the company sawmill where, dead tired, aching and impatient to be finished for the day, they then endured the prop inspection process. When the superintendent sauntered out at his leisure, he scratched an "X" on the logs he rejected, leaving the good ones unmarked, with undetectable differences between one and the other. After this, the whole load was appropriated and loaded on a waiting railroad car by Sus and José Francisco, who were then paid only for those without the "X. Along with these, the rejected timbers rolled away, a free gift to the company at the expense of the woodcutters. Young Torres was convinced the superintendent got a kickback on the excess props. During those times of standing around, José Francisco became aware of a nagging ache low in his side that continued to hurt off and on. But since the pain always went away, he dismissed it as transient and unimportant. This ache would come back to haunt him later. Outraged seventy years afterward at the treatment he and his fathers had to endure, Judge Torres labeled the system as "the most blatantly galling and dishonest tactics of a conscienceless industry,"

José Francisco simmered with impotent fury at the cynical cheating prevalent where no one had the power to oppose the practice. He saw it as nothing less than common thievery, countenanced by law, with the local Spanish the victims as had been the case in the post-Stonewall take over of valley lands. A deep and burning ambition to do something about such injustice reinforced itself in his mind.

However comfortable their homes, miners daily faced life-endangering hazards in their work. Unstable mine tunnels, equipment accidents, explosions of deadly gasses or misplaced dynamite, as well as constant breathing of coal dust brought disability, and sudden or prolonged death to countless men. A gas explosion in the Primero mine killed twenty four men in 1907, another in 1909 killed seventy-nine and in 1911, a particularly bad explosion in another ASARCO mine near Cokedale took an even larger number of lives. These disasters typified the sorry record of most mines and stirred the first organized agitation for legally enforced mining safety measures.

That most feared danger, explosion, came in the actual hand digging of coal, the same tunnel work which also led to black lung disease which developed insidiously over months and years. Once the coal was out of the ground, the next step involved using frequently erratic and poorly maintained machinery for sorting, weighing, crushing and washing unstable piles of coal before delivery to the coke ovens. This added broken bones and mashed bodies. In the final processing phase, coke oven workers suffered from extended contact with the noxious smoke fumes produced in coking, added to the continual heavy lifting associated with each step of extraction and refining, all culminating in ruined backs and prematurely worn bodies. Every part of the process carried its own dangers for which management felt no responsibility, and conveniently saw as merely "part of the job."

When fired up, the three hundred fifty Cokedale ovens would light the night sky all the way to Trinidad before the doors were closed for the final burn required to produce finished coke. At the end point, watering down the ovens prevented the coke from flaring up when air rushed in as the doors were opened for cooling. The product then was loaded on train cars for transport to smelters owned by ASARCO. Although none were killed outright, Torres family members who worked the mines lived shortened lives from injuries and black lung. No health or disability insurance to care for ill and crippled workers, nor any life insurance compensated the workers and their families.

Crusita's Uncle Alfred Long at unidentified mine.

Fully aware of this, Sus Torres, weary of cutting props only to be cheated, gave it up and took a job as a coker for ASARCO. Once hired, he moved his family into one of the comfortable Cokedale company houses. Eva found the conveniences in her new home to her liking, and her children enjoyed the company furnished celebrations. Convinced he had done the best he could for his own, Sus settled into the demanding, dirty work until some twenty years later he was forced to quit by his own case of black lung.

With Sus on the new job and not needing help, it became a time of casting about for José Francisco. Intellectually curious, academically gifted, and wanting more than the valley offered, he had no real idea of how to go forward. In the meantime, he picked up extra money helping neighbors stack hay, or shooting prairie dogs to rid horse pastures of their dangerous burrows, or assisting these people at round up for the branding, dehorning and castrating of calves. As he worked, he mentally gazed into the distance, the specifics of realizing his unfocused goals eluding him. Always, he read for ideas, for clues, knowing that the self direction embedded in his being would not allow his life to depend on the orders of others.

4

THE DIFFERENT ONE

When José Francisco turned sixteen years old in 1913, it was obvious to Sus and Eva that they had parented a son who in no way fit the pattern of the Purgatoire valley. While the other late teen teenagers of the community went to work in the mines, played baseball, and flirted with the pretty girls, reading and studies claimed José Francisco's interest. Tall and lean, but well muscled, he showed no inclination to settle into any of the venues open: coal mining, working on a ranch, wood cutting, or farming. None appealed. He knew it all, could do any of the work, but the valley life was not for him.

Even though he loved the upper Purgatoire, its rhythms and its people, and recognized the prejudice existing outside it, trips to Trinidad gave José Francisco enticing glimpses of the world beyond, standing as a sort of gateway between where he was and where he wanted to go. While the Declaration of Independence, the Constitution, and the Bill of Rights guaranteed equal opportunity for all, the fact that this so often failed to be the case did not invalidate the rightness of the principle, José Francisco reasoned, and never doubted that preparation, hard work, and high values could reinforce what they stated. The way to work for this was not yet clear, but it existed somewhere.

How unschooled and unsophisticated country parents produced a son of such brilliance is an open question, but solid, practical Eva sensed far more in José Francisco than Sus, who found him inexplicable. Aware of her son's lofty aspirations, Eva worried about the prejudice and risks he would face if he followed his dream and knew they would lose him from the close family circle in the valley if he did. Could not his own community offer a satisfactory life, she questioned? He listened respectfully, but did not accept her fears or suggestions.

After puzzling and praying over the problem, Eva hit upon the idea that he should become a priest. She ventured down to Trinidad where she talked to Fr. Richard di Palma, priest at Holy Trinity Church who, after a few probing questions, gave assent that José Francisco could begin studies. Back home, she told Sus who, having no better alternative, agreed to his wife's plan.

José Francisco saw this as a chance to advance his goals. Priests were educated, carried out duties in the church, instructed, and worked to do good wherever they were placed, much the way he envisioned his life should be. Her hopes high, Eva dispatched him down to Trinidad to prepare for the religious life.

At first, José Francisco found the newness interesting: a spartan room, meals under the critical eye of a priest, the prayers and formal mass, and the demands of his studies. Before long, however, the strict atmosphere with control over every detail and the rigid rules grew irksome. Reprimanded severely by the priest one day over some trifle in which José Francisco felt he had done no wrong and his sense of justice greatly offended, he decided that he did not care for the place, its restrictions and demands, and never would.

When he announced his intention to quit, Fr. di Palma tried to dissuade him with a lecture on discipline as necessary to a pious life. José Francisco countered that discipline was indeed needed, but it must be an inward control, not imposed by someone else. Unwilling to discuss it further and risk having his arguments successfully countered, di Palma sent the rebel on to the Mother Superior at the convent who told him: "You cannot quit. Your mother wants you to stay." Politely, young Torres replied, "No, I am going home," and went, certain the decision was the right one for him, but uneasy at facing displeased parents who had not sanctioned his action.

Once home, where a disappointed Eva bluntly asked him what he planned to do with his life now, José Francisco surprised her with a plan. His options were limited, but to start his attack against the wrongs he saw all around, he needed to use his mind rather than his muscles. In working toward this end, he would teach, molding young minds to grasp the ideas of justice and equality. With the few schools in the valley offering limited instruction, and with his own fluency in both Spanish and English, his grade school education and extensive reading, he would add a needed educational opportunity in his own community. He never doubted his ability to succeed. His *Tio* Juan, a certified teacher in an up-river school, warned his nephew that teaching was not easy, and that until he turned eighteen, José Francisco could not be certified to teach in the public schools, which paid better and furnished up to date teaching materials. Until then, he would have to find his own instructional supplies and do it all himself.

Undaunted, José Francisco elected to open a fee school. Optimism sent him out soliciting parents until he had a small classroom of prospective students signed up for a seven month term at a dollar a month per child. He located a vacant building in Weston and set up a classroom, bringing his own worn textbooks to use. He was seventeen years old when he walked to school and rang the first bell for classes in early October, 1914, to embark on his teaching career. Recalling this, Judge Torres laughed at his own audacity. "I didn't have any authority, but I knew my material and those kids learned their subjects." It foretold a lifetime of teaching, no matter where he was or what he did.

In spite of authority contests arising from his being no older than the oldest students, age and ability differences among the pupils, discipline problems, and learning to teach by trial and error, he finished the year with parents pleased at the progress of their children, and José Francisco given confidence by success. Now eighteen years old, he took and passed the teacher certification test, to be hired promptly as teacher for the public school at Molino Canyon. He soon gained a reputation there for teaching the basics, firm discipline and getting even the most reluctant to do their work. As a result, he was hired away from Molino Canyon the next year to teach at Burro Canyon where idlers turned up to disrupt classes and test his mettle.

Ending the school year, he spent the summer of 1916 studying at the Normal School in Gunnison, Colorado, where he immersed himself in teaching methodology and materials and ignored the subtle and slighting differences in the way he was treated among mostly Anglo students. Following this, his teaching moved him progressively through larger valley schools, advancing to become a principal where, along with the usual problems, rowdy young miners invaded the school grounds to flirt with the older girls. José Francisco physically ejected the amorous swains as needed, and classes went forward. His reputation grew, earning him the title of *"El Profesor"* among the parents of the valley, although those outside had no interest in someone who taught "Mex Kids." In 1917, he moved up again to head the Jansen school, the most modern in the valley, located between Cokedale and Trinidad. That year, he did not walk to school, but caught the Trinidad streetcar at Cokedale and returned from the classroom the same way in the evening.

As he taught, his resentment increased that he and all Spanish were labeled as lazy, stupid, unimportant Mexicans by the society around them. Even though their forebears had chalked up two hundred years of solid achievement on American soil, they were dismissed as inferior. José Francisco recognized a barrier wall he could see through but which offered no gateway for passage beyond it. This wall of prejudice held people captive, on the one side denying individual dreams and gifts, and on the other forcing those to assume superiority, projecting onto their own ordinariness the appearance of excellence. Prejudice, thereby, controlled each side's existence, crippling the society in which they jointly lived. America did not need such walls and he resolved to breach this one, which, in so doing, could move him onward toward where he wished to be. But the how of doing it was yet lacking.

He knew the deficiencies in society, but remained convinced that if he worked hard enough, he could make a difference. With this in mind, he attended an organizational visit to Trinidad by Frank Farrell, Field Secretary for the Boy Scouts of America and hosted by the local Knights of Columbus. Here he found the idealism in action he sought, and began one of his life's most enduring interests. The scouting goal of building character in young boys through teaching service, responsibility, moral development and patriotism sounded a clarion call to help shape boys in honor, self-reliance, and citizenship. Under the sponsorship of Holy Trinity Catholic Church, two troops were authorized that same night, with Troop 7 to be led by newly appointed Scoutmaster, José Francisco Torres. Shortly fifteen promising lads recruited from his Jansen school were following Scoutmaster Torres on excursions up the river and in the mountains, learning wood lore, survival skills, and civic responsibility. In 1919, the local newspaper published a news item that Troop 7 and its Scoutmaster had fought a fire in Jansen, saving adjacent buildings from destruction. Torres relished every minute as he set out to improve the world, one boy at a time.

El Profesor Torres continued to enjoy his students and scouting, but, at odd moments, it was not enough. He came to the realization that raising up independent and self-directed young men would assault the solidly built wall of discrimination only slowly. He pledged himself to find more active areas of combat against this poison, mentally enlarging his efforts to encompass all races and conditions of people. Additionally, events occurring in the wider world made him eager to be a part in meeting the challenges and contributing to solutions. Colorado's "bone dry" law in 1916, had brought prohibition and bootleggers in well ahead of the Constitutional Amendment which produced the same negative results nationally. Other events also brought change in the world. Mexico ousted despotic dictator Porfirio Diaz, and Pancho Villa led scraggly troops on a raid across the U.S. border, shooting up and burning tiny Columbus, New Mexico. The most serious and far reaching problems were instigated by Germany's aggression, which plunged western Europe into war. He watched developments as isolationists and interventionists in Congress heatedly debated whether the United States should become involved in the conflict. Was it right that one country be allowed to overrun others? Was isolationism the best course for this nation? He thought not. When human rights were trampled anywhere, failing to act gave permission for the same to be duplicated elsewhere.

5
OUT OF THE VALLEY

In 1917 José Francisco lost his most important mentor, Grandfather Antonio Domingo Torres. More than a decade earlier, this "pied piper" of his childhood, grown weary of the changes in the valley brought about by industrial expansion, loss of land and the self reliant, unconfined life he cherished, had moved to the Gallina Valley some thirty-five miles northeast of Las Vegas, New Mexico. Here, he had lived in the old traditional way, raising sheep on his grassy acres, content with Thomasita D'Arsenaus, his friendly and hospitable second wife and their small children, and with blued, distant views of the mountains he loved.

José Francisco had visited him there, riding the train south from Trinidad to Shoemaker, a crossing on the Mora River near Watrous, to be met by Antonio Domingo who would drive a team and wagon some twenty miles to fetch him. After catching up on family news, the old man always encouraged his grandson to speak of his dreams and ambitions, counseling him to work to become all he could be if he hoped to gain lasting satisfaction in life. At the end of two or three days of visiting, José Francisco would catch the train back north. From visit to visit, Antonio Domingo grew slower and stiffer in his movements. But the grey gaze still was steady as he spoke of his life drawing to a close. New life ever went forward while the old receded into the distance behind. He died on March 9, 1917, at age eighty-three, and after the funeral mass at Santo Santiago Church, was buried in the little cemetery there, under the immense New Mexico sky, to become a part of the wide and lonely distances he loved so well.

José Francisco felt the loss as this chapter in his life closed, but recognized that, although the heroic figure of his childhood was gone, his grandfather's wisdom remained for him to use. Rarely insightful for a twenty year old, he applied these ideals in teaching, broadening his focus beyond academics to building character and confidence. He worked to instill in his students the belief that they were as good as anyone else, and urged that they work to win whatever they tried. He entered them in any and all competitions for scholastic and athletic honors, emphasizing that if they applied mental discipline and worked, they could outdo those who did less. It was good experience for facing the ups and downs of life, he felt, and, hopefully, would give them confidence to oppose the discrimination he knew they faced. It resulted in his Jansen school pupils holding their own against all comers. His years of teaching also instilled him with confidence, insights and focus, but he never considered a classroom the final step in his career.

As World War I intensified in Europe, it stirred a life-long respect and admiration for the military and a wish to do his patriotic duty After the Kaiser unleashed guns against neighboring Austria in 1914, three years of fierce debate at all levels of government passed before the United States government achieved agreement to declare war against Germany. Young men enlisted at hastily set up recruiting offices and the first company out of Trinidad in 1917 was the Spanish Volunteers. When the school term ended, José Francisco Torres also answered the call to arms only to be rejected at the recruiting office when, during the pre-induction physical, the doctor discovered an abdominal hernia. Although he argued that it would not bother him, the doctor was unimpressed and Torres returned home in disappointment, belatedly recognizing the significance of the nagging ache that started when he worked with Sus cutting and delivering props for the mining company.

However, his hopes of becoming a soldier were reignited not long after when, as the war intensified, a national draft was put in place. Torres hastened to register and waited impatiently for his name to be drawn. The call-up came on August 22, 1918, and gave him just five days to get his affairs in shape and report to the draft office in Trinidad. Young enough to be caught up in the drama and adventure of it, he felt keen anticipation. When he reported in, he was handed a War Department special order that, recognizing his education and leadership, named him as special officer to take charge of the other draftees on the trip to their assignment at Camp Lewis near Tacoma, Washington. After carefully reading over the orders and regulations, Torres called his group to attention for a march to the train waiting on the siding. Some went awkwardly, some fearfully, some innocently curious, but José Francisco stepped on the train with confidence and purpose, prepared to serve to the best of his abilities. He was proud to be a soldier.

On the troop train, between reveille, meals and taps, he watched the changing landscape as mountains, arid plateaus, sandstone country, farms, grasslands, forests, logging and mining camps, came and went past the train window until the locomotive huffed into Camp Lewis five days later. After they unloaded on a plank platform, Torres gathered his men and marched them off to an assigned barracks where they awaited further orders. The first to come was the required physical exam for all new recruits. During this check, his old hernia was quickly spotted and again brought rejection. Two days later Torres watched his men go on to basic training while he took the train back to Trinidad, thwarted in not doing his citizen's duty while someone else would have to fight in his stead.

Back home to Cokedale, the war effort brought prosperous times to the Torres family by greatly increased demand for coal and coke amid a shortage of laborers and resulting soaring wages. The war ended in November 1918, yet long after the heat and noise of battle stopped, failure to have been a part of the action still nagged at Torres. Restless but uncertain of change, José Francisco returned to teaching for the next two years. At war or at peace, a country needed educated people to create a just and balanced society, and teaching would be his contribution even as he laid the groundwork for taking the long anticipated step out of the valley.

Idealistic and ambitious, José Francisco looked for more in life than spending it teaching unruly children academic skills and worthwhile aspirations. There was satisfaction, of course, in guiding the development of young lives, but he had craved a more immediate role in bringing remedy to the wrongs he saw around him. He burned to make a difference, to affect the here and now. And he wanted to test himself, unlabeled, equal, accepted as an individual, to rise or fall according to his own ability.

He now harbored a dream of becoming a lawyer and investigated how this might be accomplished. From the time the outlaw shot his dog, the concept of law as the dispenser of justice and equality had stayed in the back of his mind. Now, ten years later, the idea asserted itself in full blown determination. He read everything pertaining to law he could get his hands on, followed court cases and verdicts, gaining a grasp of what law involved. A legal career would give him the tools and chance to weigh in personally on the side of justice, to uphold, to interpret, to frame law, all of which seemed to him fascinating, worthwhile and exactly what he wanted to do. But how to get there? Friendly advice came from one of his acquaintances, Trinidad lawyer Eusebio Chacón, a son of Major Raphael Chacón, who had benefited from his military father's connections in higher circles. Unfortunately, this route was not available to the children of simple farmers.

Eusebio gave him information on law school requirements and, learning that Torres lacked a high school diploma, advised that he improve his credentials. He also felt Frank should aim for admittance to the University of Denver school of law. The institution was well regarded, convenient, and less expensive than out of state schools. "If you don't try," the Notre Dame educated Eusebio observed, "it can never happen."

José Francisco's decision to go meant coming up with the money and leaving home to attend law school. Although he looked forward to new places and challenges, despite savings from his teaching years, he remained short on cash and knew this would be an ongoing problem. He would have to hold a job in addition to going to school, but he knew how to work, how to make do on a minimum.

By 1920, Torres was set to follow his dream and enter the world of law without further delay. He had heard from others that the ivied institutions of higher education too frequently excluded Spanish people, generally perceiving them as incapable of college academics. Somehow, he would have to deal with that. When Jansen school ended for the summer, he went off to Denver to begin his quest.

Denver held the law school and Denver, too, held the opportunity for improving his odds for getting in to it. His Uncle Juan Torres offered a place in his home, sharing a room with his cousin, Juanito. The warm acceptance by his uncle and cousin unfortunately was offset when he felt the sting of his querulous aunt's snide complaints on the cost of feeding him even though he contributed cash toward his share. He had not anticipated this and made a note to find a place of his own as soon as possible.

José Francisco secured a job waiting tables in a small restaurant and enrolled in a banking course at Central Business College. While not interested, then or ever, in the intricacies of finance and banking, he knew money frequently was the focus of legal cases. Additionally, the discipline of study would be useful in law school. All business school really involved, he found, was methods and procedures that failed to call forth creative thinking or ideas, at least for him. After returning to his Jansen classroom for a final winter, he easily completed the banking course in Denver the next summer.

His limited time in the big city already had made clear the universal nature of society's inequities. If the Spanish had been pushed back in Trinidad, the situation perhaps was worse in Denver where they worked at the lowest jobs, received the lowest pay and were treated as the lowest by their fellow citizens. With his concept of justice, sharpened by observation and experience, the prevailing social climate offended his vision of a true democracy operating on the guarantees of the Constitution and the Bill of Rights. The challenge presented to all fair-minded citizens, he believed, was to enforce the law, raise concrete objections when it was not upheld, and, where needed, change the law itself to ensure that what was legal and lawful applied equally to everyone. This required just lawyers, judges, and politicians for which existing need seemed to far exceed supply.

The early 1920s had brought extremes and challenges in the country, and José Francisco accommodated himself to the changes in society without sacrificing his values. Indeed, unrest occurred throughout the world, and in the U. S., the headlines reported controversy over war veteran's benefits, ranchers reacting with guns when the government tried to enforce mandatory dipping of all cattle, and temperance societies pushed through the Eighteenth Amendment to the Constitution. Soon bootleggers and speakeasies dispensing whiskey and bathtub gin operated with impunity. In another change, the Nineteenth Amendment finally granted women the right to vote.

José Francisco objected strongly to the flouting of Prohibition law. To his mind, there was no such thing as breaking the law a little bit, you either respected and obeyed it or you didn't. Although he never used alcohol himself, he did not condemn responsible use of liquor by others, but could not respect those who abused strong drink, exchanging hard earned money for drunken befuddlement. Excessive drinking also led to problem behavior and hardship where the drinker became a burden on family, and society suffered. Such waste of talent and resources made no sense to him. Trinidad was no exception in the problem, with bootleggers selling "rot gut" in fruit jars to the thirsty householders and miners of the valley. Worse still, to his mind, was the rise of the Ku Klux Klan, a white supremacist organization that had come into being after the Civil War and which Torres viewed as blatantly racist.

Such were the times when José Francisco Torres put to the test his dream of becoming a lawyer. He had finished the banking course and he judged the time was as right as it ever would get. Accordingly, early one summer morning in 1922 he presented himself at the University of Denver Law School dean's office to enroll. Left there by the secretary, he stood at the office door for perhaps an hour while the Dean purposefully ignored him before fixing him with a hard stare and asking what he wanted. When Torres stepped though the door and explained, the Dean favored him with a contemptuous eye, then dismissed him with calculated insult to "get out of here because we don't want any of your kind in our school."

Stunned at the rejection and rigid with anger at the slur, José Francisco drew himself up and replied with icy courtesy, "All right, sir, but remember this, a day will come when I receive my degree from Denver University." Those words, spoken from the hurt of rejection and with no basis for his prediction would prove, in time, a remarkable precognition on his part. But as an old man, Torres still remembered the feeling of disbelief, disillusionment and pain so carelessly inflicted.

Even with the Dean's slur that encompassed Torres, his family, his ancestors and his culture still an echo in his ears, José Francisco was unready to accept defeat. There was another accredited law school in Denver at Westminister College. Determined to find out all at once how things were going to be, he caught a westbound streetcar across town.

Entering the solid red brick building that housed the Westminister law school, he was escorted by a friendly secretary into an office where Dean Hamlet J. Barry, greeted him with courteous interest, motioned him into a chair and asked what he could do for him. As Torres spoke, the dean sized him up as a bright and unusual young man, possessed of the idealism and determination necessary to make a positive contribution to the practice of law. Although Barry approved of him, lack of the required high school diploma stood in his way. But if Torres could make up this deficiency in time, he would be allowed to enroll for the winter term.

Then the Dean asked a surprising question: "Do you believe in the Doctrine of the Strenuous Life as advocated by Teddy Roosevelt?" Since the old Rough Rider's philosophy of meeting life head-on and pitting one's self against all odds was exactly the life that appealed most to young Torres, the answer was a ringing "yes." Torres in return, after explaining that his English came from a Spanish-English dictionary, asked his own question, would his accent be a hindrance? The Dean laughed. The law was the law no matter the accent or language, he assured, and lawyers were needed from every group and background for the law to be even-handed and just, without bias or favor. He then referred the overjoyed young man to the State office of Public Instruction where the Superintendent, Mary C.C. Bradford, would test him and set up the required course of study for a high school diploma. Writing a note of introduction to Mrs. Bradford, Barry shook his hand and escorted him to the door with the encouraging words that he would see his new student in January. At that moment Torres fell in love with the place.

After the graying, motherly looking Mrs. Bradford tested him, she wrote out course requirements, handing them to him along with the assurance that she knew he could do it. Torres remembered that fall as "working like a beaver" and at the end passing the tests in late November. He then quit his job at the restaurant and jubilantly went home to Cokedale at Christmas to share his excitement with his family.

After the holiday and back in Denver, he found a better job as off-hours bellhop and waiter in the dining room at Capitol Hill's elegant Albany Hotel. Included were meals and a small room. He moved there knowing he would not miss his aunt's barbs and could study better in his own place. By education and experience, he qualified for any number of higher level jobs, but Spanish were not even considered as applicants for those positions. He wasted no time on futile resentment. He was entering law school.

6
Law School

In early January, 1922, José Francisco Torres, age twenty-four, entered Westminister School of Law, attending its night classes. As the only Spanish American in the entering class, Torres neither pushed forward nor shrank back, waiting to see the nature of his reception. The first day a couple of young men hailed him, introducing themselves as Ralph Platt and Frank Wachob and welcoming him as a fellow classmate. The days following revealed that Westminister lived by its churchly heritage, allowing no room for discrimination. If once in a while some person displayed stand-offishness, the prevailing attitude remained one of easy good will among equals. Fulfilling Torres' highest hopes, for the first time in his life he was welcomed without hesitation as one in a group where ethnic origin was not an issue.

His classmates immediately dispensed with the name, "José Francisco," replacing it with "Frank." The switch suited him and reflected his new status. He was not going into law as a professional Spaniard, different from his classmates, but to compete one on one where achievement, devoid of label, was the yardstick. While proud of his heritage, he found a tremendous sense of freedom in not being boxed into an ethnic niche. He could focus his concentration on gaining the education needed to attack the wrongs of prejudice on all legal fronts anywhere he encountered separation, labeling, and discrimination. To fight successfully for his own Spanish people, he had to use the same standards for all others or his own actions would defeat his convictions. He had a rule, he said, he never drew lines against people because that created opposing sides. The line must be drawn, instead, between right and wrong only.

Frank plunged in eagerly to master the complex material, entered class activities, methodically read his way through the law library, and attended every lecture. While competitive sports never interested him, academic challenge brought out a compulsion to win.

In contrast to the academic harmony at Westminister, his job at the Albany, a favorite hangout for legislators and well to do businessmen, produced on-going bigotry that made the work harder since service workers presented an easy, safe target for racism and ill will. He held his temper, mindful of his need for the job but once in a while his control slipped. When he was called a donkey by one man he labeled a "real jerk," Frank responded with false civility, "Yes sir, I was born in a stable, and every time I see you it makes me homesick." Another time, the same man came in late as usual to order just as breakfast ended, Torres and the cook took over-due revenge by serving the unsuspecting fellow a spotless plateful of eggs, bacon, fried potatoes and toast salvaged from the garbage pail, and then gleefully stood by the kitchen door to watch him chew it down.

Fortunately another man helped make up for that denigration. This was the legendary W. I. Hallett, a pioneer cattleman and leading Denver figure who had come west, settled in Estes Park and had Hallett's Peak and Hallet's Glacier named for him in recognition of his mountain explorations and discoveries. An active widower in his eighties at the time, Hallet lived at the hotel, furnishing material to Western writers and advising Hollywood directors on accurate portrayal of the Old West. He developed a liking for Torres and during meals shared his tales with the history loving, yellow-eyed waiter, according him respect as an individual.

Frank pursued his studies with single-minded intensity, doing equally well and earning high grades both on written work and in oral argument. Accent or not, he was verbally gifted, delighting in words and winning debates and moot court cases by the simple expedient of having a better command of language and an uncanny ability to focus when under pressure. He developed lasting friendships during bull sessions and in the casual camaraderie that existed among those sharing the stiff academic demands at Westminister. Their number included future Colorado Governor Teller Ammons, Secretary of the Interior Oscar Chapman, Senator J. Edward Chenowith and Army General Paul V. Schriver, as well as the daring World War I balloonist, Frank Wachob.

Frank gloried in the intellectual challenge, open and equal standing, and holding his own among his peers. At Westminister, for the first time he was casually accepted for himself and his abilities without reference to race, creed or color. As he saw it, this was what democracy was meant to be. Nevertheless, away from law school the ethnic digs, assumptions of superiority by smug bigots, treatment as a stereotype, all were part of his days. Although far from easy on his pride, Torres met all instances with formidable control. His intellect advised him that the sure way to turn the tables on these attitudes was to be better than those who displayed them. Without conceit, he knew himself to be intellectually superior to most and the future would provide answers on position and status.

To ease the habitual pinch for money, Frank took on a second job as a hasher at the YWCA, where extended dining hours enabled him to work a second shift. In the new position, Torres' sincerity and willingness to work gained him friendly acceptance among the other help. One of these was June Nelson, a small blonde girl who struck up an acquaintance with the tall, intense young law student. June worked as dining room cashier to support herself. Frank liked her eagerness to learn, her friendliness and idealism. He also noted that she was pretty.

As the two talked during slow times, Frank enjoyed her interest and willingness to listen. He came to know and care for the petite girl who appealed to his latent chivalry. It was a new experience. His life, until then intensely focused on the future, left him with neither time nor inclination toward acquiring a girl friend. But in the middle of work, mutual attraction grew.

As schedules permitted, they attended lectures and free concerts, enjoying the beauty of the city with its soaring mountain backdrop. Spinning unformed visions of a future after Frank finished his law degree and set up practice, the two drifted through a happy interlude, filled with hope for a time in the future when all dreams would come true.

Immersed in the demands of law school, Frank read extensively, once finding and copying down a philosophy that guided his life in the years to come. It read: "The good are befriended even by weakness and defeat . . . Our strength grows out of our weakness. Not until we are pricked and stung and sorely shot at, awakens the indignation which arms itself with secret forces. A great man is always willing to be little. Whilst he sits on the cushion of advantages, he goes to sleep. When he is pushed, tormented, defeated, he has a chance to learn something; he has been put on his wits, on his manhood. He has gained facts, learned his ignorance, is cured of the insanity of conceit, has got moderation and real skill . . . Blame is safer than praise . . . In general, every evil to which we do not succumb is a benefactor . . I learn the wisdom of St. Bernard, 'nothing can work me damage except myself. The harm that I sustain, I carry about with me, and never am a real sufferer but by my own fault." He did not record the author but claimed the piece for his own, the tough, no excuses credo his guide.

The piece fitted him. He did not shy from hard facts, indulged in no self-pity and wasted no time lamenting what might have been. Deeply embedded in his being, Frank held to moral values, courage, strong effort and resolve, applying them in all things with conscious dedication. While he immersed himself in criminal and civil procedure, constitutional law, torts, liability, wills, fraud, the whole spectrum of law, he also worked on the yearbook and participated in the jousts at moot court over ridiculous situations designed to contain serious legal questions.

The future lawyers heatedly argued issues of the day with newspapers and the new commercial radio furnishing fuel for their bouts of opinion and legal theory. The twelve hour work day, child labor, union activity, radical labor organizations, and Communist activity in America, all gave the Westminister students much to debate. Torres, a good Catholic, could not accept the godless Communist doctrine and further believed that the mass regimentation it demanded opened the door for massive misuse of power against the people under it. Classmates who differed gave him vigorous arguments.

Although he carried a man-killing schedule, Torres never flinched nor faltered. He served endless meals, studied endless hours, went without sleep, money and recreation in a single-minded dedication to achieving his dream, realistically recognizing that it was this way or not at all. Stretching himself further, he made time to pitch in for the betterment of those around him, donating part of his "free" time to help build a new church in the Spanish section of Denver where the residents either went some distance to a dubiously welcoming Anglo church or worshiped in their own homes.

A gift of both land and money from the wealthy and prominent Denver Catholic, John Kernan Mullens, enabled the future parishioners to build their own church, doing most of the labor themselves including altar, pews, confessionals, and carved crucifixes and stations of the Cross. Law student Torres saw to the legal details of city permits, building codes and contracts, as well as giving ideas in planning parish use. The resulting finished structure was named St. Cajetan's in honor of a sixteenth century monk. Such hard work and devotion by the people to gain their own parish underscored the deep and unmet need that had existed among them.

Not long after, however, his studies were of little help as Frank joined an investigation into the murder of his cousin, Juanito Torres, son of *Tío* Juan Torres in whose home Frank had lived. No arrest was made and he felt that the police were not making the death of a "Mexican" as high a priority as they might have had he been an Anglo. Frank spent hours gathering evidence, questioning possible witnesses, trying to reconstruct the crime, but in the end it fizzled out when the prime suspect fled to Mexico. The experience rankled in his mind as more evidence of the ever present discrimination.

Politics also claimed the law student's attention since the elective process determined who governed and how. Frank actively participated in campaigns during his years at Westminister, laying the groundwork for political involvement later. He firmly believed that citizens who took no part in the political process had no right to complain about its failures. True to the Spanish tradition of the time, he enrolled as a Republican. Denver party leaders, eager to win, found the fiery Torres useful in appealing to Spanish voters. Their new advocate soon tangled with entrenched politicians over the Ku Klux Klan, opposing it even though the organization seemed acceptable to the party rank and file.

In addition to the ideas espoused by the Klan, he was offended by what he saw as the Klan's adoption and perversion of Christian symbolism in the burning of crosses. The cross, he said, was redemptive and inclusive, not partisan and vindictive. Frank spoke against the KKK at political rallies, pointing out his belief that the organization violated the Bill of Rights, engaged in intimidation, and delivered a racist message. His Republican party tried to get him to soften his rhetoric and the KKK made thinly veiled threats, at one time sending a dozen or so robed and hooded members in an attempt to physically block Torres from a political rally. Frank arrived at the meeting with those he referred to as his "Anglo cowboy friends" roughly shoving a path through, giving as good as they got in an exchange of insults and muscle with the Klansmen. Frank continued to hammer away against the KKK, not about to abandon his principles for any party.

He worked hard for his candidates as election day approached, choosing man over party. Because of Democrat Morrison Shafroth's unequivocal opposition to the KKK, Frank supported his bid for Congress, writing a letter to the Spanish language paper, *El Defensor Popular*, outlining his reasons and raising the ire of fellow Republicans. While they saw this as defection, Torres saw electing the best man, regardless of party, as responsible citizenship.

The weeks and months moved along where the pressure of studies, work, student activities, and politics left Frank an observer of the Roaring Twenties rather than a participant. Not given to fads or excesses, he quietly watched the giddy era unfold, although for most young people it was a daring time of kicking over the traces and outraging the older generation. Flappers bobbed their hair, wore shockingly short skirts and, with their beaus, danced the Charleston or rattled along dusty roads in touring cars and drank gin from pocket flasks concealed in oversized raccoon skin coats. Really daring ones went up for rides in open cockpit airplanes flown by barnstorming pilots, but Frank stayed focused on his goals. However, he found time to share his lodging with a South American student who had entered Westminister, instructing him in the English language and tutoring him in the principles of law. This resulted in a life-long friendship after the student went back home.

Special events leading up to graduation began in November of 1924, when the Westminister alumni feted the graduating class at the popular Alpine Rose restaurant. Frank brought June Nelson as his guest for a rare evening of dining, dancing and speeches. At Christmas, Frank again took June to a dinner by Westminister's President and Mrs. Murray and hosted at their own home. After the holiday the academic grind resumed until final exams. Frank studied hard and passed them with high marks, finishing his studies in the top of his twenty-six member class, well ahead of his more privileged classmates who hadn't worked two jobs and lived with racism. Dean Barry personally congratulated Frank on his accomplishments.

Graduation brought more activities and recognition. J. F. Torres' class picture reveals a serious faced young man with intense light eyes looking out at the world from beneath a slightly slanted mortar board. Graduation was June second, followed by a reception for Westminister faculty, students and alumni, given by the college dean and the Murrays. Then came the graduation banquet addressed by Colorado Congressman Hilliard. Although neither Frank nor June was feeling well that week, missing this was unthinkable.

Their studies behind them, the jubilant new lawyers celebrated and planned their futures. Frank felt a deep surge of joy, of release from a burden no longer carried. Only he actually had believed he would ever earn acceptance and membership in the legal world. The glass wall had vanished, destroyed by his own determination never again to be trapped behind it.

His elation however was tempered by an uneasy concern. He had relegated to the back of his mind an almost continual cough, low energy, and the tiredness which dogged him as he made the round of graduation activities. It worried him, too, that June also coughed, tired easily, and appeared frail. For graduation, she gave Frank the book, *Compensation*, by Ralph Waldo Emerson, a slim green leather bound, moiré lined, volume inscribed to "J.F. Torres, LLB, Westminister Law School, Denver, Colorado. Graduation Compliments from June Nelson, Denver, Colorado, 1925." Torres kept the book, worn from many readings, to the end of his days.

With law degree in hand, the new graduates faced a final hurdle, passing the Colorado State Bar Examination to be licensed to practice, without which a law degree became only an expensive piece of paper.

Frank prepared to take it mid-summer in 1925, ignoring his waning strength as he reviewed, invented legal questions, and worked to solve each according to the appropriate principle of law.

Graduating from Westminister Law School.

Torres reported in on test day among the rest of Colorado's new law school graduates. Examination booklets were handed out and the room settled down to the silence of intense concentration. Ignoring the protests of his body, Frank focused on the questions to frame the correct answers. Nevertheless, a quarter of the way through pain and nausea forced him to leave the room. His friend, Ralph Platt, came out at a break to find Frank slumped on the floor, hemorrhaging from his nose and mouth. He quickly explained the problem to test officials who permitted him to take Frank to the nearest doctor and finish his test afterward.

The physician looked, thumped, asked questions, and, at the end gave a brief diagnosis. Torres had a far advanced and likely incurable case of tuberculosis.

Back in his room, Frank lay on the bed stunned disbelief floating through his haze of misery. How could this happen to him now? The doctor had told him to forget the bar examination, ordering extended bed rest as his only hope for immediate survival. Sick as he was, Torres dragged himself out two days later to prevail upon the doctor and the bar board to allow him a chance to finish the test. Undoubtedly believing that what Frank did or did not do made little difference at this point, doctor and board agreed for him to finish up under medical supervision. Although this took sixteen days of forcing mind over body, the effort again paid off, and he passed with a top of the class score.

A few weeks later, coughing blood and barely able to stand upright, Torres took the oath of profession and gained admission to the Colorado State Bar along with sixty-five other young men and women from Colorado's three schools of law. Disappointingly, illness kept June Nelson from witnessing this landmark event. Afterward, he paid his twenty dollar state bar fee and forced himself to attend the luncheon given by the Denver Bar Association. The featured speaker, Justice James A. Teller of the Colorado Supreme Court, gave pungent advice on the need for moral standards in the practice of law while Frank sat not touching the excellent meal but soaking up the words and ideas. He saved his copy of the speech because it fit completely with what he believed.

7
A Battle For Life

The formalities over, J. Frank Torres now was legally entitled to practice law in the state of Colorado. His dream had almost come true, except for this one final daunting obstacle. The grind through Westminster had extracted its toll, and now he faced a battle for his own life. Not giving up, but unable to work or care for himself, he realized the only one place where he could fight it out was home with his parents in Cokedale. At his parting with June Nelson whose health also had failed, each tried to reassure the other, but out of their mutual extremity, neither had certain nor solid hope to offer. His friend, Ralph Platt, drove him to Union Station and deposited Frank on a south bound train, vowing to keep in touch.

Torres slumped against the green plush seat, wedging himself into the corner by the window as the train whistled, puffed a plume of smoke and with the hiss of brakes unlocking, eased into motion. Alternately sleeping and awakening as the miles of track rolled away, his mind and spirit rebelled against what his body told him was true. He only roused to be dimly aware and profoundly comforted as the train pulled into Trinidad. It was August, 1925.

In bed under his parent's roof, Sus and Eva watched him with inarticulate concern, knowing tuberculosis and its too frequent ending. Their José Francisco appeared so thin, so pale, and the bloody cough terrible in its implications. Was this what his dreams had brought him to? Although, weak, listless, and kept to bed, Frank still retained determination for the future. Disappointment at being unable to hang up his law shingle must not divert him from getting well enough to achieve that end. But as the weeks went by and he stayed in bed, eating the bland food the doctor prescribed, there was no discernable progress. The bloody cough intensified and he lost strength day to day. Anxious to check the progress of the disease, he had his father take him to the doctor in Trinidad. After examining the wasted body, the physician gently informed Frank that the tuberculosis was so far advanced that he had less than three months to live. He was sorry.

Sorry! The young man stumbled to his feet saying, "If that's all you can do, let me have my jacket, I'm not ready to die yet!" and walked unsteadily out of the office. Returning to his bed, Frank analyzed his options and settled on a course of action to beat the verdict. In an effort born of spirit overcoming flesh, he propped himself up in bed and laid out a plan to his mother.

He believed in the intangible power of mind over body, that ultimately the mind controlled, and by unequivocally willing himself back to health and living to that standard, he would get well. He once had come across fitness expert Bernard McFadden's ideas of health through exercise, natural foods, herbs and mental discipline that had struck him as making a lot of sense. Passively awaiting the end was unacceptable. He would use McFadden's formula to cure himself, would not vary from it, and would not fail.

Frank began sleeping with a window open, got up each morning whatever the effort, took a daily cold water bath, ate only natural foods, drank only water. He measured his limits as he walked outside, adding one step further each day no matter how he felt. He had Eva consult the old timers on the natural *remedios* that had cured ailments for the pioneers and had his mother prepare chest poultices, teas, and infusions from these herbs. Always compulsively neat, he became more so. McFadden's rule of scrupulous cleanliness made sense, for disease thrived where sanitation was lacking. His bedding and clothing were washed every day. Eva grasped at any chance to help bring back health. She prayed for him each day, did the washing on her steel washboard, and cooked simple foods, strong beef broth, beans and chile, tortillas and stews, solid food straight from the earth to replace the bland diet the doctors insisted on.

No real improvement occurred through the first winter. His body remained weak but his mind firm as he shivered through a morning bath. Little by little, something changed and with this came reinforced hope. When sunny late spring arrived, he found a secluded spot and began taking nude sunbaths, absorbing the rays and warmth. His eyes twinkled as he recalled, "I made sure I was where no one would look!" Little by little, he felt improvement, allowing no questions or negatives to enter his mind. Getting out of bed in the morning became slightly easier, he coughed up less blood, he appreciated food, and could walk half a mile a day. The regimen continued through summer and another winter.

A blow fell almost two years into this exercise of hope and healing. One of his law school friends sent him a note and brief clipping that June Nelson had died of tuberculosis in Denver. The reality of it rocked Torres although unconsciously he had feared this. They had written each other hopeful notes that ignored the question of whether there would be any future for them. Why, he asked himself, could the God he believed in allow this? There was no answer.

With his sense of loss came an insight, that she had confirmed his deepest belief in the basic equality of all people; that it was the individual who mattered not where the person came from. His law school classmates and June had valued him for himself alone. With this came a kind of peace. What had happened had happened and it was done. For whatever reason, life still was his, and to be lived worthily.

From this turning point, he concentrated even more intensely on the goal of healing rapidly and totally so that he could meet the future head on. He walked farther, he began lifting weights, using cloth bags his mother made and filled with the sparkling pink, tan and white mosaic bits of sand from river banks, his appetite grew mightily, and June Nelson gradually faded into a bittersweet memory. They had been two struggling and hopeful young people, brought together by chance, who through the depth of winter had dreamed of spring. He now focused on the positives of his youth, education, and vision. As for love, if it ever were to happen, it could find him. He would leave it at that.

The third year after law school found Frank much stronger. He roamed the hills to build his muscles, helped with chores and small jobs, read and studied legal texts to keep his edge. Early in 1928, one of his political friends, an influential Denver attorney and member of the

Westminister Law School faculty sent a confidential letter that he had recommended Torres for a position on the United States Land Board at Santa Fe. With this support, the position would be his for the asking. Tempting as he found the offer of a challenging job at an excellent salary, he used his invariable method of evaluating its requirements that led to the conclusion that his health remained too fragile to carry a full work load. Determined to be able to put forth his best before assuming any job, Torres politely declined the position when the job offer letter appeared in the mail.

From that time on, the path back to health became ever surer and with it came the itch of denied impatience to be out and doing. Six months later, in midsummer of 1928, he knew himself ready. After three years of healing, he had gained weight from a low of one hundred fifteen pounds on his six foot frame to a still lean but solid one hundred forty-eight pounds. His body bronzed from the sun, his muscles strong, his breathing deep and even, he felt fit and eager. He received another letter, this one from his law school friend Ralph Platt who wrote offering him a partner's position in Platt's thriving law practice in Berwin, Illinois. While touched by the gesture of confidence and enduring friendship, Frank was not seriously tempted. "You take care of your part of the world," he wrote back, "and I will see to improving mine." His place was among his people up the valley and in his beloved Trinidad.

Since transportation was an essential for practicing law in sprawling Las Animas County, Frank bought a Model A Ford coupe with rumble seat and drove down to Trinidad to open his law office. First, however, he gave himself the satisfaction of visiting the doctor who had told him he would die. The physician looked at him in astonishment, remarking in a puzzled voice, "I don't understand this." Frank concurred. What the man knew of medicine had nothing to do with the recovery. Back out on the street he ran into his old friend, District Attorney Eusebio Chacón who looked him over with approval and observed, "Frank, you are the most tenacious man I ever met." This came close to understatement.

The hard times, the deprivations, the testings that Torres had experienced only made him stronger, keener, more determined to meet adversity head on. One of Frank's favorite passages from Emerson summed up his affirmative philosophy. "The good are befriended even by weakness and defeat. Our strength grows out of our weakness. Not until we are pricked and stung and sorely shot at, awakens the indignation which arms itself with secret forces." This ruled out self pity, or giving up.

8
AN OFFICE IN TRINIDAD

Frank selected an office on Main Street in downtown Trinidad, easy to reach, not far from the abstract office, the bank and other businesses, and within walking distance of the Las Animas county courthouse. He paid the rent, acquired the key and a listing in the 1929 Trinidad City Directory as "José F. Torres, a lawyer from Cokedale with offices in town." As Torres opened his practice the name José Francisco or simply José, as he still was known locally, disappeared for good. "Frank" suited him better and, as it had in law school, his signature became J. Frank Torres for all purposes and people.

He installed a desk, a book case for his law books, a file cabinet and a couple of chairs in his new office and hung on the wall his Westminster diploma and his certificate of admission the Colorado State Bar. He had a large agenda staked out. He was ready to represent clients, ready to right the wrongs of society, particularly against the Spanish, and to be an active citizen for the benefit of his world.

Once launched, he did not wait for a practice to come to him, he went after it. People responded, first a few cases up the river, then a few in town, and then more. He worked long and hard and won nearly all of them. His old friend Eusebio Chacón also made use of him for contract work in the District Attorney's office. Mostly cases were small, land transactions, contracts, or petty criminal offenses, but they honed Torres' courtroom skills and gave him a reputation for winning. His meticulous researching and preparation and a compulsion to do the best job possible combined to make him a tough opponent for other lawyers to go up against.

The seriousness of law, however, occasionally turned to farce. In one remembered case from the District Attorney's office involving the illegal sale of bootleg whiskey, a sizeable quantity of evidence had been seized and held. A schoolhouse janitor, commissioned by the sheriff, was retained to guard the contraband until trial. That day dawned sunny, warm and full of good omen for attorney Torres who had studied the reports, lined up witnesses and established, in his own mind, an open and shut case for guilty as charged. To his chagrined surprise, he lost it. When the court convened and time came to introduce the evidence, a flustered bailiff appeared, propelling before him a roaring drunk janitor and reporting that all the booze had disappeared. With this lynchpin evidence against the defendant consumed by the toping constable, a speedy verdict followed: case dismissed for lack of evidence.

Pent up ambition propelled Frank into causes and activities where he felt he could make the greatest contribution, in the process cultivating contacts and broadening his recognition across Las Animas County. He used his time to its limit, leading a Boy Scout troop, joining the Spanish American Club of Colorado, investigating the new credit union movement and also looking into the ideas of the Alianza Hispano Americana, a Tucson based Spanish fraternal organization. He became active in the local Republican Party. All were piled on top of his growing, if not yet lucrative, law practice. Nor did he neglect his bent for self-improvement, reading widely in literature, philosophy and astronomy that had interested him from childhood on.

Additionally, Torres kept abreast of the happenings around the world. Across the United States good times prevailed, and in Las Animas County bumper crops and favorable livestock prices brought prosperity to the rural areas, while in-town businesses and services thrived. No one caught an inkling of the crash to come. Herbert Hoover was president, the Communist party was causing controversy, Al Capone won notoriety for the St. Valentine's Day Massacre in Chicago, and the race issue heated up with a focus on the Scottsboro Case in Alabama where in a significant first, although blacks were convicted, they were not executed in a time when lynching still existed. Overseas, Hitler had seized power in Germany and Mussolini in Italy, while in Russia Josef Stalin pushed out premier Vladimir Lenin and drove Leon Trotsky into exile. Great Britain ineffectively tried to quell unrest in its African and Indian colonies. In Mexico, persecution of the Catholic Church worsened after the assassination of General Alvaro Obregón in 1928. Torres was too busy to do more than absorb the facts, which from where he stood, were not factors in his frame of action.

Everything stayed promising for the up and coming Torres until the Friday, October 28, 1929 stock market crash and beginning of the Great Depression. For months after that date, stunned and disbelieving Americans could not come to grips with the fact that an end had come to seemingly unending prosperity. Effects of the crash filtered through all levels of society. For his part, Torres found the bad times quickly produced more clients but without means to pay for his services. Most cases resulted from default on loans, foreclosure on property, or government seizure and sale of lands for back taxes. He worked tirelessly for his client's interests, saddened for those caught in the downturn with their livelihood and independence wiped out by the Depression's grim march. But Frank still retained his optimism, certain that with necessary economic adjustments the country's abundant resources and citizen vision, with commitment, hard work, and faith, the situation could not be permanent.

Life in Trinidad pleased Torres in spite of hard times. Busy Main Street where he knew everyone, the houses on the hills, the up and down streets, Fisher's Peak standing sentinel to the south, it was his own, and he recommitted himself to make a difference there. Spanish political influence mainly was limited to a few political offices in the small Spanish villages where a respected Spaniard would be installed as the political boss who then had the responsibility of faithfully delivering whatever Spanish vote existed to a pre-ordained slate. True, one person had made it through this invisible curtain and gained higher office in the unique case of Trinidad State Senator Casimiro Barela. There was no outside encouragement for others to go and do likewise.

As a founding member who recognized the benefits which could be gained, Torres had driven to Denver in 1928 to help organize the Spanish American Club of Colorado which focused on educating and enlisting the Spanish people in the struggle to secure equal rights as citizens by getting them out to vote. Torres helped author the club's organizational statement as a call for full political participation by Spanish Americans. It stated: "Whereas, the purpose of this organization is to seek proper and legitimate ways and means of securing just treatment and our constitutional rights protected and respected, seeking no special privileges, but resenting discrimination of race, color, or religion. Be it Resolved, That we, pledge ourselves to stand united politically or otherwise to the end that our government, national, state and municipal, will recognize our rights as native American citizens whose ancestors blazed the trails and planted the first seed of civilization in this our native land; who have stood unflinchingly and undivided in every combat for the only flag we have ever known: the Stars and Stripes. And be it further Resolved, that we invite the cooperation of every Spanish speaking citizen to unite in this just cause."

Frank felt it a good start, although the changes the document demanded would take time and dedicated effort. By "Seeking a liberal interpretation of the Constitution of the United States and that of Colorado in connection with granting equal rights in all civic matters," they had formalized their goal. Armed with his law degree and years of pent up frustration, he eagerly took up the challenge to organize his fellow citizens to fight for their Constitutional rights. Back in Trinidad, Torres enlisted a few other leaders in the Spanish community and held an initial meeting toward forming a Spanish American Club of Southern Colorado. A large and interested crowd attended to listen to straight talk, including the point that failure to vote in elections had left them to suffer the injustice of their children being relegated into inferior schools, the output of which could be cited to reinforce the stereotype

Formation of the Spanish American Club in Trinidad was a positive response to the initial battle call to overturn the status quo in an arena of delayed promises. The new organization then set up a Spanish American Club regional headquarters in centrally located La Junta, Colorado. With the structure in place, Frank turned to educating his people on how to use the ballot box in their own best interests. Spanish American clubs appeared throughout southern Colorado in the next couple of years with Torres doing almost all of the setting up. The *Walsenburg Independent* on April 15, 1930 reported that Frank had spoken to a standing room only meeting on Easter Sunday afternoon at the Eagles hall there, using his trademark fiery oratory, "If we were good enough to shoulder the rifle and defend the flag which represents our nation, if we are good enough to pay our taxes, then we are equally good enough to defend and demand our rights and share in the fruits of the nation. This we can do by the united representation of our vote as citizens at election time." He articulated a strategy which has been used successfully by ethnic, racial, political and professional organizations, labor unions and other interest groups to vote as a block for persons and propositions which represented their own needs and interests.

At the spring convention of the clubs in La Junta, the eloquent young lawyer brought the delegates out of their seats to applaud when he spoke. "We are descendants of the original settlers of this country. We are here to fight our own battles. To this end, we must get together, we must educate ourselves and the public that as Americans we were born, our fathers and grandfathers were also born; as such we wish to behave, and as such we wish to be treated." Torres assailed a political system that denied one group of citizens the privileges granted others and kept them largely out of the political process. To accomplish this, the political parties maintained the machinery necessary to enable their chosen people, once in office, to remain there indefinitely. At every meeting, reformer Torres inveighed against the comfortable continuation of this wrong, trying to provoke thoughtful evaluation, ignite determination, and reinforce hope to inspire his listeners into unified action on their own behalf. Many heard his message and responded to it, registering to vote, speaking up at public meetings and running for public office in mixed districts. The active movement toward needed change was begun.

Frank was devoid of self-seeking in his efforts to involve his own people in the political process. His rhetoric sprang from his own experience from birth onward with the bitter pill of discrimination and bias. He first had seen how this evil blighted and warped lives in his own family; had to stand powerless as Sus was routinely cheated in cutting props for the mine. As an individual he rejected discrimination anywhere, ignoring or crossing ethnic boundaries his whole life long. Under the Constitution, all possessed equal rights, and such he claimed for everyone, working continually to make people see the positive gains for all which resulted from an equal society. This was, he believed, the only way to build a stable community and productive nation that benefited from the efforts of each citizen.

Frank wore his Spanish heritage comfortably and proudly but never became a "professional" Hispanic, using ethnic origin as a club to get his own way. He also rejected doing a cross-over to become a pseudo-Anglo, seeking personal benefit by joining forces with the discriminators. He remained himself, an independent individual with a keen awareness of the injustice against his own people, or against anyone else so treated. To challenge this negative element, his most effective weapons were education and organization on the one hand and the law on the other. When clearly exposed, the costs of prejudice and discrimination spoke against their continuance. The law, when impartially applied, must consider only facts not personal heritage. Bring out the evidence, apply the law, he averred, and the verdict must reinforce the cause of freedom and equality.

His fellow Spanish frequently failed to appreciate Frank's egalitarian attitude. Recognizing his remarkable strength, ability, and dedication, many felt he should be a partisan spokesman for themselves alone. But Torres held his ground, knowing that justice, ultimately, had to be blind, and its application for the good of the whole. Working for partisan ends inevitably resulted in more injustice. Separation into closed, narrow interest groups ultimately set up a competition between such, each bent on its own agenda, and would end up placing its goals in conflict with those of others. A country could not accommodate the demands of all pressure groups and continue as a unified whole. Separatism only led to more conflict and new discrimination against somebody else.

Additionally, Frank's unyielding stand did not go down well with the non-Spanish political establishment in Las Animas County that used and profited from its own exclusionary tactics. Those politicians, interested in men who would work for them rather than for causes, marked him as a trouble maker. It would not do for that "high falutin' Mexican lawyer" to gain any significant political influences, but such was his strength they could not ignore him either.

With his commitment to helping the poor secure justice in court,

Torres' law practice grew steadily. Farmers, ranchers, workers, businessmen, the Spanish and a number of independent Anglos, his clients came from all across the area in response to his reputation for honesty, hard work and knowledge of law. In the aftermath of the crash of 1929, these people's need for legal representation increased as they coped with no jobs, no money, lost lands and without the cushion of unemployment insurance or welfare assistance which would be available only years later. Of these hard hit people, and through all his years of practice, Torres never turned away a single honest person who needed legal help, although he would not touch the cases of those whom he sensed were lying to him. How could one, he asked, advocate or defend if the truth was not there to begin with? He well understood everyday foibles and failings, but drew the line at representing deliberate dishonesty.

The hard-pressed Spanish, hit by the Depression and given short shrift in opportunity by the Anglo dominated establishment, brought their tangled affairs to Torres. Without money for legal fees, they paid what they could in roughly equal amounts of produce and gratitude. He was touched by their efforts, moved by their need, and, at his deepest level, knew money never could be allowed to interfere with or influence his dedication to the law. He did what he felt called to do, what he had studied to do, what he had taken an oath to do, and, come what may, he would keep on doing it. An equal society brought more benefit than any rich lawyer did.

Fulfilling as Frank's practice and volunteer efforts were, another area in his life felt a lack. His parents, brothers and sister all were busy with their own lives and homes, but his own contained an empty spot. The time had come when he began to dream of a home and family of his own. June Nelson had faded to a fondly remembered shadow in the past. Yet, the women he chanced to meet failed to interest him and he developed a half-formed notion of someone special out there if he could find her, and he would settle for no less. Urged on by a need for completion in his life, he began taking a more active interest in community social events.

In the meantime, he continued working to improve the society around him. When he made his career choice, he had recognized that there were two types of law, moral and civil. Moral law was self-imposed, requiring voluntary obedience and self discipline and tended to occur randomly. Although Frank was ruled by moral law, he recognized that from lack of proper home, lack of schooling and church, or lack of inclination, many others were not so governed. To make an equitable, stable society, there had to be universal, enforceable rules and these, not ordained by religion or moral values, must be man-produced in the form of civil law.

Civil law, the necessary foundation and control of society had to enforce obedience, whether or not personally subscribed to by each individual within that society. Law carried the power to raise standards and influence positive behavior for a better society. If the law proved outdated, or contained errors or omissions, citizens were free to change it, using the means of election and recall. Frank Torres loved the law, and in the worst of days when he felt thwarted, insulted, put down, he never lost sight of his vision of what law represented.

Political action provided a proven way to gain equality. Frank was a Republican as had been his father and grandfather and even as a youth, as well as in college, he had paid attention to politics. He witnessed unscrupulous and unqualified men elected to office while good men often were carefully slandered into defeat. For many, the process was simply a game of playing "ins and outs," of conniving and scheming to get the better of the other side, no matter the means. Such a flawed method for selecting representative government ultimately failed everyone. Having watched cross burnings and intimidation by the Ku Klux Klan during the election in Denver, Frank was displeased to find that the Republican party in Trinidad did not disassociate itself from the Klan. Accordingly, he launched an attack within the local precincts against this organization. He knew he courted trouble in doing so.

Torres noted that across the border in New Mexico, politically wily Senator Bronson Cutting had incorporated the Spanish into the Young Men's Republican Clubs, producing great success for the Republicans at election time. Frank did not doubt this could be duplicated in Southern Colorado by a political party sensitive to the constitutional rights and ambitions of the Spanish. To force the party to be more responsive to a standard of equality, Frank pushed the Trinidad Republicans to get rid of the Klan influence, and also to utilize the power of the young Republicans for just purposes. His name began to be mentioned as a possible candidate and it was only a matter of time before he became one.

Frank's first run for office came after the 1928 primary election when one Albert Clamp, withdrew from the campaign, leaving a candidate vacancy on the Republican ticket for the office of State Representative. Although close to the end of the campaign, the chance was too tempting to ignore, and Frank quickly announced his candidacy for which the local newspaper accorded him a neutral biographical story. Although young and having no established base of support or any real clout in the established political circles, he still possessed solid qualification for public office. The Italian and Spanish communities welcomed a new face and his old neighbors up river weighed in solidly to support him. The entrenched powers, however, found him brash and unwilling to accommodate the existing political structure. Accordingly, they sat on the sidelines during the campaign, indirectly encouraging the opposition. By entering the campaign so late, with little money, and lacking an endorsement by the party, he had three strikes against him. Added to that, he was Spanish. Accepting the odds, Frank and his friend, J. Edgar Chenowith, who was running for the senate, campaigned together, keeping the contest clean, sticking to the issues and refraining from running down their opposition.

Torres presented a strong platform, pushing for a Trinidad junior college. Up to this time, Trinidad's young people who wanted to attend college had to leave home and bear the resulting extra financial cost. Those who could not swing the needed money stayed home, their formal education at an end. Frank had breached the invisible but terribly real wall of lack of education the hard way, through his own tireless, solitary pursuit of learning, but few had the inner dedication to confront the task by that route. Frank argued that for the good of the individual, the community, and society, education had to be easier to come by. Other items in his platform were lowering taxes, better roads and quality rural elementary and secondary education.

Election day arrived, an in-between early November day, with the biting chill of late autumn winds off the mountains. The diminishing sun didn't warm against the cut of the air and gust-blown yellow leaves swirled away from shedding trees, golden discs scattered against a pale grey-blue sky. Along the river willows slowly arced to and fro in the wind, showering brown and russet flecks of color on the Purgatoire's clear, shallow waters. Relishing the zest of the day, Frank went early to the polls and cast his vote, youthful optimism that he just might pull it off vying against practical knowledge that winning would be a long shot. Although Chenowith won his position, the rest of the Republican ticket fared less well, with Frank among the losers. He was not particularly dismayed. This had not been his year but other elections lay ahead.

His run brought into clear focus Frank's problem with a Republican party which he saw as bogged down in reactionary policies and unwilling to take a firm stand for right. Added to this, he laughingly reminisced, one campaign experience alone came close to providing an incentive to abandon the party totally. Accompanied by two others, one of them huge and grossly fat, Torres had driven his Ford to Trinchera for a Republican political rally. After several hours of speeches, food and dancing while private politicking went on in corners, it was time to return home. The big fat fellow had disappeared and, after an extended search of the grounds, Torres finally located him in the outhouse where his excess weight had collapsed the seat, plummeting him down into the muck beneath, and he remained wedged in, unable to extricate himself. Holding their noses, Frank and his friend extended a plank and hoisted him out, deposited him, reeking, in the rumble seat and drove swiftly back to Trinidad, keeping the car ahead of the fumes while the fellow complained that they had not retrieved his hat. Although concentrated on issues and goals, sufficient of such foibles and follies occurred on the political scene to still amuse the Judge years later.

Torres' displeasure with the Republican Party increased over its continued coziness with the detested Ku Klux Klan, its failure to represent all groups, a closed agenda and blatant cronyism continued. His outspoken opposition to the Klan netted him anonymous threats in the mail that he would be tarred and feathered and run out of the state of Colorado or carried out in a box unless he silenced himself on the subject. His answer to this attempted intimidation was, "You are wrong, I am right, and I will not be silent." Despite a public offer from Frank, the KKK would not meet him face to face in a debate on political and social philosophy.

Making clear his dissatisfaction with the party's silence on the KKK, Torres stepped down from the presidency of the Republican Spanish American Clubs of Colorado that he had organized so successfully. No one picked up on this rebellion or attempted to discuss his reasons. As the Republicans continued on a path he would not follow, he deemed further participation a waste of his time. Therefore, one day in early 1929, he walked into the County Clerk's office to change his political affiliation and the same evening attended a Democratic Party meeting. Well acquainted with his organizational abilities, the Democrats welcomed the new recruit into their camp, apparently willing to take in the young firebrand and unaware they could be setting themselves up for future problems of their own. Idealism can be difficult to accommodate in a pragmatic and practical world, and the Democratic Party's latest recruit lived his idealism. Busy in his new party of choice, Frank was gratified by a gradual and general disenchantment with the KKK all across Colorado and its fading out of the political picture. Never the less, passing years never dimmed Torres' contempt for what he saw as an organization that dealt in bigotry and cowardice.

While Frank remained a registered Democrat for the rest of his life, he never blindly followed anyone elses dictates in elections, but did his own evaluation of which candidates to support. He studied the record of each man and issue before making up his mind, crossing party lines, never voting for the party, but for the person most qualified to fill the position as the only course a responsible citizen could follow.

9

COURTSHIP AND MARRIAGE

In the spring of 1930, Frank welcomed the change of seasons. By the last of April, Fisher's peak remained rimmed at the top with pure white snow, and up on the pass, the wind still carried a chill. Below, the land stepped downward, evergreens dotting the hillside, the red-brown oak brush not yet out, but in the lower mountain meadows, rosy slabs of rock, fresh scrubbed from the storms of winter, stood out soft and somnolent on the hillsides, and fresh grass grew in incredible greenness across meadow bottoms. Sunlight bathed the town in a soft, warmth of renewed life and possibilities. Along the streets elms thrust forth fresh leaves and a flowering crabapple stood, covered in deep rose pink bloom. Overhead the intense light blue sky stretched to infinity, starkly streaked with windblown white tatters of cloud. Through Trinidad, the Purgatoire ran deep in run-off, swift and muddy, sharply eddying in and out of narrow riffles as it flowed beneath the town bridge. The seasons changed, a man's life moved. Wind and water, dark and light, cold and warm, all in its time, all part of the great eternal circle. Frank felt the renewal and responded with a sort of expectant discontent. All his family had homes of their own, he had a law office. Life held more for him, he knew, and he was impatient to move forward.

As he looked to fill another dimension in his life, Frank was moved to try to express that which spoke to his feelings rather than his reason. Music conveyed in sound what words were unable to say, although he had never progressed beyond group singing, dances, church hymns and concerts. True, the new medium of radio brought musical variety, from jazz to classical, yet music heard from the outside only echoed the music felt within.

Thus, he set out to learn to play the violin as its unique range fit any music, whether played solo or with other instruments. Frank applied action to idea bought an instrument and looked up the town's best known music teacher, presenting himself to the elderly gentleman, one Mr. John Kimball. He explained his hope and Mr. Kimball, as he was addressed by all, after studying him carefully, agreed to give him lessons. Taking up his own violin, Kimball initiated the new student into the rudiments of technique, the appropriate way to hold the instrument, proper positions for his fingers, and how to apply the bow to bring forth music. Attempting to copy the teacher's technique, with fingers tentatively searching and bow flattened across the strings, Frank produced a discordant squawk.

Torres practiced diligently and got through three lessons, aware that Mr. Kimball frowned over his efforts. At the end of the fourth session Mr. Kimball shook his head saying, "I haven't the patience to try to make you into the violinist you will never be. It is a waste of your money and my time. However, I do have something for you to do. I want you to marry my daughter, Crusita!" For once speechless, Torres' yellow eyes reflected startled surprise and swift consideration of the idea. He already knew who she was, and some of her background which included strong individuals and significant achievement much as his own did.

Although the earliest ancestors of Crusita Kimball had arrived in New Mexico with Oñate in 1598, the beginning of family records came with *Taoseño*, George Horace Long. He first arrived in Taos from Kentucky in 1833 accompanying a caravan of traders. The young adventurer liked Taos and its people, and remained to negotiate a marriage with Juan Anacleto de Herrera for his daughter, Juana María de Herrera, which allied him with one of the established old Taos families. The marriage produced four children, a daughter, Guadalupe and sons Manuel, George and Benito.

According to historical references, Long cultivated a vineyard, and operated a distillery, producing the hot, raw Taos Lightning whiskey and selling it at a public tavern he kept in a separate wing of the house away from family quarters. From this lucrative enterprise, he branched out to serve as a justice of the peace, and became a leading Taos citizen. Guadalupe, his daughter married Alfred Bent, son of the first Territorial Governor, Charles Bent, and bore him two sons before Alfred was killed in a card game with a drifter and former camel driver for the United States Army known as Greek George. Bent was shot at point blank range and in the confusion, Greek George fled. He was pursued by Kit Carson, uncle of Guadalupe, but managed to escape in the darkness to live the rest of his life out in California.

Not long after this and tired of the turmoil in New Mexico, Long sold out in Taos, took his family including Guadalupe and the two grandsons, and moved into southern Colorado to settle on the upper Purgatoire River at a spot which came to be known as Long's Canyon. In short order, he again emerged as one of the area's prominent citizens. His sons went out on their own as homesteaders and Long negotiated an advantageous marriage for Guadalupe with wealthy and influential rancher-politician, George Thompson.

Before the move, Long had arranged the marriage of his Santa Fe educated son, José Manuel, to Cresencia Martínez, who was related to the controversial Taos priest, Padre Antonio Martínez. Children born to Manuel and Cresencia were Berenice, Esther, Jesse, Alfred, Marina and Abe. Esther Long, Crusita Kimball's mother, was born on May 5, 1891 in the Long's Canyon home. An early photograph of Esther and her sister Berenice clad in long dark dresses shows two very attractive young women with a strong resemblance to their mother. Another photograph from the same time, reveals brothers Jesse and Alfred as handsome young bucks in suits and stylish starched collars, their expressions a mixture of mischief and high good humor.

When Esther turned eighteen in 1908, her parents arranged a marriage for her to Porfirio Montoya, an upstanding young man with a job in the coal mines. The couple's first child, daughter María Crusita, arrived on October 8, 1909, and a son, Lawrence, followed on August 3, 1913. Four months after the latter birth, Porfirio was lost in the deadly explosion at the Dawson coal mine on October 22, which killed over two hundred miners. He was buried in the Dawson graveyard, joining scores of fellow miners who earlier had died the same way. He left a small competency to his wife, inadequate to take care of the rearing and educating his children.

Esther was left to cope with her tragic loss as the mining situation turned increasingly ugly. Deplorable working conditions increasingly strained relations between management and miners throughout southern Colorado and northern New Mexico. Union organization gave miners the strength to confront company management and try to force change. Industry, reaping record profits and expanding rapidly, balked at granting any substantive concessions and met unionization with hostility. Violence broke out with bombings and vandalism on the side of the miners and beatings and intimidation from industry. Government, caught in the middle, wrung its hands and made ineffectual motions at maintaining public order, but seemed to find itself perpetually on the side of industrial money and power rather then the valid rights of the Spanish. The flamboyant eighty-two year old avowed socialist Mary Harris, known as "Mother Jones" by miners, arrived on the scene to act her usual part of "disturber." She traveled from coast to coast, exhorting miners to organize and also, from coast to coast, found herself locked up in local jails for disturbing the peace. In deference to her age and sex, she served her jail time in Trinidad mostly in custody at Mt. St. Raphael hospital. Upon release, she steamed straight back to the coal fields, glorying in every minute of her confrontations.

An inevitable showdown between labor and management took place during 1913-14, some fifteen miles north of Trinidad at Ludlow where the rebel miner's tent city was attacked on April 20, 1914 by the Colorado State Militia who torched the camp, trapping and killing women and children under the flaming tents. With both sides shocked by the event, a truce was negotiated which improved, but did not correct all wrongs against the mine workers, nor did it stop random confrontations. But the "Ludlow Massacre" as it came to be known served as a rallying cry throughout the mine fields giving impetus to unions and reform. Reflecting on the situation, Judge Torres observed that unjust working conditions made unionization necessary to act in the interests of powerless citizens economically trapped by the greed and indifference of industrial management. Still he deplored the violence and loss of life that occurred before needed remedial legislation was passed, noting that it was the law that finally brought a measure of fairness and justice, not acts of violence.

From the tragedy of losing her husband and the ugliness in the coal business, Esther Long Montoya carried a hatred and fear of the mines the rest of her life, refusing to allow any member of her family to work in them. Widowed at age twenty-three with two small children, Esther had few options and found the most practical solution was to acquire another husband. In 1915, she married widower John B. Kimball, Trinidad's most prominent musician. Kimball, a stiff and serious man, twenty-three years older than Esther, adopted her children, gave her an established position, a home in town, more children and a settled life under the restraints of genteel poverty.

Kimball had been born one of two sons of an Anglo Fort Union soldier, Henry Martin Kimball, who abandoned his local Spanish wife and his children a few years after the marriage in the familiar sorry tale that left an impoverished family to bear the life-long scar of rejection. The oldest son, John, taught himself to play a homemade violin while still a child, helping support his mother and brother by playing for pennies at the stage coach stop in Wagon Mound and later the railroad stop there, before moving the family to Trinidad during his teenage years. By the time he confronted Frank Torres with the startling offer of his daughter Crusita, Kimball not only gave music lessons, played at weddings and special events, but directed the choir in the Catholic Church and also the municipal orchestra. In addition to adopting Crusita and Lawrence, he fathered six more children with Esther, John Henry, Catherine, Manuel, Carmen, Theresa and Charlotte.

Kimball is remembered by his son John Henry as a rigid and demanding elderly parent and husband, over-compensating for the lack of a father in his own life by attempting to shape his children along rigorous moral and religious values. Sweet and loving Esther made a patient and self-sacrificing wife and mother, relying more and more on her eldest, Crusita, for assistance and companionship.

Lack of funds dictated that Crusita go to public high school instead of Holy Trinity where her friends went, but she accepted the family limitations, and made excellent grades there, helped her mother with the extended family, became a skilled pianist, and lived obediently under Mr. Kimball's rigid supervision, dressing modestly and eschewing the dates and parties enjoyed by her peers. Her high school graduation picture reveals a lovely young woman of true natural beauty, facing the camera with a slightly impish smile. Her wide-spaced dark eyes sparkle beneath graceful, level brows, and her dark hair is cut in a fashionable short bob. There is honesty, openness and trust, without artifice, and a vivacious aliveness in her young face. After high school, she took a course in pre-school education at the newly launched Trinidad Junior College, for which Frank had campaigned, and was hired as a kindergarten teacher where she worked at the time Kimball made his startling offer to Torres.

Given the social standard of the day which accorded single women small respect, and the fact that she was twenty years old, decided Mr. Kimball that the time had come for her to marry. Another consideration was his own advancing age, where, if Crusita were settled in an advantageous marriage, she could assist her mother and siblings after he was gone. All he needed was the right man, and when Frank Torres appeared in his studio to assault his ears with scrapes and squawks on the violin, Mr. Kimball ran a list of the young man's qualifications through his mind: from a solid old family, highly educated, healthy, strong, totally ethical, Catholic from birth, and making a name for himself in his law practice, politics and community service. This was the right man. Torres would be a responsible husband, a successful lawyer with a reliable income and Crusita would hold a position of respect in the community. A father could do no better for his daughter.

Although Kimball's blunt proposition caught Torres unprepared, Frank was interested. Crusita, among the local girls, stood out in her natural refinement and innate elegance. She was exactly what Frank wanted, he realized in a flash of revelation, and Kimball's proposal opened an answer to the unfilled dimension in his life. Marriage and family would give balance and meaning to it. Yes, he told Mr. Kimball, he would be willing if Crusita agreed. Mr. Kimball assured him she would.

What did Crusita think of the idea? After the first shock, her reaction was obedience to the man who had given her home, fatherly attention, and a loving family. She knew he only looked to what he saw as best for her and she owed him too much to go against his wishes. She said all that was respectful, but she experienced inward uncertainty. She knew who Frank Torres was, but she had never exchanged a single word with him and what she felt for this man was precisely nothing.

However, such arranged marriage contracts had not yet been entirely discarded among the local families. Although the idea might have been a bit antiquated in the late 1920s, Mr. Kimball remained a rigid product of the old school, firmly believing that such unions usually succeeded better than the impulsive and transient attractions which were forged into the romantic marriages ushered in by the flapper era. Hundreds of years of happy homes and close family units showed the system resulted in stability and order. Crusita decided all she could do was wait and see what developed.

Frank took up his courting with advance assurance that his suit would be accepted, but he was no fool. Crusita scarcely knew who he was, so he would give her time for he refused to take an unwilling bride. Never considering the possibility of failure, he determined to win her for himself. Although by nature impatient, uncomfortable with what he saw as the pointless artifice of the social scene, Frank duly presented himself on the Kimball doorstep to begin his campaign. Crusita greeted him with perfect courtesy.

As the courtship proceeded, Crusita began to find she genuinely admired his idealism, his goals for a better world and his unfailing courtesy. Frank, in turn, came to enjoy Crusita's lively and independent mind, as well as her beauty and charm, and in the process fell deeply in love for all time. This was no vague, distant dream, this was immediate, solid and true. Mr. Kimball had set the idea in motion, but what carried Frank and Crusita to the altar was far more substantial than a simple contract.

J. Frank Torres and Crusita Kimball were married on December 26, 1930 at Holy Trinity church with Crusita's favorite uncle Jesse Long and his wife, cousin Sallie Kimball Long, as witnesses to the quiet ceremony. The pinch of the Depression failed to keep Frank from taking Crusita to Denver for a brief honeymoon where he showed her the city and introduced her to friends from law school. Typically Frank, they took in places of cultural interest, ate in good restaurants, but skipped the glittering nightclubs that he disapprovingly considered a mindless waste of time and a dubious moral atmosphere. The newlyweds came back to set up housekeeping in Trinidad in a neat white bungalow at 1116 Grant Avenue on a street of well kept homes.

10

MARRIED LIFE

The marriage was good from the beginning. Frank vastly enjoyed being a husband and head of household. It gave his work an extra dimension of meaning, something that was uniquely his own. Crusita, too, found happiness in her situation, felt pride in her new husband, delighted in a home of her own., although there were adjustments for both. By virtue of being thirteen years older than she, Frank endlessly, and somewhat unsuccessfully, attempted to guide and direct his petite wife. But the dutiful daughter did not translate automatically into the dutiful spouse.

Crusita claimed the adult right to be her own person and although Frank was quick to issue orders, she never felt compelled to obey them unquestioningly. To Frank's bafflement, he would find, after the fact, that although she politely listened to his mandates, the point of difference had been resolved according to her wishes. Opposing viewpoints, however, were not a continual circumstance, since husband and wife agreed on the basics: family, politics, and values. Most of the time, Crusita agreed with Frank's views, and for his part Frank found that amazingly no all-out disasters resulted from his wife's independence and, in time, he came to have faith in her judgment. Through an inner core of compassionate strength, Crusita connected the self-contained Frank with his own humanness, enjoying the challenge of his impatient brilliance. Realistically, she would have lived a life of frustration with a lesser man while the demanding Frank would have crushed a weaker woman.

Crusita soon took over Frank's law office, serving as receptionist and secretary for his growing practice which, by then, extended west into the San Luis Valley, as well as to Aguilar, and Walsenberg to the north and other Las Animas Country towns east of the Divide. The wealthy

Salazar family in San Luis retained Torres to represent them, and this prominent family's endorsement brought cases from other residents of the valley who felt comfortable to have one of their own as lawyer. To be accessible to his clients, Frank leased a small adobe house in San Luis, enjoying the familiar and unspoiled Spanish ambiance of the oldest town in Colorado. The picturesque village still had a "common" on which all could graze their animals, and daily life kept the friendly and unhurried pace of bygone days.

Frank was paid cash by the Salazars, but among the poorer residents of San Luis, he accepted whatever they could manage, ranging from livestock to chickens, fruit and vegetables. But, no matter what, all received the legal representation they needed.

One money pinched client whom he had successfully defended presented Torres with a large hog as payment. Undaunted, he had the pig slaughtered and took home a couple of hundred pounds of fresh pork for his young wife to put up. Crusita was dubious but game and Frank volunteered to help with the canning and curing of the meat. They also made *chicharrones*, his favorite snack, rendering the fat out of the cut up pieces of skin in a skillet over a hot fire until they achieved puffy, tasty crispness. Several evenings passed before all was done, the loin cooked and pressure sealed in glass jars, hams and bacon placed in a brine cure to be deposited later in the family smokehouse. Sausage also was made using a hand grinder, then seasoned and packed in casings to be smoked. For a long time after, Frank confessed, he was so heartily sick of the heavy, oily smell of pork that he could not face bacon, much less, *chicharrones*. Still, the meat made a welcome addition to the Torres larder in those pinched Depression times.

Poor people formed the bulk of Torres' clients, and that was the way he wanted it. They were the ones most in need of help and least apt to receive justice. In a representative case, he defended a Basque sheepherder accused of murdering a man who tried to run the sheep out of their pasture. Frank presented his case that the man acted in self-defense. He justified this defense by arguing that the sheepherder, as a simple, uneducated man who reacted protectively against the threat to his flock, had followed emotion rather than reason and restraint. This gained a reduced sentence with early parole, avoiding the death penalty. For his efforts, Frank received a choice lamb from the man's family. Those Torres served were honest people, meeting their responsibilities as best they could, and they needed him. This was why he had studied law in the first place.

Frank's interpretation of good citizenship required support, work and perseverence for right causes, prominent among these, his long-term commitment to equal rights and opportunity for the Spanish. In addition to his law practice, much of what he did was for free or at marginal rates, he traveled and organized for the Democrat Spanish American Club, and also involved himself in local and state politics. He became intensely interested in the new credit union movement, attending an informational meeting in Denver to learn for himself how these institutions operated. He also began working in the Alianza Hispano Americana, an insurance and fraternal organization for the Spanish, and, faithful to his conviction that youth must be shaped for responsible adulthood, he led a perpetual troop of Boy Scouts.

Scouting gave Torres his most enduring activity. During his teaching years he had found that his scouts continually achieved better academically than those not in the program, acquired new skills and conducted themselves with more confidence. From their experience in scouting, his boys would be better able to lead in the community and work to improve life around them as they grew to manhood. He saw his troop as Trinidad's future in that scouting taught integrity, service to God, to Country and to fellow man. He also endorsed the Girl Scouts program as producing the same results through exposure to needed role models and instruction.

Frank concentrated on teaching, disciplining and enjoying the variety of his scouts, and they rewarded his efforts with enthusiasm, application to their projects and fierce loyalty to Torres himself. Talking to his former scouts, now elderly men, they recalled that he never squelched their fun, but maintained firm control, requiring each to act constructively, with due consideration for the person and property of others. In their scouting days, the boys had quoted their leader as the final word in any argument and adopted his speech patterns and mannerisms. In this mutually happy relationship Torres believed he gained more from the boys than they did from him.

With increasingly varied and complex cases in his law practice, Frank frequently spent after-hours working at home. A baffling murder case brought forth this effort. He took the defense of one George Córdova, accused of slaying a Mrs. Katerina Toller at the Toller general store near the village of Hastings, Colorado. Mrs. Toller, daughter-in-law of a wealthy family, had been gunned down in her and her husband's store by three bullets from a 25 caliber automatic fired by an unknown assailant. Community outrage demanded prompt action, and proceeding on a tip by a local named Allen Box that Córdova had been in the store at the time of the shooting, police arrested him as a prime suspect.

By the time Torres met his client, newspapers had sensationalized the case far beyond Hastings, reporting that during interrogation by the local sheriff, Córdova had changed details of his story more than once, even accusing the tipster, Allen Box, of having committed the murder for the eleven dollars and twenty cents stolen from the cash register during the crime. Box, who also had been at the store, denied it. With an acceptable suspect in hand, the sheriff had no inclination to pursue other leads. The case, which had generated high interest and partisan emotions for a speedy conviction, rested on circumstantial evidence only. Given the prevailing social order of the day, and the fact that the victim as well as the tipster were Anglo, there was no doubt in the Anglo public mind that the "Mexican" had done it. With local sentiment on his side, the District Attorney prepared to ask for the death penalty, knowing a guilty verdict would advance his political career as being tough on crime.

The Córdova family, long time residents of the community, expressed to Torres their certainty that their son would never commit murder. Frank arrived at the jail to question his client and found a badly frightened young man, incapable of relating a coherent tale. Listening to the accused still left the question up in the air; possibly Córdova was guilty, equally possible, he was not, but by law he was innocent until proven guilty. Frank was convinced that unverifiable circumstantial evidence could never be sufficient to invoke the death penalty.

As Frank reviewed the evidence establishing his argument, he recognized that the taint of racism made a case for acquittal almost impossible. Still, he counseled Córdova to enter a plea of not guilty. This done before the all Anglo jury, the trial opened to newspaper headlines and a crowded courtroom.

The District Attorney cited his slim circumstantial evidence, assuring the jury it all pointed directly at Córdova as the cold-blooded murderer. Attorney Torres in defense exposed discrepancies, emphasized that the evidence was circumstantial only and based solely on the testimony of Box. At the end of days of testimony and legal sparring, the jury found Córdova guilty with a death sentence hanging over the prisoner.

Torres immediately filed a motion for a new trial charging the verdict was not supported by evidence, contrary to applicable law, contrary to the law of evidence, and the court had erred in instructions to the jury and in allowing statements made by Córdova to be used against him. The judge rejected the motion but, conceding that Torres raised reasonable doubt, denied the death penalty, imposing life imprisonment. Córdova served fourteen years before receiving parole. The unanswered questions in the case stirred up interest far beyond the little community where the crime occurred, with the murder and trial written up in *Famous Detective Stories* magazine under the title "Who Killed Katarina?" On the road home from Denver sometime later, Torres experienced the odd coincidence of stopping in Pueblo for gas and there spotting the newly released George Córdova at the filling station. He greeted his former client and drove him home to his family. The magazine's question still remains.

A sameness marked the bulk of Frank's cases: real estate transactions, foreclosures, petty crime, business contracts, wills and estates and, once in a while, one involving him emotionally as well as professionally. Such was the case when a Fermín Martínez was brought to trial in District Court at Trinidad for the murder of Frank's cousin, Alfredo Torres, son of his uncle Juan Bautista Torres. After a wedding celebration attended by Fermín Martínez, Alfredo and his brother, Juan Bautista, Jr., went with Martínez to his home where Alfredo and Fermín subsequently got into a dispute. Wanting no part of it, Juan left, getting as far as the front yard when he heard a yelled threat by Fermín and a gunshot. Juan dashed back inside to find his brother mortally wounded, shot at close range.

Working for the District Attorney, Torres prosecuted the case where the gun, owned by Martínez, the bullet, powder burns on the victim, and testimony of Juan all implicated Fermín. Faced with solid evidence, the defense attorneys angered Frank with attempts to intimidate the witness Juan Bautista Jr. by placing in the courtroom within Juan's range of vision Fermín's family members who had threatened Juan. Torres won the case and a life sentence for Martínez, but sadly reflected that legal justice could not undo the price Martínez and Alfredo paid for losing their tempers. The fact that alcohol probably contributed to the crime confirmed Frank's belief that if liquor were kept out of the equation, society would function more harmoniously and countless lives would be spared. Although sentiment did not rule his practice, sensitivity marked all his work. Legal cases involved flesh and blood people, of infinite variety, gifts and limitations, advantages and disadvantages, and all this weighed in whatever problem the lawyer attempted to resolve.

Away from Frank's law office, Crusita busied herself with the couple's home while Frank gave attention to politics as an essential in building a more just society. Law was tied to legislation enacted by elected politicians but those from Trinidad still failed to include the rights of the Spanish in any amendment or initiation of laws. Highly articulate in both Spanish and English, Frank strongly presented his ideas vocally and in writing: First testing his arguments on Crusita, he then delivered impassioned speeches at political meetings and sent out carefully reasoned letters to the local papers advocating positions and reforms. For many politicians, involvement in politics mainly offered power and financial reward for themselves and their friends. Not so Torres who saw this as a perversion of the process. His long time Trinidad friend, Lloyd Romero, observed that unfailingly the more Frank insisted on the high road, the more his political opposition took the low road against him.

The few office holders and politicians who held almost permanent control of Las Animas County politics sized Frank up as no "yes-man" and manipulated to keep him on the outside, useful but not of the inner circle of influence. Lacking approval by the local machine, he faced party opposition if he struck out on his own. Still believing that if he proved himself he would have to be fully accepted by his party, Frank worked hard in the Young Democratic League of Las Animas County, while still privately rejecting a blind, straight-ticket, party above all, knee jerk vote. He and Crusita studied the issues, evaluated candidates, and then voted for the ones with best qualifications and highest standards, whether Democrat, Republican, or even an occasional Independent. Frank avoided political factions and had no respect for those who evaded issues and used the process for their own gain. As he pithily observed, "The pigs all lie in the muck together but when one pig gets up and walks around, the common dirt still sticks."

After experiencing politics at close hand, Crusita hoisted a flag. She did not like what it involved, wanted nothing to do with campaigning and political functions, sending Frank off on his own into a world with the less than admirable ambitions and agendas it so frequently involved. Politics, she acknowledged, was necessary in a democracy, but also could represent the worst in the governing process, acquiring a life of its own, complete with reincarnation taking place after what appeared to be natural death at the polls.

11
LIFE IN THE DEPRESSION

Although the Depression continued, Frank and Crusita did not delay parenthood by waiting for a better time and their first child, Frank, Jr., was born on September 9, 1931. Wearing paternity as a badge of honor, Frank confidently faced its challenges and worked harder to improve the world in which his son would grow up.

Financially pinched by Depression realities, Frank took on as many jobs in the legal area as he could find, earning a listing in the 1931 Trinidad City Directory as deputy city clerk. As he juggled clients and city business, he remained optimistic for the future, convinced so large and varied a country as America could find solutions to its problems. Although yet unseen, forces of coming change already cast their shadows. Franklin Delano Roosevelt was the Democratic candidate for president in 1932, and Torres, committed to the changes Roosevelt promised, campaigned for him throughout Las Animas County, particularly in the Spanish American Clubs. Roosevelt's ideas sparked widespread enthusiasm across the country for his proposals, with countless hard-pressed people switching parties from Republican to Democrat. Riding the wave of popularity, Roosevelt surged to victory over Herbert Hoover. By and large, the voters who switched party remained Democrats and, in so doing, changed the national political balance of power for years to come.

Recognizing Frank Torres' pivotal role in setting up the Colorado Democratic Spanish American Clubs, the members elected him president of their organization in 1932. At a banquet held in his honor in Trinidad, the new president waved aside cheers to deliver a down to earth speech that now was not a time to sit on their laurels but, instead, to build on their successes, use their vote, raise their issues. Crusita stayed quietly by Frank's side, proud and glad for him, but more spectator than participant.

These years brought changes, happy and sad, to the Torres family. Crusita's brother, nineteen year old Lawrence, died of uremic poisoning on March 12, 1932. A second son, promptly named Lawrence, was born to Crusita and Frank on September 17, the same year. Less than twelve months later, on July 18, 1933, Mr. Kimball died at age 65 after a brief illness. As the families grieved their losses, Esther faced the problem of raising a growing family with less money than the task demanded. This was precisely the situation Mr. Kimball had planned against and, as he had hoped, brought Frank and Crusita to the aid of Esther. Frank, in addition to monetary help for the family, became a substitute father to the Kimball children, and Crusita a strong assistant to ease her mother's daily burden of work and worry.

Frank, Crusita, Frank Jr. and Lawrence.

The year, 1933, found Torres busier than ever. The deepening Depression brought more foreclosures on land and homes with some one third of all American farmers losing their properties to banks and moneyed investors who acquired the distressed acreage and assets at rock bottom prices. When the Depression finally turned, these opportunists grew wealthier still. But for the victims, this catastrophe changed the face and future of rural life in America. New government regulations and subsidies initiated to give relief gradually became entrenched as a part of farming. These subsidies, and later enacted tax breaks, enticed big business in and opened the door for corporate agricultural investment and brought long range decline for the family farm.

J. Frank Torres searched for better outcomes and did his best on legal problems of people in outlying towns and rural areas of Las Animas County, but the law was the law. New government programs promised relief, and new ideas for change proliferated but nothing had yet reached Trinidad. The most controversial of these ideas, Communism, gained strength in American intellectual circles, particularly college campuses, and created bitter political division. Although totalitarian in method, this new philosophy appealed to idealism and anti-Fascism. Frank was bothered by its tenets, believing absolute subservience to the state would conflict with the human need for individual freedom. He found it ironic, also, that adherents of anti-church Marxism set out like aggressive evangelicals to convert the world. Unless he was badly mistaken, giving power to Communism would create more social problems and conflicts than it would solve. People needed more freedom rather than less, and so he stated in discussions.

Frank added another obligation to his busy schedule when he was elected in 1933 to Syndico, the governing board of the Alianza Hispano Americana (AHA), a Tucson based Spanish fraternal and insurance organization that he had joined in the late 1920s and for which he had served as organizer in the Spanish communities of Colorado. The stated goals of this organization, to provide savings through life insurance and foster social and cultural identity through its activities, if realized, would bring the Spanish members a large step forward into equality in financial services and recognition of their citizen's rights. These were high among Frank's priorities as he found it totally unacceptable that the Spanish, accounted bad risks by existing institutions, were routinely denied life insurance or savings and loan services. The AHA, as the society was known, offered a remedy for this problem that, in Frank's opinion, made it well worth his extra effort to work for the organization's growth and influence.

Frank also became city attorney for the town of Aguilar, northwest of Trinidad, helping it apply for federal assistance programs. His whole focus was to reduce the Depression-spawned difficulties and disruptions in the lives of suffering people in Southern Colorado. It was a matter of justice.

Aside from providing a dependable income for Crusita and their two boys, Frank Torres was not overly disturbed by being pinched for cash. If others were poor through no fault of their own, he saw no corollary that he should be enriched because of their misfortune. He was doing what he wanted to do, what needed to be done, and what would secure equal treatment for those who came to him, and that was enough.

Since the Depression posed the most immediate and formidable problem confronting the nation, Roosevelt used his "brain trust" of advisors to come up with a national recovery program. This group laid out a plan to use federal work projects to bolster the economy. These were launched as a series of alphabet lettered government agencies, the NRA, National Recovery Act, the WPA, Works Progress Act, the CCC, Civilian Conservation Corps, and the AAA, Agriculture Adjustment Act, to launch what was called the "New Deal," a massive, jobs producing approach to end the Depression.

During this time, Frank was appointed Las Animas County Attorney, in charge of civil and criminal complaints. One remembered case handed him a legal hot potato. A young girl in her mid-teens claimed to have been raped by what Torres termed a "well connected young blade in his twenties" who came from a prominent family. The young man's parents exerted strong pressure for Frank to drop the case, letting it be known they would be most appreciative if he had it dismissed. Torres firmly rejected the hint of a bribe. The angry parents then spread the story that the girl willingly participated, hoping to trap their son into marriage and, that in effect, she asked for it, an old, familiar charge.

Frank interrogated both plaintiff and defendant, evaluating what rang true, what sounded false. He considered the age of the girl, her lack of experience and infatuation. Against this, he balanced the young man's ill concealed contempt for the girl and lack of remorse, blaming the girl and confident his parents' money would get him off. From the evidence, Frank became convinced the girl had been romantically foolish, the innocent victim of a conceited, irresponsible older male who took advantage of her. He pursued the case with vigor, winning a verdict of guilty and a prison term for the young man. The parents vindictively used every opportunity thereafter to try to damage Torres politically or professionally but without effect.

In Frank's life the limitations of the twenty-four hour day served as the only real check-rein on his schedule. Through it all, he managed to remain in close touch with his parents in Cokedale where they, too, struggled with the problems of the Depression. Miners and cokers like Sus worked an average of one day a week and residents relied on home gardens, rabbits and chickens for food, selling eggs and vegetables and fall-gathered piñon nuts for small amounts of cash. Everyone watched his pennies but none went hungry or lost his home.

In Las Animas County, as elsewhere, crime and gangster activity had accelerated during Prohibition and going dry had not turned off drinking. The thirsty simply went outside the law for their alcohol, yielding enormous profits to bootleggers. After watching a decade of futile efforts to close down liquor sources and suppliers, Torres favored repeal of the Amendment. Better not to have a law at all rather than an unenforceable one that encouraged disrespect and disregard for all law. Consumption of alcohol actually appeared to increase as people found breaking the law somehow daring and fun. Compounding the problem, bootleg rotgut liquor could disable or kill.

The Eighteenth Amendment demonstrably had not worked and Roosevelt persuaded Congress to pass the Twenty-first Amendment ending the failed crusade. The ensuing challenge, as Frank saw it, would be to frame laws which allowed citizens the right to drink but also would set up rules controlling appropriate use of alcohol and establishing penalties for breaking those laws. These turned out to be a long time in coming.

Torres had become known as a leader well beyond Trinidad for his organizational work on political issues and social problems as well as for his law practice. With this in mind, Colorado's U.S. Senator, Alva B. Adams wrote him in June, 1935, that he had recommended Frank's appointment as attorney for the southern Otero County Land Readjustment Project. This was tantamount to approval that quickly came. The newly created agency attempted to help farmers retain their land, and later was absorbed into another New Deal project. During his tenure in the position, Torres worked hard at securing loans on more lenient terms, avoiding bankruptcy claims and enrolling farmers in government programs that helped them hang on. He was convinced that to have these people reduced to indigent status served no beneficial cause and created serious social problems for the future.

As the Blue Eagle emblem of the NRA flew across the skies of America proclaiming, "We Do Our Part," Frank Torres' name quickly surfaced as the man to head the WPA as Labor Relations Manager and get projects running in Las Animas and Huerfano Counties. Frank received a call from General Paul Shriver, active in Roosevelt's administration and a friend from Westminister Law School, who asked Torres to accept the position. Frank listened, then told his old friend that he did not want it. When Shriver inquired why not, Frank explained that as he read the position it was clear the job would be hemmed in by so many procedural regulations the program inevitably would bog down in red tape and, besides, he had a busy law practice. Persuasively, Shriver assured him the job was flexible enough to allow for his legal commitments, so to quit worrying, ignore the regulations, and get on with it. He would be given a free hand. When Torres asked, "Where's the office?" Shriver replied, "There is none yet, just go hang your hat where you can find a place." Aware of the desperate need for jobs in his area, Torres finally agreed but stated his terms, "I'll do it, but I'll do it my own way!"

He quickly rented a downtown, second story office, hired staff and set to work with characteristic zeal, buying the initial office supplies out of his own pocket. Frank met with out-of- work men for an already approved construction project at Trinidad Junior College, evaluated their qualifications and hired a crew, choosing from among them a superintendent for the job. To head the needed design work in the WPA office, he also hired one E. J. Roberts as chief engineer.

Frank was pleased to be able to improve the college that he saw as a vital community asset, and promptly set his men to work there. As he got into the operations of the WPA, he tried to locate a project in each community of both counties as a means of distributing jobs fairly. In eastern Colorado's blackest and dirtiest dust bowl days, his men built a new schoolhouse for the small plains town of Kim. They also constructed the handsome Memorial Square Heritage Center in Trinidad, a bold and romantic medieval castle style complex, adding to the town a structure of lasting charm.

Pushed by multiple demands, Torres spent minimum time in his WPA office, leaving it under the direction of his efficient young secretary Sarah Cunningham while he oversaw work in the field. Sarah, recalling that time, said of Frank, "He was a perfect gentleman with nothing false about him." His engineer Roberts, in charge of design work supplied the blueprints as Torres spent long hours tracking from job to job and snatching time where he could to attend to his other responsibilities. His exacting standards dictated that nothing be ignored, nothing neglected, and this included his own family.

Frank sometimes ran into problems that hindered the work, and his short fused temper flared each time, be it stupidity, laziness, dishonesty, or his old archenemy, racism. Every once in a while, he admitted, he had the urge to punch someone out, but although his fists itched, brawling was not in his rational style. He fought best using his mind and words and dealt with each situation after investigating coolly and carefully. Worthwhile achievement demanded effort and discipline of body, mind and spirit directed to the benefit of others.

He kept to this principle when he instigated a new program, unconnected to WPA work, by taking on the task of providing temporary assistance to homeless hoboes. Many of them wound up in Trinidad, which was a transportation crossroads. These were men who had hit bottom and hopped a ride in whatever direction the road and rails went, hoping for a break. The hobo rejects of a crippled society were hungry, dirty, and defeated, and created a civic nuisance with panhandling and petty thievery. Frank could not remedy their situation as jobs were reserved for county residents, but by hitting up agencies, churches, and civic groups, pointing out that here was a clear chance to provide help for the most needy victims of a national crisis beyond their control. He succeeded in pulling together enough money to rent space in a vacant downtown building and he opened its doors to the men on the street.

What the derelicts met there were typical Torres conditions and rules; each must submit to delousing and a bath with clothes taken to be washed. No alcohol was permitted and civility must be maintained. They received a clean bed, three meals a day for three days to rest and regroup. Their tattered clothes were mended and, as needed, replacement garments were supplied by the local WPA women's sewing project. Operations at the new shelter were unpredictable; the cook got drunk on vanilla extract and, with the contrariness of human nature, some hoboes drew a line at submitting to delousing and a bath, departing in a huff. Frank's shelter could not solve problems or produce jobs where there were none, but he felt that in a small way it helped give back to each a temporary measure of self-respect as on the fourth day the drifters took back to the rails and the roads. This early one-man program anticipated the efficient homeless shelters of today.

The "Dust Bowl" added another negative to the Depression's grip. Prolonged drought and stunted vegetation on plowed up land exposed to the perpetual plains winds produced black blizzards where choking, air borne dust obscured the midday sun, producing an eerie twilight mood of hopeless misery. In those tough times the WPA projects jobs became the economic salvation of Las Animas and Huerfano counties. Cash paid those working on the various jobs began to circulate, people began to hope. Another major long term gain came in 1936-37 when the WPA issued everyone in Las Animas County a social security number from the newly enacted federal law which, through a federal tax on earnings, enabled people to accumulate funds for their old age.

Torres hired more workers as more WPA projects were approved. The local newspaper printed an admiring article on the work being done, writing that the WPA had provided "Many beautiful and outstanding school structures, public buildings, improved recreational grounds, highways, bridges, and many other civic advantages and modernistic developments." These were long term community benefits, and Torres kept his workmen aware that no money would be wasted on malingerers.

Generally, his crews did their jobs with only a rare dust up. However, one incident was in tipsy progress when Frank drove out to a bridge project at Aguilar to find his men boisterously drinking and partying, their tools and equipment idle. Angrily calling them together, he pointedly reviewed the terms of their employment, offering the chance to quit the job if they didn't like it, or get to work and not let the lapse recur if they wished to retain it. For good measure he fired the project manager and replaced him on the spot. This created outrage because the new appointee, although well qualified, happened to be Anglo while the man he replaced was Spanish. A majority Spanish crew viewed this as treason from one of their own. The scrupulously non-discriminating Torres, as usual, had ignored ethnicity and looked only at ability, but the result was a near riot. Frank refused to be intimidated and faced down the shouting and fist waving men. This was America, he reminded them, where all men enjoyed equality under the law without fear or favor. Their job was to help build that America, not tear it down. He didn't care what they did on their own time, but in no way would he countenance any action that interfered with their performance during work hours. He then repeated his offer of either get to work or get out. They eyed him resentfully as all got back to work.

One of his favorite projects was at Monument Lake, thirty-five miles up river from Trinidad where he built a modern recreation complex just above Stonewall, the sentinel upright dike that cuts across the high mountain valley. The lake is perhaps a half-mile in length, rimmed on three sides by evergreens, and the air is refreshingly cool from the snowy peaks above. Long used by locals for fishing and camping, Torres' workmen enlarged the lake with a small dam on the North Fork of the Purgatoire, improved road access and built pueblo style adobe cabins, a recreation hall and other conveniences for visitors. It provided a lasting economic boost. Las Animas County outdoor lovers flocked to the new facility and ever since tourists have found their way up the valley, stayed to enjoy the water and mountains and, departing, left cash in the local tills.

12
THE BUSY TIMES

Filling WPA jobs gave Frank the thankless task of selecting those most eligible for work among the many who needed the positions so urgently. He tried to squeeze as many as possible into the programs from an area that overflowed with the jobless. Among the needy ones who qualified under federal guidelines was Frank's mother in law, the widowed Esther Long Kimball. Although not a robust woman, Esther had scrambled after Mr. Kimball's death to keep the family clothed and fed by taking in washing and ironing. However, the housewives who had employed her began to do the work themselves to save money and she was called less and less. Frank found her a job in the WPA sewing project that turned out simple garments for distribution to the poor in the community. Esther, always before dependent on men, drew a regular paycheck for the first time in her life. It brought security to the family and gave a boost to Esther's diminished feelings of self-worth.

As each Kimball child graduated from high school, they went to work. Catherine, with Frank's help, found a job at the county courthouse. Years later younger brother, John Henry spoke of the times. "After I graduated from Trinity High in nineteen thirty-seven, I worked on building a school in Hoehne, just east of Trinidad. Then Frank helped me get a job in nineteen forty, to compile a history of all local churches, using County Courthouse records and interviewing Spanish old timers who remembered the original churches. I turned in the completed records to my immediate supervisor and often wondered what became of them."

Frank and Crusita weathered the Depression years by hard work, conscious thrift and strong faith in the future. Although luxuries were foregone, the family never went without the necessities of a properly ordered home. High-minded Frank continually involved himself in any idealistic project that came up. Torn between exasperation and pride,

Crusita noted that his lofty principles all too frequently got in the way of his profit. While he was out upholding justice, liberty and equality and frequently receiving no pay for his efforts, Crusita coped with home and family, knowing her decisions usually would be subjected to stringent review. Daily reality sometimes produced a clash with saintly values. Crusita once laughingly remarked that she and the children frequently felt like the traditional preacher's kids who harbored a compelling urge to do something naughty just to express their own identity.

The strong willed husband and the equally strong willed wife gradually forged a distinctive and close relationship of mutual respect and equality. But the smoothed path did not come automatically or immediately. During the early years, Frank dominated as head of house and breadwinner, with Crusita occupied as homemaker and guardian of the peace. Exacting and authoritative husband met challenges from spirited and independent wife. Frank took things seriously while Crusita frequently saw them as funny, puncturing Frank's stiff, starched sobriety with the pointed shaft of quick wit. Frank found politics frustrating but fascinating and essential. Crusita disliked the process and kept aloof from it. Frank fretted over Crusita's irrepressible, free-spirited approach to life, Crusita found irksome her straight-laced husband's legalistic deliberations over even trivial issues. But when problems and challenges confronted the two, they loyally pulled together.

His sense of parental responsibility brought Frank back to the Catholic Church after a lapse of more than ten years. Disillusionment had come from the fact that during the three years of fighting back from a tuberculosis death sentence, no priest had come to see him even once. This hurt grew into anger, resentment and balking at going where the preaching was not followed in practice. By Frank's reasoning, the priest probably avoided his pastoral duty out of fear of the disease, rationalizing that Frank was not going to be around long. Frank also felt that a poor Spanish man did not merit the attention afforded prominent parishioners of other ethnic background. Although the omission rankled for years, Torres' faith in God held firm even while he remained forever skeptical of the institutional church.

However, Torres could not ignore the benefits of religious affiliation and wanted his children to be given the education, solid moral values and spiritual strength found there. Moved to give them this, Frank went back to Holy Trinity and became a parish leader, although remaining skittish on total acceptance of infallibility in the priesthood. He continued to rely on his own perceptions, make his own judgments, guided by personal prayer rather than by a cleric.

Lacking any inclination toward religiosity, Torres' inner faith prohibited wearing piety as a public badge. Content to leave the mystery of life to God, Frank's beliefs were for the here and now. Sin, as he saw it, was anything that enticed a person from the path of his highest good or forced him from it. To Frank, the Ten Commandments formed an exemplary moral code for any society which, along with the Eleventh Commandment that "thou shalt love thy neighbor as thyself", if followed would leave little need for armies or police.

Holy Trinity Church, where the Torres family worshiped, is an architectural gem that lifts its single, graceful, gold cross topped spire above the rooftops of downtown Trinidad. Built in the late 1800s of hand cut stone and local red brick, the serene beauty of the church interior is bathed in varicolored light from stained glass windows. It reveals marble floors, decorative wood, a vaulted ceiling with gold ornamented, supporting ivory arches, wall hung Stations of the Cross and life-sized figures of the twelve Apostles which form the gently curved back wall behind the sanctuary. Votive candles burn and the thick walls speak of peace and solid, enduring faith, a lingering sense of the endless progression of devotions and prayer hangs in the air. Adjoining it on the south and west are the rectory and parochial schools grounds.

In church as elsewhere, Frank was a stickler for proper behavior. Crusita's brother, John Kimball, remembered a Christmas Eve mass at Holy Trinity where, although Frank and Crusita were caught up in the liturgy, their preschool aged sons were not. After shoving and exchanging looks, Frank, Jr., hit Lawrence a whack bringing an outburst of tears and parental attention. Turning a meaningful fatherly eye on his eldest, Frank marched him out for a brisk spanking, returning him to their seats beside a now angelic Lawrence. It did not happen again.

Frank also perceived the church as a vehicle for accomplishing good in every day society. He joined the Knights of Columbus and continued to lead his Holy Trinity Boy Scout troop. In addition to regular attendance at mass, he sent each Torres child to Holy Trinity School, recognizing that in times of changing values they easily might lose the solid and secure faith he had received from his grandfathers and which now sustained him. Torres saw church as a place for moral instruction and character building in the young, which along with quality education, constituted a first priority for society. A Trinidad educator who knew him well explained: "Torres understood children. He had experienced all the shame, humiliation and pain children live with and he never forgot it." He, indeed, had lived through slights and insults, but he had no place for self-pity, deeming it a "corrosive emotion," and, instead, carried on a lifelong crusade to improve the lot of children. When childless old people of Trinidad asked him where they should leave their money or property, he always suggested the Holy Trinity schools as the best place to help children and the community through one and the same gift.

In 1933 the nation flocked to the Chicago World's Fair and a new spirit of hope permeated the country. Across the Atlantic, Adolf Hitler became chancellor of Germany and eminent Jewish scientist Albert Einstein fled to the United States. Wars and rumors of wars cropped up in the newspapers. The League of Nations failed to persuade Japan to return Manchuria to China, Germany pulled out of the League, while Russia attempted to gain admission there. As frequently happens, the United States Congress was immobilized by partisan politics and failed to get agreement to join the League. Boxing, baseball, car racing and tennis emerged as national pastimes and fan dancer Sally Rand's censured performance at the World's Fair brought her national fame. As the New Deal rolled forward, American ebullience came back. Informed and busy, Frank Torres carried out his professional and volunteer obligations while serving as the mainstay for his extended family of Torres and Kimballs in town and up river.

Frank, Crusita and the boys now lived at 325 East Topeka, a pleasant, tree lined street near the Trinidad Junior College campus and a good location for growing children. But there, he and Crusita experienced another loss. In October of 1934, Crusita delivered a weak and tiny baby daughter who died a month after birth, leaving Crusita with lingering health problems and depression. Frank, accepting that sorrow came, lived with it, and went on, while looking to the high promise of his two healthy sons.

Mortality struck again on February 3, 1935, when Eva Bustos de Torres, the supportive center for the Torres family bled to death after attempting to excise a growth from her left hand with a razor sharp kitchen knife. It slipped, severing an artery and frantic attempts to save her failed. Loss of Eva left Sus unable to cope. He already coughed from black lung disease, and noting his ineffective efforts to manage on his own, Crusita and Frank invited him to live with them. He accepted and became the adored grandfather to the Torres children.

For all his civic work and family orientation, J. Frank Torres was, at bottom, a very private person, a loner who did not display his feelings openly and felt uneasy in social situations. Only Crusita really knew the man for who and what he was. His uncompromising standards, intellect, education and position caused the average people of Trinidad to regard him with respect and a near awe, never achieving a closer relationship. Crusita recognized and accepted this but Frank, unaware, would have been shocked to realize it.

The pair enjoyed their town in all seasons, warm and growing in summer's glow, secure and snug during dark days of icy wind-driven winter snows when the dimmed rays of a south dipping sun provided no warmth. Fisher's Peak, standing sentinel above the town, changed with the seasons, from brown to white to green. Trinidad had endured through the good times and the bad, had claimed Torres' imagination from childhood on, and he felt satisfaction in daily life there. If he could do good, it must be among his people there.

Turn of the century buildings, including the elegant Victorian age, Columbian Hotel, the brick paved streets, all contributed a settled feeling, their materials and architecture far more interesting and enduring than the modernistic, economy-of-statement buildings which cropped up in vacant spaces. The Purgatoire, flowing through town provided charm and definition. Its waters gave life and vitality along the banks, descending in unstructured loops and curves from headwaters located to the west in the twelve thousand foot Sangre de Cristos. Ice crusted, snow rimmed, silent waters of winter turned to vigorous spring runoff, flowed a low and sluggish brown-green in late summer, but it could roil and race with fierce energy after summer downpours, on occasion washing out bridges in its path. The creatures of the wild and the resilient humans along its grassy, tree edged valley, all lived, sustained by the stream as it flowed away to be lost in the trackless, muted distance of the plains to the east.

However busy, Frank remained in the political fray with an unshakable resolve to root out corruption and strengthen democracy in any way he could. To maintain representative government, power continually needed to be taken from the elected few and redistributed among the many, he said. Politics too frequently resembled a battle of the victor claiming the spoils, but, it did not have to be that way. If a person made it successfully through a campaign, nothing save greed and self interest would prevent him from responding to the legitimate needs of the working public. In Frank's political skirmishes with entrenched indifference to representative government, he predictably encountered bigoted opposition from a self-perpetuating political hierarchy. He met this on-going ethnic insult and scheming with dignity and countered with unyielding principle, at one time assuring a political caucus that, as he read it, the U. S. Constitution made no provision for either privilege or exclusion based on race or ethnic background. A dishonest government could expect dishonesty from its citizens, he believed. The importance of the vote; to have it and to use it wisely, was an area of greatest need.

When he set up the Young Democrats, the County Party Chair had delicately explained that it was fine for him to organize the Spanish, but to do it primarily for the purpose of having them fall in line at election time with a party line block vote. It was better if major decisions were made by educated men of higher social standing. Torres ignored the directive. A block vote could be an effective tool, but only when it advanced the interests of those voting. Many potential voters of that time had failed to receive formal education but this had no bearing on native intelligence. His purpose was to organize every day people to think about the issues, to recognize their own political power, to reject empty promises, to evaluate what was best for themselves and their communities and to vote accordingly. He also urged these people to speak out and to run for office themselves. The popularity of his message among the young voters and their families brought a measure of success to his efforts.

In 1936, with the Democrats in the saddle and prepared to stay there for a long ride, the Roosevelt re-election campaign rolled into Trinidad. Under Frank's leadership, the Young Democrats turned out a record crowd to greet the caravan, and provided a parade escort for the entourage where floats, bands and cheering onlookers stretched from downtown to the city limits. The New Deal programs had brought jobs and money to Las Animas County, so that Roosevelt's party and policies held an insurmountable advantage that year. At the official welcome from the mayor and other community figures, the crowd stood sidewalk deep to hear the candidates, and also a talk by Attorney J. F. Torres, Labor Relations Manager for the area WPA projects. Torres predictably appealed to citizenship rather than partisanship. Speaking in Spanish, he pointed to the progress already made, the problems yet to be solved, and ended by urging his fellow citizens to study the issues, be informed and vote the best interests for the country, the community and ultimately, for themselves. Roosevelt and the Democrats carried Las Animas County in a landslide the following November.

Frank, celebrating his fortieth birthday in 1937, found life good, his work, his home and family deeply satisfying. He and Crusita had forged a strong and supportive relationship, he watched his growing sons with fatherly pride, and money had ceased to be a worry that plagued his days. He was at the peak of his abilities and the future never looked brighter.

In 1938, Frank took his delegation of Spanish Young Democrats, to the Colorado State Democratic Convention in Glenwood Springs. They went, determined to be equal partners in the state's business, solidly unified in their support for a natural gas tax and a permanent public works program derived from the existing WPA, CCC, and NYA. The recommended natural gas tax was accepted and later legislated into law, but the farmer's and rancher's deep-seated suspicion of big government prevented serious consideration of permanent public works. The young politicians came home satisfied that they had made a difference, and determined to continue to play a meaningful role in state politics. It was a significant forward step by the Spanish Americans of Southern Colorado toward political recognition and strength, toward where they ought to be, Frank felt.

Elected in 1939 as third vice-president of the Colorado Young Democrats, Torres soon ran into a political complication. Big Ed Johnson, then governor of Colorado, openly coveted the United States Senate seat held by fellow Democrat, Edward P. Costigan. The Young Democrats caucused; they liked Costigan's record in Congress, but also knew that Big Ed was doing a good job in the governor's chair. Torres and his Young Democrat officers felt that a primary battle for the same office between the two equally-liked incumbents would be detrimental to party unity and could lead to defeat in November, losing either the governor's office or the senate seat as part of the damage. Accordingly, the Young Democrats framed and unanimously passed a resolution stating, "We know of no better assurance of continued good government than the return to their respective offices these experienced leaders of demonstrated ability and unquestioned integrity."

Despite complaints from the Johnson forces that the Young Democrats favored Costigan and intentionally forced Johnson out of contention for the senate, the Young Democrats endorsed the re-election of Johnson, Costigan, Senator Alva B. Adams, Congressmen Lawrence Lewis and Fred Cummings to the positions they held. It proved a winning ticket.

With the 1939 outbreak of World War II disrupting Europe, the convention also advocated broad neutrality legislation to "enlarge the effectiveness of embargoes and regulate trade with neutral countries." At the same convention, Torres urged legislation to qualify Colorado for inclusion in the national Social Security Act that he saw as an essential safety net for elderly working people. This support strengthened the governor's call for a special session on old age security, which then passed enabling legislation and opened a Social Security office in Colorado. Torres chalked up another gain for Spanish security as equal citizens.

The militant Young Democrats additionally took a firm stand in favor of the graduated income tax, placing the cost of government on the people in direct proportion to ability to pay. At the same time, Torres and his group vigorously opposed a sales tax, arguing that it constituted double taxation and increased the cost of necessities for the poor. But after open debate, they recognized the opposition as too strong and tabled their recommendation. However, they came out forcefully for the merit system in state employment and flatly opposed four year terms for state officials as contributing to entrenchment of power. A number of the stands then taken by the Young Democrats still are argued over.

13

THE FIRST CREDIT UNION

Frank stayed deeply involved in politics, believing there needed to be new leadership, new ideas and new programs to accomplish full economic recovery, particularly among the Spanish Americans. Still, the political process did not move swiftly and, while he was confident that justice would prevail if everyone pressed the issues, there would be a period of stalling and half measures. In searching for means to speed up the process, he became convinced that the credit union movement and the Alianza Hispano Americana were two necessary organizations for bringing about beneficial change and opportunity. Each offered services denied the Spanish elsewhere but which were readily available to the Anglo population. Torres was determined that in free and equal America these should be open to every citizen, regardless of origin.

In the early thirties, Torres had become interested in the credit union movement which then was pushing aggressively across the country from its beginnings some twenty years earlier on the east coast. Frank had gone as a delegate to the historic national organizational conference in Estes Park, Colorado in August, 1934. Surrounded by mountains and housed in the elegant Stanley Hotel there, the delegates hammered out the legal framework for a national organization to guide expansion of credit unions across the country. Practical visionary, Edward W. Filene, Boston department store magnate, who earlier had started the first credit union in America at his own store, presided over the meeting. Filene had then helped secure enactment of the first credit union law in the country, pushing the Massachusetts state legislature to adopt one in 1909. In 1921, the growing movement met again to establish model by-laws that have remained largely unchanged down to the present. Filene believed unions answered the problems created by changes in the economics of labor.

The transition from hand labor to machine power, and from individual enterprise to big industry brought with it the need for labor advocacy and a different approach to personal finance. When a man no longer worked for himself on his own land, but at the will of a corporate boss, protective action became imperative to prevent worker exploitation and give financial security.

As a result of the Estes Park meeting and union pressure, enabling legislation for credit unions to operate throughout the nation was passed by the federal government in 1934. Under this law, some one hundred ninety existing credit unions rapidly mushroomed up to over a thousand, now subject to governmental oversight. The credit union movement's credo, "There is no death to a real service rendered. There is no death to kindness. There is no end to the influence of good life," echoed Frank's belief that what one person did, for good or evil, went ever outward in its influence on the lives of others. As he listened to the talks, Frank determined he would spread the message of credit unions wherever he could gain a hearing, beginning in Trinidad.

Very likely, most credit unions and their millions of members today never consider their debt to the early trailblazers sent out by Filene and exemplified by J. Frank Torres who, identifying a need, always worked to provide a remedy. The credit union was a powerful new tool to deal with the financial inequities in society, and which would open doors to the working poor, including the marginalized Spanish Americans.

As Torres tackled his home town with the new concept, he prudently enlisted the help of Father Heller, the priest at Holy Trinity Church, who persuaded a few other influential Catholic townsmen to help back the new idea. By 1938, the hope had become a reality when Trinidad's first credit union opened its doors for business. While strongly supported by the church, this credit union never functioned directly under Holy Trinity Church, but operated as an independent corporation, even though charter membership was restricted to parishioners of the church. Father Heller worked closely with Frank in setting up the operation and appointing a board of directors. Heading up the new organization, named the Holy Trinity Credit Union, Father Heller placed Torres in charge of operations. Characteristically, Frank dived in, working overtime, explaining benefits, enlisting new members, building confidence and growth in the institution.

To promote credit unions, Frank visited towns throughout Colorado; out of the way hamlets, county seats and trading centers; spoke at countless meetings, always seeking to awaken his listeners to the vision of a better life, lived under the rules of democracy with equal opportunity for all. To his Spanish audiences, he expounded on ideas and policies, urging them to band together and work for their own long term good by setting up credit unions. He was not anti-Anglo in his efforts, rather he simply looked to apply support where greatest need existed.

In his earnestness, however, he retained an ironic sense of humor and could laugh at himself. In one incident he recalled, his reflexive courtesy, acquired from early home instruction in manners, made him ridiculous. In Gunnison for a credit union organizational meeting, he walked down a narrow street, rehearsing his talk. Absent-mindedly polite, he tipped his hat to anyone approaching. In the middle of his ruminations, an indistinct black and white form came toward him, triggering a mental image of a saintly nun, and, not looking twice, Frank raised his hat only to discover he had saluted a wandering Holstein heifer. Still, he observed, better to be absently mindedly well mannered than rude by default.

In taking on the credit union management, Frank held to the principles of the Declaration of Independence, the Bill of Rights, the Constitution, and the precepts of the Bible, employing them in the new venture. As the organization moved beyond development stage and proved its value in the community, Frank pushed for more democratic by-laws, firmly arguing that membership, then allowing only Catholics, should be open to any qualifying applicant, extending impartial help to all workers, regardless of race, creed or affiliation. After considerable board discussion, Torres prevailed and the change was adopted. For an enrollment fee of five dollars, Holy Trinity Credit Union offered both savings accounts and loans to members. These were geared to the resources of the average working person where most need for the service existed. The organization picked up new members rapidly.

Long time nurse and health educator in Trinidad, Gertrude

Brunelli, evaluated the early years of the credit union. Torres, as director, she stated, ran the organization with scrupulous honesty and meticulous bookkeeping, encouraged people to save whatever they could spare, however little, thereby receiving the benefit of earned interest. This discipline, creating initiative and responsibility, set members on the track of financial solvency and eventual security. He instructed all members in their duties, the advantages of disciplined saving, and the necessity of meeting obligations.

Not long into operations, Trinidad's two banks saw the credit union as a rival and made strong effort to weaken it in the community. However, it did not take acute perception for the credit union's members to see that if their institution went under, they would be back at the mercy of the banks who historically had shown interest only in amassing profits. Banks admittedly had their legitimate place, Frank granted, but so did credit unions. This attempt to discredit met with failure because the excellence and human quality of the credit union services was unassailable.

Lloyd Romero, a friend of Torres since childhood, saw Frank committed to total and complete honesty. If an applicant did not check out according to his standards, Frank would have nothing to do with him. The strict credit union rules were a major part of its success, Romero believed. To emphasize its human quality, the institution also developed a social side. The regular Sunday afternoon meetings of the board and membership instituted by Torres encouraged personal participation and always ended with a potluck supper. Crusita organized these affairs, giving people a chance to socialize and develop a sense of shared community.

Personally investigating each application, Frank attended to the smallest details, assessing the character and life situation of those applying for loans to be sure they met requirements. He did not allow default, in fact, was deeply offended by the idea. Responsibility and honesty were required to lead a successful life. For those unable to keep up monthly payments, Torres was eminently fair when he worked with the debtor, evaluating what could be paid and setting time constraints for doing so. The credit union was there to help people, but could not fulfill its purpose on unpaid loans. He was relentless on the point that one honored one's contracts, carrying out what was agreed upon at the time the loan was made. He was uncompromising in his conviction that without honesty on the part of all, the credit union would fail and everyone associated with it would lose.

J. Frank Torres also allowed no discrimination in the credit union, with its services impartially available to anyone in the community. Each received the same courtesy and respect, with no special attention or consideration for the more influential nor any additional requirements for the less so. Actually, he made it a point to be particularly attentive to the down trodden, those whose expectations had been hammered so low they lacked courage to stand on their rights. All people were created equal, although he did not deceive himself that all talents, abilities and status of birth were equal. Far from it. Still, this had no bearing on the dignity and respect to be afforded each human. At credit union meetings, everyone was encouraged to speak, but anyone overstepping the bounds of courtesy received a pointed rebuke. Frank had no patience with bad manners, pomposity, conniving or dishonest dealing anywhere, and zero tolerance when confronted with these offenses in his credit union.

Frank disliked superficiality, worked best among straight-forward people of real ideas, problems, or solutions. Socializing for its own sake he privately considered a waste of time. The idle chit-chat of parties bored him as irrelevant in his perpetual bent for learning and doing. If necessary to achieve an end, as in the Sunday afternoon credit union meetings and potluck dinners, where he would socialize, slyly using the time to educate and persuade as he mixed casually in the group. His most polite social demeanor simply masked his on-going quest to counter problems and frame solutions.

This high mindedness did not always endear him to his board members. Some worked against him, pushing for more rapid credit union growth through easier loan terms, rather than continuing the prudent, slower gains that Torres advocated. This, he saw as a prescription for corporate failure, and, relishing the challenge of debate, met the arguments head on, giving chapter and verse on approaches and outcomes, demolishing the get rich quick schemes and winning a majority vote of support from the board. Fr. Heller stood solidly behind Frank whom he had put in office for the lawyer's strength of person, honesty, and soundness of ideas.

In addition to managing the Trinidad office, Torres traveled around southern Colorado spreading the credit union message, recruiting, organizing, giving legal advice on charters, and education on risk management. Initially, some people viewed the idea with suspicion, but Torres long since had proven a relentless persuader. One by one, he helped groups get started. Gaining acceptance for the idea took time and education, but he never doubted the rightness of what he did, deriving intense satisfaction as each new credit union opened its doors.

Within the Torres marriage, Crusita added her own dimension of thoughtful practicality to her husband's lofty, impatient idealism. She never forgot her growing up years in the financially strapped Kimball family and did not plan to duplicate the experience within her own. Unusual ability in mathematics and a growing grasp on the complexities of economics and money management enabled Crusita to take control of family finances, skillfully balancing income against expense to build family savings. However indifferent he might be to money, Frank did appreciate gracious living, and gladly turned the matter over to his wife. He never doubted her ability, nor had he cause ever to regret it. Through the years, Crusita's skills gave him a cultured home, funds for the children's education, and a secure retirement. Through it all, she remained in the background, kept the home, helped at the credit union, participated in church and civic life and lived with her high-minded husband's crusades and campaigns. Respecting her ideas, Frank increasingly used her advice and skills in day to day credit union decisions.

Busy as he was trying to improve society, Frank still had time for individual's plights and problems, one of them long term. With the death of Mr. Kimball, Frank stepped in as father figure to the Kimball brood much the way the old man had envisioned when he arranged Crusita's marriage. He kept an eye on young John Kimball who, with his sisters, had started up a locally popular dance band that charged five dollars for each night's engagement. When a dance hall owner in La Junta refused to pay the band its fee, Frank came to the youngster's rescue by writing the man a terse letter to either pay or face legal action. The money came forth.

But once in a while Torres' principled stands came to nothing as when Holy Trinity's basketball team won the parochial schools state championship in 1937 to qualify for the regional tournament in Chicago. With each team allowed just seven players, star varsity player, John Kimball, sidelined by a severely sprain ankle, was told he would not be included. Badly disappointed, John felt he had earned the right to go, but the parish priest decided to fill the seventh slot himself. When Torres confronted him, the cleric offered the defense that he never had gone beyond Trinidad where he had been born, educated, and entered the priesthood and therefore deserved the trip. Frank pointed out that John's standout play had contributed greatly to the team's winning this chance. At that point, the priest drew his rank and sharply reminded Frank that as Holy Trinity's priest, he was in charge, was going, and that ended it. Since the priest's trip came at the expense of one of his own young parishioners, Torres observed that it was no wonder he never got beyond his own doorstep, because he set his sights too low.

Always on the alert to educate, with time and weather permitting, Frank often cranked up his car for an outing, taking Crusita, the children and any friend who might gain from the experience. As the family sedan chugged over the miles, these occasions expanded into a classroom exercise, covering history, points of interest, and geography as they passed. A trip to Taos permitted Esther to visit her youngest sister Marina, reared there by her grandparents. Another excursion took in historic Santa Fe, a run to Texas brought them to the bedside of terminally ill Uncle Ned Kimball, and another carried them to California in 1937, visiting Los Angeles and San Diego, before heading back home through Tucson. No educational opportunity ever was ignored.

Local affairs provided entertainment, civic spirit and frequently a glimpse of history, as when Frank portrayed Coronado in Trinidad's 1937 Conquistador historical parade, recalling to mind the Spanish origins of the town. Torres believed people needed to know their heritage, recognize the greatness of the past's people and their achievements and apply those strengths and values to the present. Accomplished horseman

Torres happily donned a replica of three hundred year earlier military raiment and rode a white horse to head the parade. Crusita's brother, John, was assigned a supporting role, to walk behind as a Franciscan friar.

Meanwhile, the WPA projects continued to occupy a fair share of Frank's attention. Although local employment picked up, spurred by war in Europe, jobs still were limited. The unemployed easily equaled the number of the employed as the federal government cranked out more programs. But it was not enough to employ all which led to an ironic instance when Frank's careful education of voters on political action techniques was turned against him. Resentful of the continuing lack of total employment for everyone and determined to force action, the local WPA workers, the unemployed, and their families and friends organized a protest. On a Tuesday evening early in October, 1939, they gathered at the Las Animas County courthouse to demand immediate remedy. The overflow crowd also attracted political office holders hoping to enhance their images, as well as J. F. Torres, head of the local WPA. A spokesman demanded more jobs, followed by other speakers who brought up old grievances of the Spanish, and several voiced threats of unspecified retaliatory action if their demands were unmet. The politicians gave unspecific promises and reassurances of bettering the worker's lots. Torres listened, irritation rising at this attempt to coerce ill advised and unachievable action that could reflect negatively on all the work in progress.

When the last politician sat down, Frank rose and, by contrast, did not hold out any easy answers or glib promises but set forth the facts of the situation. He stressed the importance of citizens knowing how their government operated, explained the objectives and guide lines for WPA projects. He pointed out that government works programs already had furnished substantial monetary benefit in Trinidad that paralleled a slow but definite upturn in the national economy. He emphasized the dangers of attempting to manipulate class distinctions and thinking in terms of a particular group, that individual welfare inevitably was tied up with the welfare of the whole. No one was in it alone.

Torres acknowledged a need for more jobs, but reminded them

that their community was not unique in this, and that the local situation required a united, unselfish community effort. Still, he asked, were not most of them better off than they had been in 1932? The money paid into Las Animas and Huerfano counties from WPA projects increased overall income for both individuals and the business community. When someone belligerently interrupted him with a demand for action at once, Frank informed the speaker that the word "demand" implied threat of force, and suggested that "request" was a better word to use. No one cheered at the end, but all went home with a clearer view of what was possible because Torres had educated them on the realities of the situation.

As some WPA projects finished up, others began, and these, combined with the spur to the national economy by war in Europe, increased employment. Rains came, farming turned profitable again, and by 1939 Las Animas County gradually turned the corner, away from the lingering effects of the great Depression.

How Torres so efficiently managed all he did remains a question. Whatever his time constraints, he never neglected family or Boy Scouts, and combined both as his sons grew to scouting age. Shaping unformed boys into responsible manhood was of utmost importance in a democracy and by then, in addition to leading his own group of boys, he was overseeing leadership and activities of three other troops as well.

On occasion, his troop and their scout master faced unscheduled tests of preparedness, as occurred one day when they hiked out to practice woodland skills, and came upon the body of a local, small time hoodlum and cantina owner. Murdered in some underworld falling out and dumped in the tall meadow grass along the upper Purgatoire, it lay there, bloated and ghastly, in their path. The scouts remembered their training and acted correctly; not touching anything as they gingerly circled around the corpse and headed to the nearest house where Torres called state police. The experience cast both a cloud and high drama over the day as the troop headed home, reviewing the discovery in hushed tones and speculating on the murder scenario.

Another scout outing provided high farce as Torres' boys prepared a campfire meal. The old camper's standby, canned pork and beans, deposited in coals of the fire, heated up rapidly. Unfortunately, someone forgot the necessity of punching a hole in the can tops to prevent build-up of pressure as they heated. The tins went off like firecrackers, exploding in the air and spraying a hailstorm of their supper's superheated beans on hungry scouts and leader. As they marched home on empty stomachs, Frank pointed out that this was a lesson in the consequences of carelessness and not following directions.

14

THE ALIANZA HISPANO AMERICANA

In his unrelenting quest for means to help secure equal citizen's rights and respect for the Spanish, Frank's activities now included increasing involvement in the Alianza Hispano Americana. This organization offered financial and cultural opportunities for the Spanish to regain dignity and pride, and he threw himself into pushing its goals. This fraternal savings organization came into being in 1897 to give Spanish Americans the life insurance and institutional savings or loans then denied them by existing banks and insurance companies. Incorporated in 1902 at Tucson, Arizona, the Alianza grew slowly but steadily in the Spanish American Southwest.

Fraternal organizations developed out of widespread need which created efforts, both altruistic and profit motivated, to meet it. The Alianza Hispano Americana was one of several incorporated to offer these services. However, the AHA, as it was called, outpaced the others in its recruiting and programs largely because it was geared solely to the Spanish Americans, presenting a Spanish speaking and Spanish run institution that quickly gained the lead over its competitors.

In addition to providing low cost life insurance and social programs, the Alianza set itself to preserve the history and strength of the Spanish American culture. Before the entry of the United States Army into the Southwest and the subsequent flood tide of outside settlers into the territory, the Spanish held power in finance and government, with an attendant respected position in society. But by the late 1800s, prejudice and discrimination defeated Spanish American efforts to retain equal standing in the new society, leaving them thwarted and resentful. A few locally influential Spanish men and some non-Spanish who had long-time roots among them were numbered among AHA's founders. These included Carlos Tully, Bernabe Bricta, Santiago Ward and a Dr.

Odermatt. The new organization had received extensive publicity in the Tucson Spanish language newspaper *El Fronterizo*, edited and published by Carlos Ignacio Velasco until his death in 1914.

Alianza membership was held in separate local chapters, each with a rule which provided that when a male chapter member died, the rest of the chapter membership each were required to donate one dollar to the family, the assessment dropping to fifty cents for the death of a member's wife as a lesser contributor to family finances. The mainline insurance companies routinely denied service to the Spanish on the basis of low income and high incidence of job related disease among workers, particularly tuberculosis. In offering death benefits, as well as a social and political structure, the corporation expanded and by 1913, the Alianza was chartered in Arizona, California, New Mexico and Colorado. It was active not only in the American Southwest, but also had extended operations south across the Mexican border. To minimize actuarial risk and provide financial stability, prospective members had to show a source of funds sufficient to pay the small fraternal dues.

Around 1920, the Alianza admitted women as members on the same basis as men, a move approved by Tomás Serrano Cabo, AHA's historian, who noted that this move came ahead of national legislation in the USA granting the vote to women. The order's motto, "Protection, Morality and Instruction," combined with rituals reflecting strong Catholic overtones, and holding family a sacred obligation strongly appealed, as did its uncompromising position of "Spanish for Spanish" rule.

The AHA generated strong interest among the Spanish in Colorado during the Depression's early years when organizers from New Mexico came in to help launch local chapters. Frank Torres reviewed the Alianza's organizational statement and listened to the organizer's explanation of the society's goals. If these services were available on the widest possible scale, there would be major progress in confronting and overcoming existing discrimination where inequality still was apparent, including in Trinidad. As a teenager, he had burned with resentment to see his parents submit to discriminatory disrespect. He felt the AHA's attendant social programs provided a means of renewing and reinforcing the traditional Spanish American culture. Torres then joined the AHA and persuaded his extended family to become members also.

He believed that applying integrity, education and hard work to the Alianza's high goals would improve the standing of Spanish Americans, allowing them to enjoy the democratic equality to which they were Constitutionally entitled. In a democracy, past failures must be eliminated to enable future progress, and so he added AHA to his work load.

The organization also had in place a successful program, emphasizing character building and presenting uplifting activities and rituals for Spanish youth. AHA membership had dropped with the crash of 1929 and the accompanying financial crunch. However, new growth resumed by the middle thirties as the New Deal made the ground breaking move to recognize the rights of all citizens by providing equal employment in the National work programs across America. The laboring man, including the Spanish, began to come into his own, demanding his rights, starting to exert political muscle, and experience support from labor unions and other worker's organizations.

Problems to come in AHA management did not show up immediately when the Supreme Executive Council began covertly using accrued insurance monies controlled solely by themselves, to make undisclosed and illegal raids on those funds in the form of loans to themselves. According to its own charter, all insurance monies were required to be invested as a guarantee of payment of insurance benefits. Although the under the table loan practice was successfully hidden from the organization at large, one other situation threatened to produce turmoil in the organization.

From the early years, the American and the Mexican Alianzas had functioned as one operation. However, by the mid-twenties the Mexican government ordered Mexican Alianza funds to be separated out and invested in Mexico rather than be bulked in with the Tucson AHA accounts and invested in the United States. This resulted in two parallel national Alianzas, united in aims but separate in operations and finance. Mexico plunged into another revolution in 1928-29 in which Plutarcho Elias Calles, ex-president and army general, played a key role in victory for the anti-Catholic Socialists who then imposed severe restrictions on the Catholic Church. On a lesser scale, the revolution disrupted the Mexican AHA lodges, forcing the one in Ciudad Juárez to move to El Paso for security. These troubles reverberated through the Alianza north of the border where factions lined up on opposing sides in that conflict. A stalwart Catholic, Torres found Calles' actions anathema to the concepts of freedom and equality by which he lived.

Membership growth in Colorado lagged behind the rest of Alianza territory in the early 1930s until Frank Torres brought his unshakeable idealism and persuasive oratory into actively promoting the AHA. Although stretched by his management of the WPA projects, his legal practice, Boy Scouts, politics, church and family, he joined and worked actively for the Alianza. At meetings he emphasized that the organization offered immediate promise for expanding the role and rights of the Spanish, as opposed to the slower progress being made by government. Even his beloved credit unions offered no more than savings and loan services, but the AHA provided many opportunities for education and unification. As time passed, Frank gradually focused more of his time, hopes and energies on furthering the vision. He worked throughout the Spanish areas of Colorado to acquaint them with the promise of this organization and to set up local lodges in every community he could reach. He emphasized the Spanish heritage, the pride they could take in their courageous and distinguished forebears, that they were contributing citizens and worthy people who now held the numbers and power to significantly improve their lives through the help of AHA. People responded to his message in gratifying numbers. Despite competing fraternal organizations, including LULAC (League of United Latin-American Citizens), the AHA outdistanced all others in popularity.

Frank worked to bring the Young Democrats, the Spanish American Clubs and the Alianza together for maximum political clout, utilizing basically the same leadership in all three. This practical and effective move gave ballot box muscle. In addition to his other abilities, Frank was an astute political strategist, formed by his long experience of bringing legal and political challenges to the prejudice in society that he then presented as an affront to the Constitution and the Bill or Rights. Added to this, his work for AHA was made more effective by technological advances which brought changes in how people lived, particularly through improved communications and general use of the automobile. However, on another level, these advances would hasten an era where widespread use of those same benefits would be a factor in reducing the economic and political need for fraternal organizations.

As Frank visited community after community, his results began to identify him as a new star in the Alianza organization. He developed a friendly relationship with AHA Board Member, F.F. García of Albuquerque, who, impressed by Frank's work, brought him to the attention of the leaders. As a result, Torres was elected to Sindico, the governing board of AHA at the August 1933 convention in Nogales, Arizona. He had become a familiar sight as he repeatedly criss-crossed his home state in his trusty Model A Ford, launching twenty-eight new chapters with a membership of over twenty-five hundred, who then elected him as president of the Colorado AHA in 1934. To assure continued success for the movement, he prudently enlisted a cadre of dedicated local workers at each chapter house to carry on the work. He received special commendation from the Tucson headquarters at the 1936 Colorado convention that credited him alone for the outstanding progress within that state.

Torres attended a Fraternal Congress held in Santa Fe, New Mexico in 1937, mingling with his counterparts from other organizations including the Elks, Order of Moose, Woodmen of the World, LULAC, French and Greek citizen's societies, and others. He became acquainted with prominent AHA members, among them New Mexico Corporation Commissioner Bob Valdez, New Mexico Senator Bronson Cutting, and the AHA Supreme Physician, one Dr. Samaniego who lived in Las Cruces and enjoyed the additional cachet of being uncle to motion picture idol, Ramón Navarro. Frank drove back to Trinidad enthused and eager to continue his work. As he told Crusita, the signs were right, the times were right, and the Spanish stood on the threshold of regaining their full citizen' rights through their own efforts which was as it should be. Citizenship was not a gift for someone to bestow but an inherent right to be claimed.

The Alianza Hispano Americana's stated goal of improving the lot of Spanish Americans materially, politically and socially, coincided with Torres' belief that integrity, hard work, education and participation in democracy was the only route to a better life for any citizen. The needs of the Spanish were well known to him and it long had rankled to see his own people trapped in the role of second-class citizens. The inequality still was apparent everywhere, and he relished the opportunity to create a change.

Frank brought to the AHA his organizational skills honed in the development of credit unions and the Spanish American political clubs in Colorado. He had enlisted new AHA members by convincing them that without the ability to buy insurance, they were deprived of a major protection for their families, pointing out that this safeguard was freely offered to Anglo citizens. With fewer land owners than in the past and most men working for a daily wage, the lack of insurance could mean destitution for a whole family to meet funeral costs of a death within it. The AHA program took care of this and also served local communities' social and cultural needs. Because of his work, Torres, serving as president of the Colorado AHA in 1934, was appointed as Assistant Supreme Legal Counselor for the state's organization a year later. In this capacity, he attended the international AHA meeting at headquarters in Tucson that same year.

Torres was present again at the 1938 eighth national AHA convention held in Albuquerque where a vote put official organizers on essentially the same work contract as commercial insurance salesmen and instructed them to enroll younger members wherever possible. With their working years ahead of them, these were targeted as a necessary source of long term income, contrasting with older recruits paying a shorter term and collecting sooner. The organizers were paid a fixed sum for each new person enrolled that provided them a practical incentive beyond the spur of serving an idealistic concept of brotherhood. This was fine by Frank who could use the extra money but it was never his motivation. Adding to the new business-like approach, the Supreme Council purchased a corporate headquarters building in Tucson, ending the expense of rent. Growth was enhanced from another direction as discrimination against the Spanish American flourished anew nationally, fueled by radical "American" front organizations which deemed Anglo

Saxon birth an essential of full citizenship.

By the late thirties, Frank Torres was working harder than ever, keeping up his legal, credit union and government commitments but focusing his hopes for long term Spanish American betterment on the Alianza Hispano Americana. Deeply committed to the AHA's stated goals of building economic security and political power, of reinforcing moral strength and pride among the Spanish, Torres had rapidly moved upward through the ranks from member to organizer to ranking officer.

Frank, in white, as Coronado in 1940 Trinidad celebration.

During that decade, radio and motion pictures became common in daily life, providing news and entertainment. As a result, fraternal groups' social programs and activities began to take a back seat as the culture made a transition from people entertaining themselves to being entertained by others. However, the AHA still benefited from the fact that most Spanish could not regularly afford to enjoy these attractions, leaving the Alianza still an integral part of member's lives.

The 1937 Alianza Hispano Americana National Convention, held in Santa Fe in the spring marked a peak point for the organization in the New Mexico-Colorado area. While Crusita stayed home with their sons, Frank drove over from Trinidad with a car full of Alianza lodge officials. Record membership cheered the delegates and corporate financial practices, for once, did not come under question. The future promised continued growth and service, and by 1938, Trinidad boasted one of the most active lodges in all the AHA, prompting the Supreme President, Emilio H. Apodaca, to come from Tucson headquarters to visit this exemplary chapter. While there, he officially designated Trinidad host city for the AHA National Convention in 1941. This was heady stuff for Frank even as Crusita worried over changes she sensed coming.

President Apodaca, serving his second term amid major problems in administration, felt Frank could be valuable in dealing with these. Accordingly, he carried Torres' name and credentials back to Tucson for recommendation to the Supreme Council as a man of multiple abilities and qualification, including a law degree, the latter for which the AHA had urgent need.

Alianza membership in 1939 stood at a record seventeen thousand, three hundred sixty-six members named in the books and held $4,897,824 worth of life insurance, with $815,461 in assets, plus the Supreme Headquarters building in Tucson. At this high point, Frank Torres received notification of his appointment as Assistant Supreme Attorney for the corporation. By then, the WPA project work gradually eased out as war in Europe boosted the national economy, reducing bankruptcy and foreclosure cases, so that Frank's obligations there were lessened. His law practice in Trinidad would not suffer as the new AHA position did not require full time work. He accepted the Tucson assignment on a temporary basis, recognizing that serious problems awaited there but optimistic that he could cope with them.

The Alianza had a long history of questionable money management, and the executive council was torn by strife and dissension over personalities and issues. Frank believed these could and must be solved to fulfill the AHA's lofty goals and commitments to insurance holders. He had talked the new position over at length with Crusita, considering possibilities and draw-backs. Their family, home, and his practice in Trinidad suited them and offered an assured future. Tucson was strange and uncertain, the society snarled in problems. As always, Frank's idealism won out. The Spanish people throughout the Southwest still faced prejudice and resistance to their political and economic advancement. Here he could do the most good, and nothing was more important. He could adjust his work in Trinidad on a strict schedule and still be relatively free to take on the Tucson job.

Frank arrived in Tucson in 1939-40 on an interim basis, leaving Crusita, who was carrying another child in a difficult pregnancy, and his two sons at home in Trinidad while he determined to accommodate the work at both ends on flying trips back and forth. Behind his desk at AHA headquarters, he learned more about the existing power struggle with a Texas/Mexico group under the manipulations of ousted Mexican president, Elias Calles, who apparently hoped to use both the Mexican Alianza and the Tucson AHA in an ongoing attempt to regain his position as President of Mexico.

Calles, who had risen from his first job as a school teacher in a northern Sonoran desert town by supporting Obregón during the Revolution, had positioned himself to become president, succeeding Obregón. Once in office, Calles zealously enforced the 1917 Mexican constitution, attacking the Catholic church and its schools. This brought the priests out on strike, denying services, baptisms, marriages and burials in protest against the persecution. Although embracing the Revolution, most Mexican retained their Catholic faith and respect for the church, banding together in opposition to Calles who answered by calling out the army and covertly countenancing the assassination of priests.

Calles also had courted trouble with the United States by expropriating American holdings in Mexico, particularly oil properties. Although this order was amended in 1927 and tension with the U.S. lessened, he still was viewed with distrust north of the border. Political opposition at home had forced Calles to flee Mexico to the Unites States where he set up near the border awaiting some advantageous situation to use for getting back in power. He worked tirelessly, in close contact with his henchmen in Mexico.

The Alianza Hispano Americana, possessed of money and numbers, appeared ideal to use for furthering his ends. This set up an automatic clash of idealism versus personal ambition as the ex-school teacher from the Purgatoire Valley worked to counter the ex-school teacher from Sonora. The astute Calles shrewdly stayed in the background leaving his underling, José Vasconcelos, to involve himself in the Tucson Alianza affairs. This included courting members of the Board and ingratiating himself. If manipulated rightly, this popular organization might make the difference in Calles' chances of success.

Torres objected to the foreign ex-dictator meddling in the United States and set out to block his scheme which already had gained adherents within the Tucson office. He talked with like minded individuals, enlisting their support, spoke strongly against involving the organization in the affairs of a foreign government and cited the AHA's by-laws and incorporation as establishing it as an American institution to be run by and for Americans.

Although Frank had hedged his odds by leaving Crusita and the children in Trinidad, he soon found his job significantly more complex and time demanding than had been apparent from a distance. Questionable management practices involved the AHA Supreme Council in lawsuits, and Frank made fewer quick trips home, handling his Trinidad business by telephone and letter, instead. As he focused on getting AHA legal problems in order, Frank still assumed corporate good faith had blundered into honest mistakes which could be righted in the corporate board room, and, as needed, in the courtroom where he was called to answer for management problems which had attracted legal scrutiny from the State of Arizona.

In the middle of this, he made a hurried trip back to Trinidad where on October 17, 1940, Crusita gave birth to a tiny, healthy baby girl. Her parents baptized her Eva Marie, taking the name of her late paternal grandmother. The dark eyed little charmer promptly enslaved Frank for the rest of his days. As Crusita regained her strength, she faced up to the fact that Frank had full time work in Tucson, and knew neither of them wanted a long distance marriage. A family belonged together which required that they move to Arizona.

Still fired by the vision contained in the AHA's by-laws and statement of purpose, a vision which, fulfilled, could produce a better society, and believing he had made a dent in the legal snarl of Alianza affairs, Frank closed his law office. While Crusita may have been less than excited about leaving her pleasant home and all of her family in Trinidad, her husband's dream took precedence. The house was sold and she and the children moved, taking with them Sus who had become a part of the family. Amiable Sus entertained his grandchildren and made new friends during street corner and park bench conversations in Tucson. Crusita had no time for leisure, juggling roles of homemaker, mother, and gracious wife of an important and highly placed man. She accomplished it all with efficiency and charm.

As they removed from Trinidad, the war raged in Europe and Japan continued aggression across the far East Pacific rim. Torres did not buy the pacifism of some on the home front. The aggressor armies would not be satisfied to stop as they advanced to new victories, and Nazis boasted of "tomorrow the world." Accordingly, Frank supported military intervention. If Hitler and Mussolini succeeded in Europe, America would have to face the consequences at home. Additionally, Japan's armies continued to overrun its neighbors, adding to world crisis. Past enlistment age and still possessed of his nemesis hernia, Torres quelled his old dream of serving his country in the armed forces and volunteered for what he could do on the home front, selling war bonds, helping set up food and gasoline rationing and practicing strict adherence to all wartimes restrictions and codes. A citizen could do no other.

Things grew worse at AHA's Tucson office. A 1940 audit revealed fifty-four thousand dollars missing and unaccounted for on the balance sheet. With a past year of growing membership and new insurance premiums paid in, this disappearance of funds was impossible to explain. Adding to the financial problems, a gradual slowdown occurred in membership enrollment. War-generated job opportunity, and the enactment of retirement and health benefits plans gave increasing numbers of Spanish workers new options for previously unavailable financial security. This affirmed Frank's long held conviction that a democracy must be guided, legislated and steered into equal treatment for all people. However, it did not benefit the AHA as the nationwide shift showed up in declining lodge numbers and attendance. Military enlistments and the draft moved young men out of their communities and participation in AHA programs, offering them new possibilities for careers and lives, which added to the Alianza's problems.

As a result of accounting discrepancies, the Arizona State Corporation Commission placed all AHA insurance matters under its own direction, complicating difficulties already faced by the organization. Using this authority, the Arizona Corporation Commission moved to block the AHA from holding its scheduled convention in Trinidad, which Frank foresaw would be a serious blow to the morale and confidence of members. To prevent this, Frank successfully argued before the Maricopa County Superior Court judge, presenting the act as unlawful meddling in the internal affairs of a duly licensed corporation. His argument resulted in the restraining order from the commission being denied by the court.

April 1941 brought Frank and his family briefly back to Trinidad for that National AHA Convention. He was determined to present an affair that would calm worries and doubts of members. Assisted behind the scenes by Crusita, he doubled his efforts to give a memorable three days of meetings, bringing up a large class of candidates to present for initiation as members. The delegates attended business sessions where plans were formulated for expansion of AHA work into the mid-western states, ate festive meals with lavish decorations supplied by Crusita and a crew of wives, and enjoyed a grand, old time Spanish dinner and *baile* (dance) which brought the event to a close. A photograph taken at the time by the Trinidad newspaper reveals a large crowd of men and women grouped in front of the Heritage Square wall, with an enormous American flag waving overhead. Five hundred delegates and twice as many more visitors and observers had come to Trinidad to work for a better world.

Despite the good will and fellowship, serious business was given attention. The delegates heatedly debated solutions for the AHA's financial and management problems, recommending a tighter budget and stricter bookkeeping. Chandelier B. Sedillo was elected new Supreme President and plans were formulated to revamp and monitor operations, cut overhead, and restructure the Alianza to restore solvency. Back again at his Tucson office, Frank continued to learn how serious and entrenched the problems were, and perhaps that the problems were not entirely the result of honest mistakes.

The State of Arizona intervened again, making the society accountable to the state for all corporate financial and business transactions. Additionally, there was an overt push from a Mexican contingent to seize control of management in order to boost the political strength of Elias Calls. Torres was jolted further by the extent to which funds were disappearing for obscure purposes and apparently contrary to the AHA charter and by-laws. How could this happen? Frank, who had taken accounting at Central Business College in Denver, decided to look at the books himself. In reviewing the financial records, the clear evidence that the disappearance of money was neither legal nor right stared him in the face. But he needed to carefully investigate his facts before he made a case of it, after which straightforward honesty must be applied.

He began at a board meeting by requesting that his fellow officers enforce existing rules at all levels and monitor any expenditure for compliance with the by-laws. He also called for an audit, and searched his law books to find a way out of the mess in court. He demanded personal control of all legal work, and succeeded in getting the action of the Arizona State Corporation Commission temporarily stayed in favor of the Alianza, gaining a little time and slack to turn the crisis around. Although disillusioned by the obvious dishonesty in transactions, he still believed the Alianza worth salvaging.

The Arizona Corporation Commission, scrutinizing AHA operations, however, did not take into account good intentions, and when insufficient progress occurred, issued Special Order 122, assuming control over the Alianza's books, records and property until the end of 1941. Again Torres returned to the Pima County Superior Court to make his argument, pointing out the responsible, established positions in the area held by the board members as evidence of ability to return the corporation to solvency. Torres also argued that the undeclared assets, including the headquarters building, were more than adequate to cover the deficit. Again he won and upon the Corporation Commission's appeal, the lower court decision was upheld by the Arizona Supreme Court. During the months Frank spent tied up in legal arguments, President Sedillo and the Supreme Council employed emergency cost cutting measures, returning the society to temporary solvency, and getting the AHA's license reinstated by the state.

Strongly commended for his legal success over the Arizona Corporation Commission, the Supreme Council then elevated Torres to the position of Supreme Secretary where a movement developed to nominate him for the office of president at the next national convention. Torres saw the presidency as grandly ceremonial but removed from the working operations of the society. He could not summon up any interest in the position, figuring that he could accomplish more at the working level than as a figurehead on the top. However, his growing popularity among the rank and file caused antagonism among the Calles supporters on the AHA Board who weren't enthusiastic about straight forward honesty. They felt no rapport with anyone who disdained, as Frank did, the lavish AHA parties, spending his time, instead, out mingling with every day people at street fiestas, talking, listening, aligning with those the AHA professed to help. From this, his fellow officers decided he lacked the appropriately lofty attitude for high position. At this point, Crusita told him that however right his actions were, she foresaw trouble ahead because of them. The situation somehow resembled Las Animas County politics, to her mind.

Torres was a moralist of the fiber of the Old Testament prophets, which earned him an on-going problem. "Righteous" is a word currently in disrepute, implying some fanatical, judgmental assumption of moral superiority. In its older sense, however, righteous is doing right and insisting on right because it is right. Torres believed language was diminished by consigning certain words to disfavor and, by doing so, making it easier to apply relative, less definite terminology where acceptance and inclusion serve as universal positives, evading confronting the fact that choices are made, actions taken, some beneficial, some harmful.

Unfortunately, righteousness inevitably becomes the object of unrighteous opposition. Torres faced this but remained incapable of ignoring what he knew to be right, no matter the inducement to act otherwise. Still, he was flexible enough to accept that tolerance for harmless foibles was needed to live with and accept differences in people, but never simply to be applied as cheap elastic to stretch moral values.

Because of this unyielding rectitude, Torres earned the nickname of "the Jesuit" among members of the AHA governing circle. While not intended as a compliment, he actually fit the description: scholarly, exacting and moral, even though, to his detractors, the term meant unbending, moralistic and judgmental. Unwilling to reshape himself to be more accommodating, Frank soon became the odd man out.

Torres believed the AHA, as its charter stated, should be solely concerned with helping the everyday Spanish people gain equal rights and power over their own lives, but other council members, some aligned with José Vasconcelos, intended to shift control toward Elias Calles by contributing money to him and becoming actively involved in Mexican politics. An inevitable showdown shaped up between contending goals and philosophies.

Although Torres made it known he did not want the presidency, the push to put him there anyway resulted in infighting and more division among the ranks. These conflicts intruded into Frank's efforts to deal with AHA financial and management problems. All records indicated a comfortable profit being paid in through insurance premiums, but it did not show up when he examined the books. Also, he faced the continuing Calles problem. He had limited personal contact with José Vasconcelos who lived in San Antonio, Texas, but the Calles supporters were pushing to get this man invited to address the next Alianza National Convention in Tucson. Once there, they believed that Vasconcelos, skilled at exploiting the frustrations and grievances of a crowd, could enlist a following and set up a take-over for his mentor, Calles. Torres opposed, and spoke strongly against allowing Vasconcelos, whom he saw as an ambitious demagogue, to deliver a flaming emotional appeal to the divided group.

The speaker question was submitted to the board where three

members solidly supported Vasconcelos, others wavered, wanting to be on the winning side without having to take a stand. Frank and a like-minded Chilean board member, an actuary for the New York Life Insurance company in Chile, tried hard to rally opposition against Vasconcelos, but the final vote had only those two voting against extending the invitation, and five supporting Vasconcelos for speaker In that vote, Frank saw more and worse trouble coming for the AHA.

As squabbles grew more rancorous, an illuminating bombshell landed on Frank's desk. Examining a sheaf of official papers awaiting his signature as Supreme Secretary, he found one that supplied a cover up for member's long term private use of the insurance fund, which then totaled some twelve million dollars. Frank had suspected something of this sort and this was the confirmation of what amounted to outright embezzlement. He rejected the document as an illegal diversion of society monies and declined to sign it. This required courage on his part but Torres had no qualms. "Courage is necessary but it needs to receive its direction from a working brain," was his analysis of such a situation. It also required an indifference to material reward, on which he resorted to Emerson again: "The reward of a thing done well is to have done it." Fortified by a disregard for the consequences, he demanded honest answers, digging deeper into the financial records. He found there a well-established practice, which was by no means new to the organization. Instead of the funds being held in a restricted, interest bearing account for insurance policy pay-outs as legally required, the fund was being milked by high ranking officers who gave themselves loans and cash, using bogus collateral as security. Frank vehemently attacked this policy at the next board meeting, producing evidence that this illegal practice accounted for the bulk of ongoing financial difficulties in the organization and, if continued, could destroy it. No one liked or heeded the message as they simply changed the routing of their requisitions away from him.

Commenting on this later, Torres' brother-in-law, John Kimball, observed, "Of course, Frank refused to go along with their plundering the funds as he did with anything dishonest," recollecting that in 1941 when Kimball was stationed at the Vallejo, California naval hospital, the

AHA held its convention in San Francisco. There, Frank contacted John, explaining that he was skipping the dinner and festivities of the AHA because he would not be associated with the usual convention pursuits of alcohol and women. Loose morals offended him, and his values continually came in conflict with the majority, whom he saw as turning traitor to the people they purported to serve.

From then on, trouble multiplied at AHA headquarters and Torres, now a pariah on the board, became increasingly discouraged and disillusioned with the manipulation and dishonesty he encountered there. Action was taken to sideline him away from power, culminating in a vote by the board reducing his responsibilities as Supreme Secretary and eliminated finance from his duties. He could be the AHA's lawyer, but only to do their bidding. With the weight of the Supreme Council arrayed against him, he could not win and he would not play their game. He worried late into the night looking for solutions, but none came. He was powerless to prevent what he saw as willful self-destruction by the AHA board.

Tired of the scheming and squabbles, the growing strength of the Calles faction led by Vasconcelos, and a blatantly dishonest financial policy that progressively weakened the Alianza, Torres found the situation contrary to all he believed. Disillusioned and saddened by the society's failure to live up to its high goals, he concluded the only honorable course open to him was to quit. He wanted no part of an organization that ignored the law, put greed and profiteering above the interests of the people it promised to serve, using high-sounding slogans to secure dishonest ends. He had signed on with the Alianza to help people, not defraud them. Accordingly, he submitted his resignation and prepared to leave Tucson.

His letter of resignation, written in both Spanish and English, made clear his reasons. "I hereby submit my resignation from the office of Supreme Secretary of the Alianza Hispano Americana, the same to be effective forthwith. I have arrived at this decision with a great measure of regret, but in strict obedience to what I consider my clear duty under the circumstances. In fairness to everyone concerned, I must now state that gradually, as your program has evolved, it has become clearly apparent that it contains very definite tendencies of centralization of power and authority in the person of the Supreme President alone, aided by heads of departments without clearly defined jurisdictions and without proper checks and balances, so essential in a democratic form of government, such as is granted by law in our society.

Any government built around the person of one individual or motivated solely by the consuming dream of such individual, is essentially weak and undemocratic. It does not inspire confidence and does not make friends.

Under such a program, the office of Supreme Secretary has been gradually stripped of its functions, so that today it has virtually no work left to it to perform. A state of confusion and misunderstanding is bound to occur as the natural result.

I, for one, am unable to reconcile myself to such a state of affairs; with such a system as now revealed, I am entirely out of sympathy."

The letters were signed by Torres and accompanied by a letter of transmittal written in Spanish: *"Le Manda aqui inclusa copia de mi carta de renuncia como Secretario Supremo de la Alianza Hispano Americana para la informacion de los hermanos de esta honorable logia. La misma se explica de por si. Aprovecho la oportunidad papa manifactar a Un. y a todos los estimados hermanos de su logia mi mas sincero agradacimiento por us bondados cooparacion y cortesia en el pasado. Los saludos con todo carino, su hermano fraternalmente en P.M.I."*

Torres' letter was answered by a curt dismissal from the AHA's president, C.B.Sedillo. "Your resignation under date of April 20, 1942 as Supreme Secretary of the Alianza Hispano Americana to take effect forthwith has been duly received and the same is hereby accepted with the thanks of the Society for the services you rendered."

So it was over, the glorious hope of achieving lasting good for those who needed it most, the ending a collision between ethics and idealism versus unscrupulous self-interest. For one of the few times in his life, Torres felt real discouragement as he reviewed the failure of his noble cause. It could have and should have been otherwise. Torres' enthusiasm, belief and tireless organizing, his vision and high principles had provided major ingredients in the Alianza's growth and success, and had he been heeded, the society's dismal ending might have been forestalled. As it was, predictably after Frank left, the AHA continued its self-serving course, unchecked by conscience or management. Vasconcelos spoke at the convention, but Calles must have read the handwriting on the wall of AHA's coming failure and shifted his aims, as there is no record of further meddling by his supporters in the AHA. Later still, Frank would read that Vasconcelos had become a daily attendee of Mass in his home town deep in Mexico. As he read it, Frank observed dryly that it was heartening to find that sinners still repented.

Deprived of Torres' integrity and legal skills, it does not seem coincidental that the Alianza gradually slid into failure, disgrace and oblivion. Instead of correcting its practices, AHA struggled on until it ceased to exist some twenty years later. Misuse of power and funds dogged its downward path until, in 1965, Carlos McCormick, former Supreme President of the Alianza was indicted by a Pima County Arizona Grand Jury, charged with embezzlement of AHA funds, and convicted of diverting one hundred sixty-nine thousand dollars into dubious loans for his own benefit. This forced the society into receivership and the remaining insurance claims were paid out through the Arizona courts. The noble aims of the Alianza Hispano Americana ended on the sourest of notes. However, it is also true that by the time of AHA's demise, changes in society, including Social Security, more enlightened hiring practices, and employment benefits had begun to render the AHA and like organizations unnecessary and irrelevant in financial planning.

During this frustrating period for Frank, troubles also compounded in the world. Roosevelt, winning an unprecedented third term, moved the country out of its prevailing isolationist mood, convincing Congress to provide arms and aid for both Great Britain and Russia to bolster their defenses against the attacking Nazi Germans.

In Asia, Japan's invasion of China and its alignment with Germany and Italy to form the "Axis" powers further raised alarm in the United States. On December 7, 1941, dubbed "a day that will live in infamy," by Franklin Delano Roosevelt, Japanese aircraft bombed the Hawaiian U.S. Naval base at Pearl Harbor in a sneak attack. Ships were sunk, with heavy casualties among the sailors on board. Roosevelt asked

Congress for and received an immediate declaration of war. Young men left the ranks of the unemployed, deserted farms, factories, and college to enlist and, for the first time, women entered the armed forces. Putting aside his own frustrated wish to serve, Frank had to decide what came next in terms of his own family.

15
GETTING BACK HOME

Frank's resignation from the Alianza in 1942 brought him to a career crossroads. Along with his disillusionment had come uncertainty. He had put his legal practice in Trinidad on hold, had disposed of his home, and bet his all on the Alianza Hispano Americana as one key to a more equitable society. Instead, it had become simply another corrupt business. Now he needed a time out to put things in perspective. As the war raged, he easily could have secured a position as a lawyer in a government agency, but he was not inclined to take on the structure and limits of another bureaucracy. Nor was he ready to go back to Trinidad with the bad taste from Tucson still in his mouth. He was in the mood for a complete change.

With his proven ability, solid qualifications, and experience, Torres could look to a variety of options. As he put out feelers, new possibilities presented themselves. However, before he took a first step into the unknown, Frank wanted his family secure and sent Crusita, the children and Sus back to Trinidad to lodge with Esther Kimball where they could live rent free and surrounded by family while he picked up the pieces of his career. Crusita, knowing her husband, never doubted he would recoup and was satisfied to go home without him. His idealism had cost him their security and, with a family to care for, high minded causes had to take second place to personal finance. In Crusita's words, they "left Tucson stone broke."

Among other offers, Frank received an especially attractive one to work as an agent for the Clinton P. Anderson Insurance Agency in Albuquerque. This business was owned by Anderson, the long time U.S. Senator, and New Mexico's best known citizen. The opportunity was engineered by an old friend from Trinidad, Sam East, who had been made general agent for the firm when Anderson left the Senate and moved to

Washington to become Secretary of Agriculture in Roosevelt's cabinet. East, who knew both Frank's abilities and the disaster he just had come through, offered a position that carried a good salary and opportunity for advancement which Torres gratefully accepted. This well paying job took him back into home territory which, instinctively, he liked. Frank drove over, secured a room in Albuquerque and concentrated on rebuilding his bank account.

Although the separation was not one Crusita freely would have chosen in other circumstances, with the funds from the new job her husband forwarded to her, she managed sufficient economies to hold up her family's end of the expenses at Esther's and to set up a growing savings account. She enjoyed being with her mother and those siblings still at home, enrolled her boys in Holy Trinity school, allowed preschool-aged daughter, Eva, to be coddled by the clan, and took up again with life long friends and church work. But there was a major difference. Now she alone bore responsibility and made decisions for the daily life of her family. While she missed Frank beside her, where necessity drove, one must ride, and there was a challenge in it, a satisfaction in being entirely on her own. For the first time in her life, there was no man to order her actions and make decisions for her.

The marriage relationship between Frank and Crusita subtly changed at this point as she gained self confidence without her exacting husband there to press his will and wishes. In the past, she had followed the dictates of an era that decreed that husbands led and wives followed. With it all, she consciously tried to make decision of which he would approve. Frank, of course, continued to issue directives through his letters and when he drove home for weekends, but the day to day decision making was Crusita's. From his substantial paycheck earned at the Anderson Agency, Frank kept out only enough for immediate needs and the rest went to Crusita who used it carefully, saving for the future and a home of their own again.

While in Albuquerque, Torres was urged to enter Democratic politics, but he remained wary. Gilbert Espinosa, attorney, distinguished scholar, and historian of the day, ran in the primary for New Mexico Attorney General, but was defeated by what appeared to Torres as a "cheap politics" set up with party bosses calling the shots to elect a different man who would be agreeable toward their own goals. However, when Frank was pressured to run for lieutenant governor in the general election, he initially was attracted to the idea. He was qualified and the position would provide visibility and influence to push social reform, including greater attention to Spanish civil rights. Interested but cautious, he met with Charles McGrath of Las Vegas, New Mexico Democratic National Committeeman, who urged Frank to run. But later, carefully reviewing his discussion with McGrath and also studying the New Mexico political climate, Torres abandoned the idea, fearing a sell-out of himself and his principles amid backroom politics. During the same time, he managed to offend entrenched state politicians by campaigning for young Joseph Montoya for U.S. Senator against the wishes of party bosses. Fortunately "Little Joe" went on to win and spend years in Congress, remaining always grateful to his early supporter. As a non-candidate, Frank spent the rest of his time at the Anderson Agency aloof from the infighting that characterized New Mexico politics.

However, at one Albuquerque political rally in late 1942, Frank made a particularly interesting friend. This was the legendary Elfego Baca, then nearing eighty and already well incorporated into the folklore of the Southwest. Baca had grown up in raw times, becoming a skilled marksman which served him well later in his varied career of gunman, sheriff, Juárez barroom bouncer, elected official and holder of various other civic jobs. Frank was familiar with the man's most famous feat, which occurred during Baca's 1884 confrontation with some eighty trigger-happy Texas cowboys who were amusing themselves by shooting up Frisco Plaza in Socorro County. He single handedly routed the troublemakers while successfully defending the town's people and property. From this fracas, the nineteen year old emerged unscathed and an established legend in his own time.

The old man did not dwell on his colorful past in his discussions, seemingly getting more enjoyment in observing the conflicts, compromises, and characters on the New Mexico political scene. Apparently he found Frank interesting and enjoyed exchanging views and insights with another Spaniard who shared his language and culture. They met for lunch or a cup of coffee from time to time during the year Frank spent in Albuquerque. When Baca died in 1945, Torres already was gone from town. Some fifteen to twenty years later, Disney produced "The Nine Lives of Elfego Baca," which Frank made a point of watching with Crusita, but discounted the production as "fantasy entertainment that took too many liberties with the facts."

Frank Torres could have settled into a lucrative career as a corporate executive in Albuquerque, or he profitably could have pushed other men's agendas on the New Mexico political scene. The monetary rewards would have been considerable, except that such a life did not suit him. Unquestionably he could have done well continuing at it, but Frank found selling insurance boring. True, he had sold insurance for the Alianza, where it was only part of a package designed to improve all aspects of members' lives. Now, the old call to make a positive effort against the wrongs of society, to make a concrete contribution toward bettering the lives of those around him again sounded in his ear. Security was well and good, but should not displace working for one's beliefs. An insistent voice told Frank he was well able to follow the path of idealism and still provide for all the needs of his family. A man never lost when he worked for what he knew was right, he only failed when he did not try.

By nature, Torres was neither a socializer with automatic agreeable charm, nor a people pleaser. His interests lay in concepts and values and his barely leashed impatience to be about things that mattered itched him as he sat at his desk in the Anderson Agency. In addition, he sorely missed being a daily part of his children's lives, and felt the lack of Crusita at his side to serve as a sounding board for his innermost hopes, ideas and ambitions. She understood him as no one else ever had and he valued her opinions even though they did not always agree with his. Having developed an outline for the future in his mind, and with a tidy bank account saved by his resourceful wife, Frank put thought into action.

16
Rebuilding

Late in 1943, Frank politely resigned from the Anderson Agency, finished up the work on his desk, packed his bag, climbed into his car and drove north, home to Trinidad, home to his family, home to his future. He could work for a better society there as surely as in any far away metropolis, and those he knew and cared most about were the people in the land he knew best. He could tackle what needed to be done there, making a particular concern those most needing help.

His Trinidad legal, social, and political ties had not been totally dropped during his time in Tucson and Albuquerque, so that Torres reentry into Trinidad affairs came easily. He resumed his law practice full time, took up Boy Scouts again, entered into local politics, and worked for the church, serving as a member and legal counsel to the Knights of Columbus. He joined in the war effort, spoke at bond rallies and planned to offer his legal services to assist returning servicemen even though conflict still raged in Europe and the Pacific. Hopefully, but unknown to the public, scientists at a secret location in New Mexico concentrated on beating Hitler in a race to develop the atom bomb and win the war.

As if a special place had been retained for him, his old friends welcomed Torres back, clients appeared in his office, and the rightness of it all deeply gratified him. Frank and Crusita soon bought a spacious home and moved the family from the cramped quarters at Esther's, making the transition complete.

In his law practice, Frank did his best on each case, regardless of background or situation, but never hesitated to reject a client who lied, or was evasive. Such people, he said, could not be represented honestly. When he took a case, he also undertook to educate the client on the practical benefits of ethical conduct, avoiding actions leading to trouble, and seeing present problems as opportunity to seize on principle and work for a better life. Interestingly, in his whole career, Judge Torres never filed a single lawsuit in his own behalf.

The practice of law certainly did not meet fully the glowing idealism of Frank's law school days, and the games played in court could stir his wrath. But he had learned to control his temper. Early in his practice he had been angered when evidence crucial to his case was not admitted in a court hearing, and made a heated protest, which brought a cold admonition from the judge, "Mr. Torres, I suggest you hold your temper." Frank acknowledged the reprimand as justified and never forgot it, later carrying the same insistence on civility into his own courtroom. But sly shading of the law and outright dishonesty in the courtroom were too common, as was the fact that connections could take precedence over evidence in a court of law, and political cronies with friendly access to the judicial system never lost. The only cure for the situation required ethical men of highest credentials and standards to dispense justice, and this could come only through the elective process.

One other thing that raised the hackles of the non-smoking, non-drinking Torres was off-color jokes. The quality and use of language revealed much about the mind from which it came. This was brought into focus shortly after he arrived back in Trinidad when Frank was asked to join a small group of influential Democrats who lunched together every Tuesday. He accepted, assuming constructive discussions of issues and party strategy, and a chance to voice his own ideas would be the agenda, but this proved not to be the case. Rather, he found that conversations centered around local gossip, and, once, over dessert, a prominent politician told a raunchy sex joke which offended Frank greatly. As the others guffawed, he shoved back his chair and rose, saying, "You have no shame! *Sin verguenza*! (for shame.) I am out of here and you will not see me again!" At home, he irately reported to Crusita why he had quit the group. It was offensive and contrary to his principles and he would not waste his time in such activity. If politics was not clean at all levels, it undoubtedly was clean in none.

Shame, Torres explained, was a natural consequence of wrongdoing, a loss of pride and self-respect for having acted in an unworthy way. Shame could be useful in shaping character, however, prompting avoidance of actions where the person would have to face the recognition that he acted wrongly. If this became a part of the experiences of the young, the emotion would hold as a restraint on them as adults. Pride and self respect came, in part, from withstanding wrong instincts and impulses, and Frank believed that a lack of this accounted for endless laws trying to force what should be natural action to avoid shame. He believed that the absence of the two, shame and self-respect, contributed heavily to overloading in the legal system.

Life at the Torres home, while happy and harmonious, had changed. The children were older, and Crusita now possessed sufficient confidence to stand up as an equal to her opinionated husband on issues where they differed. Not that she regularly opposed him and, occasionally, in matters where she felt certain she was right, she simply acted on her own rather that provoke an argument. Frank would complain volubly when she failed to consult him, but another side of him felt pride in her independence and spirit.

Torres once again was busy leading a Boy Scouts troop. Somehow, the scholarly and staid Torres who guided with firmness and discipline also managed to create pure fun. His boys hero worshiped him, copying his mannerisms and using his opinions for authoritative quotes. In talking to his former scouts, they agree that he had inspired the best in them, and they credited his influence as a most important factor in their ability to set goals and build successful lives.

To emphasize scouting's patriotic ideals, Torres and his scouts provided the City of Trinidad with an enduring civic monument. This took money. His troop held fund raisers, collected school children's pennies, and hired out on menial jobs, until in 1950, they had acquired sufficient funds to erect a replica of the Statue of Liberty on the northwest corner of Courthouse Square. Frank then organized an impressive dedication ceremony to focus Trinidad's attention on this important symbol of Democracy and Scouting. He prevailed upon the national head of Boy Scouts, O. A. Kitterman, to come and serve as speaker, and scout troops and school bands from throughout the county marched in the parade. A scroll containing the names of the children who had given their pennies was included in a time capsule enclosed in the base of the statue.

Ten thousand people attended the occasion, and the statue still stands, surrounded by flowers in summer, capped with snow in winter, holding aloft the torch of liberty. The time capsule was opened in 2000, fifty years after installation, at another community wide ceremony organized by the Trinidad Historical Society and the County Commissioners with honored participants, J. Frank Torres daughter, Eva, and granddaughter Tara representing him.

By the mid 1940s, the Torres sons, Frank, Jr. and Lawrence attended high school at Holy Trinity, and Eva entered first grade there. Sus, his health continuing to fail, moved to Denver to live with his daughter, Juanita, and her husband Alfred Martínez. Typical of the times, Sus had no retirement benefits and Frank contributed to his care, adding enough extra so Sus would have some money to spend on his own. Frank's brother, Manuel, retired from the mines with black lung disease, also lived in Denver. The close ties of family still held with regular visiting between Trinidad and his own people. Frank believed if you did not care for your own, you undoubtedly were incapable of caring for anyone else.

Frank and Crusita enjoyed their large, white, corner lot house on South Commercial Street, only a couple of blocks from the Las Animas County Courthouse where lawyer J. F. Torres kept busy. This two story house, owned in the 1890s by the MacKenzies of the Scottish held Prairie Cattle Company, and a sometime residence of Uncle Dick Wooton, had a basement where Frank one day came across a curious relic. In the dim light, he perceived what looked like a rattlesnake, but upon closer examination, found it to be an intricately carved cane. This intriguing piece became a prized possession, carried with a flourish through his lifetime, and now to be seen in La Fonda hotel in Santa Fe, housed in a glass case dedicated by hotelier Sam Ballen to his friend Judge Torres.

Trinidad shared in the nation wide economic boom of World War II, which created full employment, overtime production pay, and unprecedented demand for farm products and natural resources. In sharp contrast to a few years earlier, everyone had money, but because of war time rationing, there were few luxuries upon which to spend it. Using the argument that leadership should not be changed in perilous times,

Franklin Delano Roosevelt was re-elected to third and fourth terms as president. Torres disapproved of this overstepping of the unwritten two term rule, seeing it as opening the door for unlimited successive terms and a possible route to de facto dictatorship.

Frank credited Roosevelt's response to the Depression crisis as appropriate and necessary, but doling out government assistance during ordinary times, he believed, set up a dependency mentality, eroding ingenuity and independence. He noted that the politically canny Roosevelt increasingly made his appeals to particular groups of people, providing them separate recognition and benefits that insured their loyalty. This was flatly wrong, Torres held, because it divided the population into competing factions, defeating the pledge of a fair and equal society. But Roosevelt's matchless rhetorical charm worked magic politically, and his method of campaigning proved so successful that it has become the norm to the present. Congress then voted to support tradition and passed a two term limit for the presidency in answer to strong voter criticism of Roosevelt's extra terms.

Soon Torres' expanding law practice outstretched his ability to handle all his in-coming cases and keep up with his other commitments. After sizing up the legal talent in Trinidad, Frank brought a young lawyer, Gilbert Sanders, into his practice. That Sanders happened to be a Jew struck some locals as an odd choice, but they prudently refrained from sharing their opinions with the senior partner who bristled at any hint of racial preference or denigration. Color or ethnicity had nothing to say to the fact that Sanders was a skilled lawyer of high principles, and there it ended. In addition to his ethical stand, Torres was not about to jeopardize his practice by being saddled with a second rate individual simply because the person's background might match his own.

In late spring of 1945, long ailing President Franklin Delano Roosevelt died at Warm Springs, Georgia and was succeeded by Vice President Harry Truman. Feisty, strong minded Truman took over the reins of government and during his tenure became admiringly known as "Give 'em hell, Harry." Torres liked Truman, respecting his honesty, and his willingness to be held accountable as stated on his desktop sign, "The buck stops here," proclaiming the new president's forthright determination to confront problems personally.

As battles were fought and air strikes carried out, German strength waned, Italy fell, and the tides of war shifted strongly in favor of the Allies. In 1944, General Eisenhower launched the successful Allied invasion of Normandy, followed by the Battle of the Bulge and the liberation of Paris, while the U.S. Eighth Air Force methodically eliminated German air power and defenses. German surrender came on May 5, 1945. Victory in the Far East followed shortly. President Truman had calculated the excessive human cost of winning the conflict against Japan through standard aerial and ground warfare and made the decision to employ the atom bomb, recently developed by scientists at Los Alamos, New Mexico. Using this new technology, which would change the entire world forever, brought surrender from Tokyo on August 15, 1945, after the U.S. dropped two atomic bombs on Japan.

With the war won, the country looked to an era of peace and prosperity as thousands of ex-soldiers, marines, airmen and sailors returned home to jobs or college. Frank gave Trinidad's servicemen free legal guidance on the use of their veteran's benefits to plan their futures, and to be certain those who had been wounded received the government medical care and disability pay to which they were entitled. His own brother Pete, a decorated combat veteran, numbered among the wounded ex-servicemen he assisted, placing him in Fitzsimmons Army Hospital in Denver for recovery.

Shortly after Torres returned to Trinidad, Fr. Joseph Heller of Holy Trinity Church had been ordered to active duty as a Navy chaplain. Before the priest left, he prevailed upon Frank to assume management of Holy Trinity Credit Union to secure its' continued successful operation in his absence, seeing the lawyer as uniquely qualified in experience, vision and honesty. The credit union was too valuable to risk any mis-handling of its' services and funds. Following the priest's directive, the board installed Frank as both treasurer and general manager in late 1943, giving him another outlet for his pragmatic altruism.

Frank managed Holy Trinity Credit Union for nearly twenty years and, under his careful direction, membership grew and assets tripled. He also traveled around Colorado helping set up more credit unions and advising on their operations. In the process he was elected president of the State Credit Unions Association. During his tenure, his long time associate in the Trinidad office, James Passerelli, assessed Frank as precise and careful in management but perhaps too outspoken for his own good. Torres would have pleased more people, Passerelli said, had he been soothing in his speech rather than always compelled to point out negative specifics wherever he saw them. As a result, Frank frequently tangled with others at credit union meetings, refusing to yield on any issue until all questions had been resolved. Good business practice rejected muddled decision making.

Neither was Torres inclined to bow to priestly authority, as Crusita and young Eva found out one day. Coming up the stairs to Frank's credit union office, they heard raised voices and, as they reached the second story hall, a hat sailed out the office door to plop to the floor at their feet. In an amused voice, Crusita murmured to Eva, "I expect we will see Father coming out shortly." Sure enough, clipped footsteps sounded and a moment later, the red in face, furious priest stalked out. He snatched up his hat, and slammed it on his head, belatedly tipping it to the mother and daughter standing in the passageway as he made for the stairs. Inside the office, an irate Torres gave them a summary of events. The priest had pressured him to relax rules and make a loan to a notorious deadbeat upon whose spiritual betterment the good Father was laboring. As the priest pressed for leniency, Frank's temper rose at the temerity of someone trying to dilute lending standards. Rules kept unsound risks off the books, avoiding the loss when such borrowers inevitably defaulted. The credit union, he had caustically explained to the equally angry cleric, helped responsible people better their temporal lives, but had no mandate in the redemption business. Crusita nodded, but little Eva never learned the answer to the all important question of who threw Father's hat?

The priest's attempt was not an exception. Board members frequently requested special consideration for a relative or good friend. These Frank flatly refused, applying the same standard to his own family and friends. If an applicant failed to meet the rules, no money was forthcoming. Rash loans would endanger the financial standing of the credit union and conflict with its own regulations. He had seen first hand in the AHA what resulted from by-passing rules and giving preferential treatment. No such thing would be allowed at Holy Trinity during his tenure.

People doing business at the credit union found Frank honest, unpretentious and an astute judge of character. However, his standards did not suit some board members who believed relaxed rules would produce more rapid growth and pushed for him to change his mind. But Frank stuck to his position and measured growth continued, supported by a favorable balance sheet.

Unexpected set-backs in jobs and the family affairs of the borrowers made lapsed loans a continual problem. Torres handled each with understanding and firmness, always allowing a one month grace period after calling the borrower in to talk the problem through, consider other necessary commitments, and arrive at a reasonable schedule for repayment. After agreement had been reached, however, no further excuses, other than a major new crisis of health or circumstance, was accepted. Financial independence depended on a realistic balancing of income and expense, with a portion, no matter how small, marked for saving. Unless this was practiced, the person never would succeed in building financial security.

Given his perfectionism and impatience, Torres was a surprisingly effective office manager. Faced by a problem, either with credit union members or with staff, he kept an unbreakable rule to always confront the individual on the issue directly but privately, so no one was embarrassed publicly. The person had to realize that a mistake had been made and must be rectified. He was there to help but not to excuse. Momentarily, this approach could be daunting, but in the long run, however upset at the time, those on the receiving end of one of Torres' consciousness raising sessions came to respect and appreciate his plain spoken candor.

17
CHANGING TIMES

The old plague of racism still continued to confront Torres, coming forward as he helped organize new credit unions around the state. One of these incidents took place at a start-up meeting of the Pueblo, Colorado, credit union where board member-organizers made it plain they had little wish for his presence. They condescended to Torres as a "Mexican" who had nothing useful to tell them on how to set up their operation. Insulting as it was, Frank had lived through the same countless times and become skilled at holding his own. That they had in mind an operation that would be favorable to their own personal use of it was apparent, and this he would not allow. During discussion he set the men straight on the point at issue, their independence to set their own rules. The credit union would go forward under the standard procedures and applicable by-laws as provided by Mr. Torres, or the State Credit Union Board, of which Frank was a member, would refuse their application. Having to take this from a perceived inferior to themselves rankled, but they dared not risk throwing him out or even ignoring him. Officers of the Colorado State Board, they discovered, had an automatic vote in any state credit union affairs. They could either enact the rules Frank stated, or abandon the idea of having their own organization. With forced smiles, they conceded. Frank left, indifferent to the fact that he had bested them but satisfied that the new union would be set up to operate honestly and fairly.

Always mindful of moral obligation and responsibility, the egalitarian Torres remained unswayed by position or ceremony. When the state board sent him as representative to a national credit union conference in New Haven, Connecticut, Frank went, eagerly expecting to gain new viewpoints and ideas. Boarding the eastbound train at Trinidad, he watched, fascinated, as more than half the continent passed by his window. But once in New Haven, he found the meetings resembled nothing as much as the ceremonial affairs of the AHA in Tucson he had been so at pains to avoid. Impatient and irked at the waste of time and the credit union's money, he endured long winded speeches, lavish banquets, and calculated courting of position. When the train returned him to Trinidad, Frank's letter of report to the state board and a verbal one to the local union were succinct, "I went, I saw, I came back." Nothing of any value to credit union management had been offered, but much was expended on the vanity of men.

Another meeting held at credit union national headquarters in Madison, Wisconsin subjected him to the subtle discrimination of invisibility. The other delegates ignored his presence, dismissing him as a Mexican nonentity who, curiously, had managed to get himself included, but could have little comprehension of the proceedings. They underestimated. Far from remaining mute in the background during discussion of issues, accomplished speaker Torres gave a lucid and precise analysis of current problems. He focused on the importance to both credit union and borrower of prompt and compassionate but firm attention to default, and outlined the methods he employed in Trinidad. Failing to act immediately, he told the group, resulted in loss of capital and of clients in the long run. The condescension stopped and while no real acceptance came for him as a person, he was treated with complete, if distant, respect. Frank brushed it off. If he had let such stop him, he would have been sidelined twenty-five years earlier.

Frank Torres' vision and his disdain for anything not democratic and moral did not make him immune to the sting of slights but allowed him to rise above them. He chose to live positively and usefully. As a member of the Colorado State Board of Credit Unions, he sat on the executive committee overseeing all Colorado credit unions, advancing to president of the group. Frank routinely out-thought, out-organized and out-performed his peers. In the face of ever-present prejudice seeking to discredit him, he proved himself the most effective man in the Colorado credit union organization. An old *dicho* of his grandfather's reminded him, "*Hace tu dilligencia y Dios te ayudara*" (Be diligent and God will help you). It worked.

The town of Trinidad remained busy and relatively stable after 1945, but the same was untrue of Torres' old home, Cokedale, which had enjoyed record prosperity during the war. The post war economic downturn and renewed union agitation for miner's benefits contributed to a drastic cutback in coal production, the town's major source of jobs and revenue. Underlying worker discontent, built up through years of exploitation and an unwillingness by the union to compromise, put Cokedale's future in doubt and posed an economic threat to all Las Animas County. Intensifying the downturn, conversion of the railroads from coal fired to diesel-powered engines brought a sharp decline in demand for coal. Faced with slumping revenues, the coal companies refused to budge and production from the mines and coke ovens gradually halted. Once again, locals lost their livelihood to the priorities of industry, the long shadow of Stonewall stretching darkly down the years.

Frank worked with Cokedale community leaders on ideas to save the town for its residents, but a lack of investment money doomed the efforts. The town was sold to a Denver company that was unable to come up with a profitable scheme for its use or disposal. In an effort to bail out of this unprofitable investment, the company in 1948 put the houses up for sale at one hundred dollars per room, plus fifty dollars additional for the lot. This was a price the tenants could swing, and the new home owners then moved for incorporation which transformed the model company town into a normal community with taxes and politics. A nostalgic hope lingered that some energy crisis would revitalize the mines and bring back the glory days to Cokedale. It did not happen and little by little, new employment in other fields and new means of support supplanted dreams of the past.

18
Parents And Children

Postwar dislocations had to be dealt with not only in Cokedale, but world wide. In 1947, the Marshall Plan was launched in Washington to aid European recovery from the devastation of World War II. In an ironic twist, the United States paid not only for fighting to win the war, but furnished capital to help reconstruct economies destroyed, including those of the perpetrators of the conflict. Frank pegged the time as a transition period with no going back to what was before.

In Trinidad, Frank and Crusita gave unstinting help as the Torres and Kimball families branched out into new careers and ventures. Crusita eased the daily burdens for her mother as Esther grew older and her health gradually failed and Frank counseled the brothers and sisters, guiding them into educational or job opportunities, serving as a fatherly friend. He encouraged the musically talented Kimballs to utilize those skills, which led John and his sisters to start a dance band. Frank also assisted his brother Pete in claiming his benefits as a permanently disabled serviceman.

However, not everyone appreciated Frank's efforts for the family. In 1947, teenaged Teresa Kimball went to California and enrolled in the Hollywood Arthur Murray School of Dance, hoping to become a professional dancer. Unfortunately, during that time, beautiful Los Angeles party girl, Virginia Short, known as the Black Dahlia, was killed in a sensational rape-murder. Reading of this in the Trinidad paper, a horrified Esther called Teresa to come home where she felt her daughter would be safe. When Teresa refused and scoffed at the notion she was in danger, Esther turned to her son-in-law for help. Frank drove to Los Angles, forced a refund of her money on the prepaid course by threatening a lawsuit when the studio balked, packed up the resentful Teresa, and drove the sulking girl back to her relieved mother.

The family in early 1950s

Gradually, the young Kimballs found their niches. John, Jr., in the Navy hospital corps during the war, returned to a civilian career in hospital work in California. Manuel did military service as a guard at the Army prisoner of war camp in Trinidad and later found a local job. Carmen married a soldier and moved to Delaware. Catherine married and lived in Albuquerque, and Charlotte also married but died early. Rebel Teresa, after her dance fling, became a novice in the Palatine Missionary Sisters, left there to enlist in the military, which she found not to her liking, and dissatisfied, drifted in and out of Trinidad, finding no clear path to a future.

Naturally, parenting their three children came first for Frank and Crusita who provided each with opportunity to explore interests and gain skills. Frank, Jr., and Lawrence, each in turn, were scouts in their father's troop. Both teenagers successfully took the required swim across Monument Lake for their Eagle Scout badges, and Crusita served as de facto den mother for the troops, with the home always open and food available in the kitchen.

Frank Torres also believed in family outings as unifying and educational, and through the school years, gathered up his wife and children to go places and see things, with enjoyment and learning pleasurably mingled. He formed the habit of after Sunday Mass taking the family on summer picnics up the Purgatoire to the mountains and scenes of his youth. It was important to him that his children knew their heritage, what the history of the family had been. Bends in the river, old houses and chapels, the fields, hills and peaks, all held stories of the past, lessons to teach, and Frank never tired of recalling the earlier days. Crusita provided hearty outdoor feasts, and afterward, the children played and explored, while Frank parked himself under a tree with a good book and Crusita kept a benign eye out to be sure no one roamed too far or got into mischief.

The mature Frank Torres probably never knew how to have simple fun. In its place, he substituted observation, evaluation and participation in activities he found educational or uplifting. Nonsense was outside the realm of his experience, although he could indulge in fanciful whimsy and spoof, once straight-facedly assuring Crusita that low clouds on the horizon were actually exhaust fumes from cars on the road. He laughed as Crusita shushed him. She knew that for all his reading of books, Frank was no scientist. He was analytical, but only in the areas of human situations, social theory, and the liberal arts, not in how lightning was produced or internal combustion engines propelled cars. He simply accepted these in generalized terms on faith.

Crusita, on the other hand, had an irrepressible funny bone with much of her amusement coming from her starched-up husband's attitudes and foibles, finding them variously trying, laughable or endearing. If Frank failed to find humor in the ongoing incongruities of life, Crusita did it for both of them. She also could draw a line. If Frank got on his verbal high horse too publicly, she could fix him with a minatory eye and say, "All right, Frank, enough is enough. You've had your say," and, with a retreating grumble or two, he would refrain from further comment.

In a formal family portrait from the late 1940s, Crusita looks very much the wife of a successful professional, wearing a simple dark dress with pearl necklace and earrings. Standing next, Eva, a slim, solemn, large eyed adolescent, bears a strong resemblance to her father who, himself dressed in impeccable dark suit, looks at the camera with a resigned impatience. Standing behind in light suits and ties are mid-teen Lawrence, who projects an open innocence and a wariness of the camera, while the older Frank, Jr., shows more confidence. At home, the family enjoyed easy companionship and unity. All gathered around the dinner table and on holidays, Frank made such occasions a learning experiences. Thanksgiving was given over to gratitude for the blessings of life and foods tied to family history were featured. Christmas brought faith and goodness, and the Fourth of July produced hot dogs, watermelon, firecrackers and community celebration, featuring patriotism, duty, and love of country.

Frank found continuing pride and satisfaction in being head of his house. The Torres family life exemplified his belief that a solid home was built on common experience, a shared history, a sense of connection and a togetherness between husband and wife for the benefit of the children. From this came an intimate mutual caring among the members that eliminated need for artifice and cunning, or maintenance of a facade to bolster an image of family unity. A true marriage and home set one free to be one's best self, not to let down and exist on tolerance or excuses.

While Frank went out to insure justice, liberty and opportunity for those around him, Crusita, equally busy, assisted at the credit union, coped with family, home, budget, social obligations, church, and anything else Frank brought into her orbit. And together, they reared their children with discipline and approving encouragement, instilling in them solid values and high standards of conduct. Crusita approached the task with flexibility and an understanding of youthful foibles, while Frank's fierce idealism made him strict and exacting. Undoubtedly, Crusita and the children sometimes chafed at living with the rules of a man seemingly above the temptations, failures, and self-indulgences of the average mortal, holding to his path regardless of obstacle. Understanding him became important.

"Your father gave you the sky, I tried to add the stars." Crusita Torres explained to her growing children, speaking both fact and metaphor. Fascinated with the night sky, Frank taught his children the constellations, but also gave them ideals and ideas, encouraged each to view life as opportunity, limitless as the sky. Crusita supplied mother love, consistent and reasonable discipline, practical advice and emotional security, seeing each family member as having special strengths and needs. If, once in a while, she quietly helped her children circumvent a rule in order to fulfill adolescent dreams, she never negated Frank's basic values and ideals. Most of all, she was at pains that the children comprehend and appreciate the ideals and remarkable talents which set their father apart. "This is what your father is about," she would say, detailing his goals and achievements, and she took care never to undercut or shortchange him in his relationship to their children.

Frank had held each as babies, listened for their first words, and guided their toddler footsteps. They were his focus of being and the overridingly important responsibilities of his life. While not overtly demonstrative, he loved each child totally, wanted for them the security of a warm and solid family, the enjoyment of growing up unpressured by premature, adult problems. And always, he worked to instill the strong religious and moral values of the Catholic faith, and to assure each received a college education. He showed, by word and example, that laziness of mind body or spirit defeated ambitions and hopes, and that a feeling of true self-worth was derived from honest work well done. Each would attend college, with their high school classes, homework and grades focused toward that goal. A college degree was a must for living equally among their peers. Each child possessed unique talents and Frank was strict that they use them. He demanded they face their mistakes squarely, not shrink from challenge, and respect the person and rights of others, regardless of race, color, creed or status, laying the foundation for them to build meaningful lives of their own.

According to Dr. Charles Cassio, Eva's childhood friend and a long time intimate of the Torres family, Frank always paid attention, whatever the needs of his children. He supported them in organizations and activities drove them to athletic events, attended school games, theatricals and special events. However, as a chaperone at school dances and parties, his strict adherence to rules earned him the title of universal wet blanket, with students groaning when his name was listed for duty. Frank happily shared his children's joys and triumphs and was there for them in disappointment and defeat. He was not a hugger and kisser, his role more nearly that of coach and cheerleader, exhorting, directing, advising and encouraging, rather than leaving them to cope on their own while he attended to his business affairs, as did many parents.

The Torres home was a popular gathering place for the children's friends. Although Crusita and Frank truly enjoyed the young people, this also gave them invaluable insight into youth activities and attitudes, allowing the couple to approve the good and prevent the undesirable. Dr. Cassio gave Crusita high marks for her cooking and open, welcoming hospitality, finding her pretty, gracious, cultured and with a sense of fun as she listened to confidences, held the line on proper behavior and fed the always hungry teenagers. Frank, a more remote and somewhat intimidating authority figure, offered considered advice, generous support and a disciplined kindness, challenging his own three and their friends to be the best they could be.

Although usually rational and balanced in dealings, Frank could act the fiercely partisan parent, taking great pride in the athletic honors of Frank, Jr., and Lawrence. Once at a Trinity High basketball game he had to be restrained by Crusita from climbing over the gymnasium balcony and punching out the referee for what he saw as unfairly calling a foul against Lawrence. Each child received their parent's undivided attention. Eva, ten years younger and the apple of Frank's eye, growing older, sometimes was taken along when he had courtroom work away from Trinidad. The pretty child was indulgently received in those places. Torres remembered how an elderly judge in Steamboat Springs invited her to sit on the bench with him, but Eva, objecting to his strong reek of cigar smoke, ducked out to stay elsewhere in the courtroom.

19
POLITICS AND COMMUNITY LIFE

Rancorous ward meetings and caucuses frequently marked Las Animas County Democrat politics which remained under the control of one particular group. Frank Torres, although prominent and highly respected in the community, remained an uncompromising outsider. No matter what personal gain he might have realized by working with these politicians, he stood by a non-partisan view for what best would serve the county's needs. On one occasion, he sided with Dr. Michael Beshoar against the machine. Active in business and Democratic politics, the elderly Dr. Beshoar, autocratic and hot tempered as ever, took orders from no one and was at the boiling point over resistance to proposed changes in the party platform which would give political voice to a broader spectrum of voters, particularly the unrecognized Spanish.

In total agreement with the doctor, Torres' temper heated up at barbed criticism suggesting Beshoar's real objective was personal gain. As the session proceeded, one of those against the change suggested that Beshoar's supporters be thrown out the window. Frank bounced to his feet and angrily announced that in such case he must be the first tossed. Then serving as the highly respected county attorney, Frank's opinion carried enough weight that Beshoar's critics quieted down. The meeting proceeded a little stiffly until someone managed to table the motion and hang onto the status quo under the label of "party unity."

Frank determined to run in the primary for state representative in 1950, feeling that Southern Colorado was being short changed in attention and benefits from the state and that the already announced candidate offered no real platform or even ideas that would profit Las Animas County. Although he decided to make the run, Torres did not care much for campaigning, seeing the activity as basically artificial although necessary for office seekers. The process of deliberately trying to impress people made him uncomfortable and he was incapable of giving an audience the time honored "only what they wished to hear," preferring to zero in on facts and issues. To court strangers with manufactured camaraderie was foreign to this private man, although he duly visited all sections of the county.

In the course of the campaign, Frank again encountered slighting reference to himself and his people. The opposing politician emphasized the race issue by managing to raise the charge that Torres could not represent true Americans because of his "Mexican" accent. This man had managed to get on the public address system at Holy Trinity School where he made mocking reference to Frank's Spanish accent. Fr. Sebastiani, priest in charge there, immediately invited Torres to give a rebuttal. Frank's reply was brief. "First, I am an American. Second, I am Spanish. Third, my language was acquired from a dictionary. My opponent speaks Spanish saying, *"Vaya con dias"*, meaning, literally, 'drop dead.' But I say, *"Vaya con Dios"*, meaning, 'go with God.' Thank you." The classrooms exploded in laughter and clapped their approval of the set down.

The politician publicly shrugged off the incident but privately complained to his friend, the District Court judge, about the encounter. However, the judge offered no consolation, instead, scolded him saying, "I have told you and told you to stay away from that Mexican, Torres. He will fight at the drop of a hat." They did not like him, but they did respect him.

For a change of pace, Frank sometimes took young Eva along on his campaign excursions, her cuteness deflecting away from himself some of the burden of socializing. Campaigning was easiest up the Purgatoire where, Eva with him, he would spend an unpressured day among old friends and relatives, catching up on what they needed and what concerned them. But as the campaigners drove home afterward, he always cautioned Eva not to tell her mother that they hadn't really campaigned. Crusita would disapprove of such an haphazard approach if he was serious about getting elected. In the end, the entrenched Democrat politicians, disapproving of his outspokenly independent views, favored the other candidate, withheld party support and Frank was not elected.

Both the good times of family life and the unhappy ones came to the Torres' family. Crusita lost Esther, her fifty-nine year old mother and best friend on February 3, 1949. Esther Long Kimball who had lived through personal tragedy, poverty, hard work, and in her later years, failing health, had slipped away, leaving Crusita, Frank and the children to mourn the courageous, uncomplaining and generous woman.

Although Frank gained increasing prominence in Las Animas County affairs, the Torres' social life was less than lively, partly from lingering prejudice and partly from his personal preferences. Finding most social affairs frivolous and devoid of interest, Frank's idea of a good time consisted of a book and a few uninterrupted hours to read it, or a rousing debate of ideas with an able opponent. The one exception to his staid preferences was that he loved dancing and learning new dances. In this pursuit, he took up square dancing which had become popular and set out to learn the fundamentals. Once he mastered the intricacies of the figures and steps, his perfectionist side asserted itself and he began pointing out other dancers' missteps. Crusita found his instructional zeal embarrassing and dragged him off the floor, telling him he was spoiling the fun for everyone else. Frank protested plaintively that the dances ought to be done right. Crusita favored him with a serene smile and prevailed.

Probably unending ethnic slurs and insults from youth on gave Frank Torres a touchy sense of self-dignity which was tested on occasion by his own children. One morning, a pet duck of Eva's followed him through an unlatched yard gate as, briefcase in hand, he headed down the sidewalk for his office. Unbeknown to Frank, the half-grown duck flapped after his familiar figure, quacking frantically. Mentally reviewing his day's work, he was unaware of his feathered follower to the amusement of people on the street until a downtown shop owner laughingly hailed him to look behind himself. He self-consciously scooped up the little creature, retraced his steps home and gave Eva a sharp scold for not confining her duck properly. Although he laughed in retelling the incident, Torres was thin-skinned about appearing ridiculous. He had an intellectual's sense of ironic situation and could see his own foibles, but this did not extend to his playing the buffoon.

Frank had worked hard for the establishment of Trinidad Junior College, constructed buildings for it as WPA projects, and supported it strongly as the needed educational opportunity for Las Animas County's young people. Accordingly, as each of his children graduated from Holy Trinity High School, they spent their first two years of college there. Frank, Jr., the first, finished there and went on to Denver University to complete his degree. His father took satisfaction that the same institution which had denied himself admission readily accepted his son. It confirmed his idealistic expectation that wrongs tended to be righted through effort and time. Frank, Jr., graduated from there with a degree in mathematics, and enlisted in the Air Force, where, after a special training course in meteorology at the Massachusetts Institute of Technology, he went on to make a career in the service. He spent the bulk of his Air Force years in Europe, marrying a girl from Liverpool, England. Frank Torres proudly followed that military career, one he could have wished for himself.

20

IN THE COURTROOM

The post World War II years kept Torres busy in his law practice. Frequently appointed by the court to either defend or prosecute, those cases ranged from routine to more complex and, at times, were distasteful to Frank's purist standards. But the concept of equality under the law was sacred in his eyes and no one, rich or poor, must be denied recourse to the legal process and justice. Acting as special prosecutor in one murder trial in San Luis, Colorado, he ran into conflicting evidence and testimony. The deceased, a man named Romero, had been running for the office of Costilla County sheriff, and the question was whether his death was by accident or constituted deliberate murder. Torres anticipated a difficult prosecution. Candidate Romero had spent the evening of his death sitting at the village bar and engaging in a heated argument with another man over the upcoming election. Voices were raised, fists swung and during the melee, Romero received a blow to the head. Witnesses testified that he fell backward from the punch, hitting his head against a table and slumped, unconscious, to the floor. A hastily summoned doctor pronounced Romero dead an hour later.

An autopsy revealed the death had been caused by concussion, and the man who struck the blow was arrested and charged with murder. The defendant pleaded not guilty and his defense attorney argued that death was caused not by the original blow, but rather from the deceased striking his head on the table as he fell. However, Torres contended that the original punch was the cause of death since the secondary blow came as a direct result of the first. After deliberating for a day, the jury chose to believe Attorney Torres, finding the defendant guilty as charged. Since the murder was unpremeditated, the convicted man received prison time rather than the death penalty. Frank was satisfied that justice had been done, since he had no appetite for capital punishment except in the rarest and most vicious of cases.

A different case, tried in Trinidad, centered around the accidental shooting of one hunter by another. Both men were respected members of the community and heated blame was assigned to each by friends of the other. Frank successfully defended the survivor, but it was not to his liking because he perceived "plain carelessness" combined with alcohol as the fault. As one who had used guns extensively and safely and as a person who did not drink, he found the death inexcusable but, nevertheless, accidental. He kept the defendant out of prison, but it left a bad taste.

Appointed by the court in another trial at Del Norte, he found himself defending a client with whom he felt no rapport. The young man who served in the Navy stood accused of getting a Del Norte girl pregnant and was being held on a paternity charge. Without enthusiasm, Torres listened in court to one of the world's oldest stories retold. Prosecution and defense questioned the witnesses who variously testified: the girl had a certain reputation, the girl was an innocent cruelly betrayed, the boy was a slick seducer, the boy was not the father. Back and forth, pro and con, the argument went, ending up in a hung jury. The court set a second trial for a month later which resulted in another hung jury. As a third hearing headed toward court, Torres found himself increasingly tired of the case where neither side had displayed standards of conduct Frank respected. During a recess in the third try for a verdict, the judge became violently ill and the court was recessed indefinitely. When the court clerk who reported the judge's indisposition asked Torres what would happen, Torres replied that the delay would cost his client the case. Questioned on this by the clerk, Torres grinned. "By the time court reconvenes, the baby will be old enough to say 'Papa!'"

With the case in limbo, Torres returned to Trinidad. In a couple of months, Torres' prediction came true. When the baby was born, the waiting apparently had taken its toll on both sides, making them eager to put the case behind them. Torres devised an out of court settlement in which the father agreed to child support and the mother to drop legal changes. Each grudgingly accepted the terms and the case closed.

Two years later, in a sequel to the story, Frank, riding on a bus, saw a young woman and small boy get on at the Las Vegas stop and then seat themselves beside him. The female was the unlamented plaintiff in the rape case who cheerfully brought him up to date on the activities of the father. Out of the Navy, the fellow had gotten into trouble in a county job in New Mexico where he was charged with embezzling funds. To avoid prosecution, he had skipped to Mexico and she was sure he would get in more trouble there. Torres shook his head over the tale. Such people, who never learned, were ready-made clients for lawyers unfortunate enough to be assigned their defense.

Sometimes even small cases centered on vital issues. In one such instance he defended a ten year old Spanish boy accused of assault with a deadly weapon and causing bodily harm. The boy, from a poor background, had been teased unmercifully about his home and family by three older boys at the school. Unable to take the bullying, he secretly took his father's gun from home and, returning to school, shot one of the tormenters wounding him slightly in an arm. Court charges were filed by the parents of the injured boy. Frank, after investigation, decided the accused boy basically was a good student, and would be greatly harmed by a guilty verdict. He defended the child strongly by arguing that being goaded beyond endurance and too young to comprehend the consequences, he had pulled the trigger only in instinctive self-defense and should not be held accountable under adult law. The jury agreed and the judge released the boy to his parents after ordering them to pay the victim's medical costs, closing the case and eliminating it from permanent record.

In contrast to the cases involving serious questions of law, a few strayed far from any valid legal moorings. The Judge recalled a trial he termed a "masterpiece of silliness" when one woman sued another claiming damages inflicted by the defendant's parrot who had an extensive vocabulary of offensive words. According to the prosecution, this bird had one day hailed the plaintiff saying "damn you," and then added a few descriptive expletives. The offended female filed charges of insult and slander against the owner who retained Frank to defend her. Torres, annoyed at being dragged into what he considered a frivolous lawsuit and believing no bird capable of deliberately insulting a specific human, had it brought into court as evidence. There the parrot obligingly squawked out curses and vulgarities, but his words were repeated mindlessly at anyone and everyone in the room. With this evidence, Frank argued that the parrot, having no understanding of meaning, merely repeated sounds it had heard. The judge agreed and ruled that as there was no malice or criminal intent on the part of the bird there was no provable damage to the human. Case dismissed after a useless waste of the court's time and money by Torres' standards.

Occasionally events could bring back reminders of one of his many and varied past clients. In one instance, memories of the 1940s were triggered by a 1979 national news story which featured the photo of a World War II bomber on a remote, high and inaccessible volcanic mesa in southeastern Colorado. Bold print topped the story of someone landing the aircraft successfully and disappearing without a trace. Evidence indicated the empty plane had been used for drug smuggling, but where the cargo came from and where it went remained a clueless, unsolved mystery.

This caught Frank's interest because, for a decade during the 1940s and 1950s, he had served as lawyer to the owner of the land, an illiterate, wealthy rancher named Porfirio Salas. The man, then into old age, had managed through hard work and shrewdness to rise from hired sheepherder to owner of a twenty-five thousand acre ranch. Aware of his lack of education, Salas put Torres in charge of all his matters involving legal knowledge, and had him draw up a will. A congenial partnership developed as Salas regaled history loving Frank with stories from many years past. Torres felt a kinship with the old sheepman that crossed age and station. Salas was a relic from the pioneer culture of work, community, family and faith into which Frank had been born. When the old man died, Frank settled the estate and relegated Salas to inactive memory until vividly brought back to mind by the newspaper headlines.

21
THE FIFTIES

Frank gained much recognition and many awards during his long and busy life, but none so cherished as the Silver Beaver medal that he received in 1952 from the Boy Scouts of America. The story was carried in the December 20th edition of the *Trinidad Chronicle-News*, noting that this highest award is given only to those who have made outstanding contribution to scouting. At that time, Torres had spent thirty-five years of faithfully leading troops and, additionally, had put in many years of service as a director on the scouts' regional council.

Accompanied by Crusita and Eva on the appointed day, Frank drove to Pueblo to receive the honor. Once there, he encountered one of the misadventures that seem to jinx such occasions. During his acceptance talk a window fell out of its frame high on the wall hitting Crusita, seated underneath, a glancing blow to the head and shoulder. Frank's speech was halted by the crash and shattering of glass. He flew off the stage to the side of his wife and was joined by a doctor from the audience who checked her reflexes before giving the opinion that her only problem would be bruises and discomfort. How Frank finished the speech he did not know. Later driving back to Trinidad with Crusita and Eva, he glanced at the medal gleaming on the dash, an unmeasurable honor given him for doing only what he wanted to do. If one looked amid the disappointments of life there was an equal balance of joy, he believed. Crusita kept to herself the fact that her shoulder and head ached, unwilling to cloud her husband's pleasure. Was his work with scouting coming to an end? Absolutely not. He had another thirty years to give.

The 1950s moved the country beyond post World War II relief by the triumph of Democracy to the reality of the Cold War, Communist aggression, and a Russian nuclear arms threat. Frank and Crusita kept up with national and global news, recognizing that what affected one area usually came to impinge on others. Far from being mindlessly complacent, as often assumed in present day folklore, the fifties produced a ferment of political and sociological change. Harry Truman won the election over a confident Thomas Dewey in 1948, and proved himself a determined and adept president. He spearheaded formation of NATO, ordered development of the hydrogen bomb, invoked the Taft-Hartley Act in the coal fields strike where he locked horns with the imperial head of the United Mine Workers (UMW), John L. Lewis, and also survived an oval office assassination attempt by Puerto Rican radicals.

Abroad, General Dwight D. Eisenhower headed the Atlantic forces in Europe, while in the Far East, China joined North Korea in combat against South Korea as pent up Third World resentments and ambitions began to stir. In response, Truman called a national emergency in 1949 and ordered military forces to stem the southward advance of Communist North Korean troops, activating the draft and sending American servicemen to bolster United Nations forces in keeping South Korea independent.

This conflict would find a Torres seeing combat. After completing high school and Trinidad Junior College, Lawrence had followed his brother Frank to the University of Denver. But the Korean War boiled up, and in 1951, Lawrence and twenty four of his college classmates enlisted in the Navy. After boot camp, he was trained as a supply officer and shipped out to the far East. He spent his total military hitch in the Pacific, a good part on board ship in the war zone. Much to Frank's delight, Lawrence met and was entertained there by his old friend from law school, General Paul Schriver, then military governor of Guam. While on the island, handsome Larry also won a walk-on part in the Dean Martin-Jerry Lewis comedy, *Sailor Beware!* which was a sell out when it showed at the Trinidad theater.

By serving in the military, both sons accomplished what Frank always had wanted. Service in the Armed Forces, he felt, was one of the responsibilities of a citizen in a democracy and he was inordinately proud of Frank, Jr. and Lawrence. Yet being a parent of a serviceman in a war, Frank found, produced a measurable difference in viewpoint. As Korean battle news came in, Frank spent wakeful nights and Crusita lived in constant apprehension.

With Seoul abandoned and Wonju given up to the advancing North Korean Army, President Truman clashed with General Douglas MacArthur, in charge of the American Military forces, and with trademark Truman feistiness, fired him, putting General Matthew Ridgeway in as replacement. Truce talks started in midsummer, 1951, dragging on indefinitely. Truman, who chose not to run for re-election in 1952, was replaced as president by Dwight D. Eisenhower. Frank voted for the General, feeling the World War II leader had the strength and experience needed in the Oval Office. The death of Josef Stalin and new leadership failed to bring abundance or end militant Communism in Russia, but did push its puppet, North Korea, into action at the peace talks. The U. S. signed a Korean truce in July 1953, and Lawrence came home to Trinidad. Crusita and Frank were overjoyed but soon recognized that their son's happy personality had almost vanished amid the gunfire and bombs he had lived through.

Frank and Crusita applied love, acceptance, and patience as Larry battled his demon, which later would be termed post traumatic stress disorder. His haunted, goalless drift ended some months later, when late one night he wrecked his car in a mountain roadside ditch. Called to the scene by the State Highway Patrol, Frank Torres pulled the critically injured Larry from the wreckage and somehow carried him to the waiting ambulance. In the following weeks, Larry was revived and patched up by the doctors at Mt. St. Rafael hospital. During his time there Lawrence had his epiphany where, enduring the pain of his injuries, he began to look to the future. Afterward, weak and pounds thinner, he left the hospital for his parent's home where he told them he was returning to Denver University. He had not escaped death in the war at sea only to kill himself on the roads of his hometown.

Back at Denver University, he billeted with a favorite cousin, Al Martínez and his friendly, outgoing wife, Aggie, while he finished his degree. During the process, he experienced the fact that bigotry and prejudice still was as firmly ensconced in Denver as in Trinidad, particularly for a bright young Spanish male looking for a job where he could use his education and experience.

Change continued in the United States. Late in 1953, President Eisenhower named Earl Warren, ex-governor of California, to the Supreme Court by this selection unknowingly affecting the justice system and social structure of the United States far into the future. A Communist scare swept across America and Soviet head Nikita Kruschev hinted that Russia led in development of the H-Bomb and held superiority in rocketry, prompting the United States to begin a crash program to catch up in both fields.

Intervention by the U.N. failed to prevent the Israeli Army's capture of the Gaza Strip and control of the Sinai in late 1957, expanding that country's hold in the hostile world encircling it. Frank Torres saw the dislike and distrust between Israel and its Muslim neighbors as too long-standing and deep seated to yield to simple remedy. Elsewhere in the world, to meet demands for freedom from colonial rule, Britain turned over its territory to form the new black nation of Ghana and, one by one, the rest of the European governments followed in departing Africa and turning rule over to each country's own citizens. Frank approved, envisioning that democratic self government could end exploitation and inequities anywhere it was applied. The question was, would democratic governments be set up or would dictators rule?

Frank equally applauded something of like importance and for the same reason, the Congressional enactment of the Civil Rights bill in August 1957. This was followed by President Eisenhower's sending troops to Little Rock, Arkansas, to enforce school desegregation and protect entering black students. To round out the decade of change, trouble continued in the Mideast as Torres had foreseen, atomic power came into commercial use, and President Fulgencio Batista was forced from Cuba by rebel Fidel Castro and his Communist soldiers. In addition, the world changed forever in September 1959 when the Soviets fired their rocket "Sputnik" into space, hitting the moon after thirty five hours of flight. This was followed by a triumphant visit to the United States and talks with President Eisenhower by Russia's Nikita Kruschev.

These mid-century years brought good to the Torres family. Their income was nicely comfortable, with Frank engrossed as in law, politics, and civic betterment. Crusita kept the home, worked at the credit union and followed the activities of her children, Frank, Jr., and Lawrence already on their own and Eva about to begin college.

Of necessity, Crusita refined her methods of dealing with her often intransigent husband. Sometimes, her sense of mischief took over as in the case of a worm infested Russian olive tree standing in the Torres front yard. Crusita wanted it out, Frank refused to give up on the tree he had planted as a sapling and which he watered daily in an effort to revive it. Crusita avoided argument, but each day after Frank had gone to his office she poured a toxic mixture of copper sulfate solution around the base of the tree. No one knew whether the copper sulfate or the worms triumphed first, but when spring came again the tree definitely was dead. Frank, who hated to lose in anything he had so diligently worked at, took the stump out with no notion that this failure most likely lay at the dainty hands of his wife.

But the Torres family experienced one more loss when Sus, nearing ninety, died in early January, 1954, at the Denver home of his daughter Juanita where he lived. The funeral and burial in Denver brought the extended family briefly together. Frank's brother, Manuel, shut out of mining with black lung, had become a foreman at Midwest Steel in Denver, and semi-invalid Pete, a decorated World War II veteran, lived in Trinidad with his artist wife and daughter. Although widely different in their interests, the Torres siblings respected and cared for each other, reaffirming the connection as they met at their father's grave.

Throughout their marriage, Frank and Crusita engaged in a never resolved argument as to the most important control for one's life and behavior. Husband held that "principle" should be the rule of what was right or wrong, while wife insisted with equal conviction that "propriety" must be the guide. Principle, Frank maintained, provided knowledge of the obligations of right conduct as a fundamental truth on which other truths depended. Propriety, Crusita countered, required conformity to established standards of behavior with appropriateness to the purpose or circumstance. Neither ever yielded the point and matching wits on the issue came almost to be a competitive game. While agreeing that behavior required rules or control, the small difference in definition of how this occurred mattered greatly to the debaters.

Eva listened to her parents with an indifferent teenaged ear. By either standard, she behaved herself properly as a matter of course. Nearly as tall as her diminutive mother, she entered Holy Trinity high school, unusually pretty, a good student, a promising ballerina, and a typical Torres who took part in all activities offered, she enjoyed the classes and her fellow students. With both sons gone, Crusita and Frank focused on all she did, supporting and encouraging her since both believed that a daughter should have the same choices and opportunities given a son.

Legal practice, civic good works, religious responsibilities, and the perpetual scouting, kept Torres as occupied as ever. His two man firm remained busy with the demands of a flourishing law office. Torres also served as Alternate Director of the National Association of Credit Unions and was elected president of the Colorado Credit Union League. As councilman from the Second Ward in Trinidad, he sat through extended night sessions, keeping a sharp watch to thwart unending attempts to manipulate city business for personal gain. This vigilance led to trouble. Among those looking to profit from the city's work was a certain Johnny Cha. Torres was well acquainted with Cha's activities that since bootlegging days had been linked to the local Mafia and unproven involvement in various crimes of that time. Although never indicted, and having stuck around Trinidad presenting himself as a civic minded, law abiding citizen, it was noted that he lived by deals rather than work. At one city meeting a councilman friend of Cha's made a motion which would give special advantage to one of Johnny's interests and Cha spoke persuasively from the floor in its favor. Recognizing the smoky slight-of-hand going on, and offended by the blatant attempt to push a private agenda through the council, Frank opposed the motion. Others joined him, and the meeting ended with the motion shelved and Cha departing in a considerable temper.

The next evening, Cha appeared at the Torres front door brandishing a gun and pushing a frightened Crusita aside as he demanded to see Frank. Upstairs in his study, Frank heard the commotion and started down to investigate. Cha swung around from his confrontation with Crusita and pointing the gun directly at Torres, snarled that he had come to change Frank's mind about the tabled motion or else. His yellow eyes icy with anger, Frank never broke stride until he stood directly in front of Cha, speaking clearly and firmly, "If you are going to pull a gun on me, you had better be prepared to use it." He then shoved the gun aside and ordered Cha to get out and never show his face around there or approach Crusita again. Confounded by the total absence of fear, Cha hesitated a moment, then slid the gun back into his pocket and, voicing a vulgar epithet, complied. To the shaken Crusita, Frank confided that the back side of a bully always revealed a coward.

During his term on city council, Frank devoted a good deal of attention to the issue of water, recognizing its crucial importance. One summer evening he came home to find Eva playing with the garden hose, gleefully dousing herself and everything else in sight. He turned off the faucet, gave her a brisk lecture on the need to save water use and called on Crucita to enforce his edict. Water was not really scarce in Trinidad at that time, but his farm upbringing made him wary of overcommitting it. Against whatever growth the town might experience was the allotment of water downstream and also the inevitable cycle of wet and dry years. He worked for building a dam on the Purgatoire above town to store runoff, seeing an additional benefit in ending the river's periodic flooding through town. Mustering support in the community and securing Federal money to construct it, the project was completed and Trinidad gained a stable water storage and flood control dam a few miles above town.

Torres was elected president of the Southern Colorado Bar Association and also served as state advocate and legal advisor to the Colorado Knights of Columbus. His personal values coincided with the Knights' religious commitment to the betterment of community life, and he had long since worked in their projects where the members served their church. In doing so, they helped each other and worked for a better society, utilizing the force of common effort linked to high moral purpose. Despite encroaching secular political and social agendas intruding into the established ecclesiastical order, Frank saw the church as a tried and true stabilizing element in a society then busily rejecting long accepted moral standards.

Determined to combat what he saw as a drift away from the historic Faith, Frank took to the road, organizing more Knights of Columbus chapters throughout Colorado, and urging the established ones to greater activity in combating the trend toward secular accommodation. Any culture enjoyed greater progress and stability when it held to a common set of moral values. Usually taking along another Knight, he visited, exhorted, and re-educated each group. As he succeeded beyond anyone's expectations save his own, the church took grateful notice.

His dedicated work earned him a trip to Philadelphia as delegate to the Knight's national convention in 1954 where he attended meetings and stretched his days to visit the historic sites of that city. It pleased him to stand on the same ground where the Declaration of Independence had been written. Again, in 1955, he was honored by an invitation from the National Knights to serve as keynote speaker at their convention in Boston. After a rousing address to the delegates gathered from across the country, he was designated leader of the St. Patrick's day parade there. For this, his name officially was changed for the day to Mr. Frank O'Torres, which when pronounced in Bostonian accents, he laughingly confided to family and friends, sounded to him as "Mr. O'Tore-Ass." He wryly observed, "Oh, my, I've been called worse things than that!"

Torres enjoyed his excursions, they provided new experiences, ideas, and people, but official gatherings never had overriding importance for their own sake, serving merely as a means of getting agreement on direction and purpose. He took pleasure in them without falling into conceit.

His work in the Knights brought a boost to Trinidad when Frank arranged for it to be chosen for the 1955 Knights' Colorado state convention with Holy Trinity as host church. Hundreds of delegates and wives registered in, filling every hotel room. The Most Rev. Willging, Bishop of Pueblo, came to celebrate the Knights' mass and administer confirmation to two hundred fifty-five new communicants. In getting the convention to Trinidad, Torres brought not only honor to Holy Trinity, but community good will and a cash windfall for the town. For years after, Frank continued to take care of Holy Trinity's legal matters and also worked as a dedicated layman while still remaining skeptical of mere institutional religion, Catholic or otherwise.

Torres diligent work also helped bring long term benefit to Las Animas County in 1956 when Trinidad became the site of Colorado's first State Home for the Aged. Many of the state's oldest citizens who had worked their whole life had no old age security. There were no pension plans and many elderly laborers, failing to understand Social Security, had not enrolled in what they suspected was a scheme to skim off part of the limited money they earned. Impoverished old people, no longer able to fend for themselves, had been dependent on the generosity of family or an incomplete and insecure patchwork of charity efforts. From his experience in providing for both Sus and Esther, and seeing others tackle the same problem, Frank had worked to remedy the lack, pressing the issue at political, credit union, and Knights of Columbus meetings. His efforts contributed measurably to the strong support building throughout the state. Politicians saw its appeal among voters and prudently voted homes for the aged into being, one of these in Trinidad. The town benefited doubly through the jobs and money brought during construction, and as a place where the elderly poor, regardless of race or background, could live out their lives in security and dignity. Frank saw this as democracy in action where Americans who saw a need could be counted on to work to meet it.

22
CIVIL RIGHTS

Frank's commitment to opposing racism and class distinctions was total. Certainly, he worked to protect the Spanish from its inequities and spent long hours trying to educate them in how to counter this evil, particularly by using their vote. He was loyal to his background and proud of his heritage. But he stood firm: he was a United States citizen first and totally. As surely as he would not tolerate being dismissed simply for being Spanish, it never would have occurred to him to seek special attention or advantage because his family history stretched back to Spain. He rejected the term "Hispanic" as too vague, neither did he accept "Latino" but stood, unbudging as "American Spanish" in that order, without further qualification. The Constitution and laws agreed, as he read them, that everyone was an individual not a group, and all deserved equal respect in their own right. Where accident of birth placed an individual could be no excuse for bigotry, racism, discrimination, preference or special consideration, or used to categorize anyone as superior or inferior, and he would fight anyone guilty of using it for any purpose.

This emotion was foremost in late summer 1955 when Frank climbed into his car for a speedy drive to Pueblo where the Daughters of the American Revolution (DAR) was attempting to remove a Spanish boy who had been chosen to carry the Colorado State flag in the opening ceremonies at the Colorado State Fair. They pronounced this boy, from an old and good Pueblo family, as not a fit "American" to carry the flag. Backed by the weight of his American ancestors whose residency in the country predated those of the DAR women, Frank drove to Pueblo and confronted the females, opening the fireworks by demanding they produce evidence that would disqualify the lad. Was he an American citizen or not? What did the Constitution say to this? Who had elected them to determine who was or was not an acceptable American?

Drawing themselves up angrily, the ladies responded that his culture and background was too different to qualify as a "true American." Torres countered that they either could withdraw the objection or be branded as un-American themselves, and he would take pleasure in bringing them to court to prove the charge. Livid at the nerve of this "Mexican" lawyer, they never-the-less quailed at the specter of being humiliatingly summoned before a judge and, with outraged dignity, withdrew from the scene. The boy held high the flag in the opening ceremonies. Although thin skinned at slight or insult to the Spanish people, Torres would have taken the same irate drive to support a person of any other ethnic designation denied his rights as an American citizen by a Spanish group. His democracy had no tolerance for bigotry from any direction.

Frank's attitude on race showed again at a Colorado State Bar convention dinner in Denver. A black man approached Torres as he sat with friends at a table in the Brown Palace Hotel. Hesitating until he made eye contact, the man then humbly knelt at Torres' feet, asking if Frank would help him find a place for his family to live since no one would rent to him. Flaring with anger, Torres erupted out of his chair. "Get up," he commanded. "I don't talk to anyone on his knees. We talk eye to eye!" If he had anything to say, he told the man, he should present himself in a business like manner as an equal. The black man was taken aback. No one ever had spoken to him in such terms. With that point cleared up, Frank sat down with him and listened to his tale of discrimination in housing. Frank offered him sympathetic encouragement, writing out a note of introduction to a Denver lawyer friend, and gave him advice on how the law applied favorably to his situation. The black man left feeling better about himself and with the hope that race relations might be improving.

At home in Trinidad, Crusita, with a mix of Anglo-Spanish ancestry in her veins and her upbringing, felt the ugly undercurrent of prejudice, but her nature was to avoid rather than confront. The continual racial slights left her with a deep-seated wariness of the social circles in town. Frank, however, met bigotry head on, countered it, rose above it, but paid a price. In many places and circumstances during his lifetime, his refusal to recognize or accommodate people by class or ethnic group weighed heavily against him. His uncompromising demands for a just and equal society made for poor politics where some of his fellow Spanish found his attitude traitorous to their own special interests and showed their resentment at the ballot box when he ran for office. This negative did not stop him. His position went far deeper than the merely philosophical. He had borne the brunt of discrimination since childhood, had seen it used to devalue his parents and their friends, and was no passivist Ghandi. While his anger blazed inwardly, it focused outwardly in the coolly precise workings of his mind. A wrathful Torres thought more clearly, focused more exactly, and, although he made no such claim, became a far more dangerous opponent than those whose rush of rage automatically brought up their fists as a solution.

Frank knew that many failed to understand him, and many found his egalitarian position inimical to their own special agendas, but he could not respect himself by merely attempting to please those around him. He never yielded in his battle to make democracy work and felt regret for those who did, for he believed that bowing to adversity however reluctantly never allowed anyone to rise above it. Still, he refused to retaliate in kind, knowing such would make him a similar demagogue, spouting his own version of the same racist invective he received and putting himself against the good, everyday people who far outnumbered the bigots in any society.

He used all his legal skills and his political influence against injustices done the Spanish but he never turned a blind eye on some of their own attitudes that he felt contributed to their problems. Frank saw many Spanish who had abandoned the self-knowledge, self-reliance, self-determination and moral values of their ancestors. Losing that vital dimension, they had come to semi-accept the loser's role assigned them and lived, too often, unproductively, passively angry and resentful of the society around them. In this self-defeating spiral, the unique Spanish family bond had suffered, and frequently the tensions these people lived with were addressed through a solacing alcohol bottle, compounding the problems rather than solving them. Both education, and political pressure on government to live up to its own guarantees were necessary for people to achieve their potential as equal citizens.

On the other hand, Frank also distrusted too much reliance on government welfare as answer to society's problems. Certainly emergency measures accomplished great good during the Depression years. Nonetheless, although temporary help had to be available for unexpected need, long term welfare dependency hindered ambition and competencies in the individual and more welfare did not alleviate the problem. At one Democratic party state meeting, he spoke on this, observing, "By the process of welfare, you keep people dependent," adding that the same amount of money spent on education and job training could produce independence for most welfare recipients. At times, he suspected that welfare became part of a political power strategy that banked on the hallowed old assumption that nobody bites the hand that feeds him. Frank advocated a more personal approach of cooperation among people in dealing with such problems. In a talk at the Museum of New Mexico, his daughter, Eva, quoted him on this: "One person should do for another person, and another for another, cooperating and helping, and if we had this kind of responsibility there wouldn't be any need for welfare." Achieving this would require an entirely different attitude in society but, undiscouraged, he worked for it. To foster individual success, Torres advocated that parents and schools work together, instilling high values, reasoning, willingness to work, alertness to opportunity, and refusal to accept others' evaluation of personal worth. He had proven the success of this approach in his own life and knew it was doable.

Frank saw the elections, which rolled around every two and four years, as the key to social progress locally and also for exerting pressure on state and national issues. Having run for office before, he knew he stood slim chance to get on the ballot, but finally could no longer ignore his inner promptings. Friends and fellow townsmen were pushing him to try for the position of Las Animas County Judge where the fairness and impartiality expected in a court of law frequently were lacking. This dereliction was a sore spot with Frank and also with the rank and file voters who routinely saw legal rights ignored in favor of political interests. Torres accordingly made a warm-up run for the county judge position in the 1956 primary election. The *Trinidad Daily Chronicle* ran a biography on him, and the local politicians took a look at what they rightly saw as a challenge to their domination.

Knowing that Frank would shake up the comfortable "politics as usual" they lived by, these men set to work immediately against him, holding lavish rallies for their own candidate and persistently holding up Torres' Spanish background as rendering him incapable of representing "everyone," something they had by no means done themselves. By their apparent definition, Spanish and "qualified" were irreconcilable terms. Although Frank stuck to the issues, avoided personalities and mud-slinging, he was out spent and painted negatively to enough credulous voters that he lost to the chosen candidate. However, his strong showing made Frank determined to try again.

Especially in the political arena, Torres showed impatience with stupidity and phoniness. He observed that those who tried hardest to parade what they knew usually proved what they did not. By contrast, he valued the native shrewdness and original thinking frequently encountered in those with little formal schooling and he listened to them. This earned loyalty to him in their ranks, and caught the attention of any who thought for themselves instead of relying on second hand, ready made opinions.

In Trinidad politics, Frank on occasion met up with his cousin, Charlie Vigil for whom he held ambivalent feelings. Charlie, also a lawyer from the Trinidad area, focused his practice exclusively on prosecution of organized crime. He had moved rapidly upward to become U.S. District Attorney for the state of Colorado, sending a number of underworld figures to the penitentiary. Frank approved and was proud of his cousin's achievements, but Charlie's quirky ego chose to ignore the good done by Frank who devoted himself to an opposite, but equally beneficial, goal of bettering the lot of common people. Poles apart in their practices, they also were equally distanced in values and behavior. Frank did not approve of Vigil who enjoyed a life-style that placed him as an habitué of Denver's cafe society. The straightlaced Torres found such unacceptable, while Charlie viewed Frank as a sober-sided spoil sport.

Basking in his position in Denver, Vigil still nurtured an odd rivalry with Frank whom he never missed a chance to needle on his visits back to Trinidad. This typically showed itself when he was a guest at a political luncheon at Mt. Carmel Catholic church. As he rose to speak, he pointedly ignored Frank when he graciously acknowledged by name all the rest of those present. Torres sat steaming at the slight, waiting until Vigil ended, then rose to his feet and announced, "Since you do not introduce me, I will do it myself," did so, and sat down to approving applause. Politics had a habit of handing out as many downs as ups, and a less dedicated idealist might have given up in disgust.

23

EMPTYING THE NEST

Although Frank encouraged his daughter to participate and compete in school, he adhered to the Spanish tradition where properly reared daughters were kept from premature romantic adventures. Later, when a suitable young man appeared and a marriage, sanctioned and blessed by the church was agreed upon, the bride could enter her new life, unsullied from past experience. In keeping to this, his parental strictures closed out much of the usual teenage socializing for Eva, totally forbidding association with boys of whom he disapproved. Neighbor young Charles Cassio, who qualified under Torres' stern requirements as both intelligent and properly reared, was allowed as Eva's childhood playmate, school chum and, in time, became a lifelong friend.

The adult Cassio, who earned a Ph. D. in music, made a career in orchestra, including choosing and directing music played at Denver Broncos' football games, held the Torres family in special affection. Frank had displayed particular friendliness toward the boy, calling him Charlie and unbending enough to joke with him. Signaling paternal approval, the boy also was included in family excursions, where Torres predictably offered mind improving commentary on places, people and history of the countryside as they wheeled along, wherever the destination. Education was available any place Frank steered the car.

Dr. Cassio remembers Crusita as the perfect wife and mother, gracious, cultured, generous and beautiful, while he found Torres, himself, an awesome figure, uncompromising in his morals and ideals. To the young Cassio, Frank had loomed "a larger than life figure who won the respect of Trinidad in a boot-strap effort, a self-made man, a paragon in all he did," who never raised his voice to berate or scold. Charlie, however, could sense disapproval when, without being any less courteous, a sort of negative electricity emanated from Torres, and while nothing might be said or done, the withdrawal of approval was tangible. In the end, Dr. Cassio saw Crusita and Frank putting their children first in everything, working to lay the foundation for each to build a life of solid achievement and sound personal relationships.

Frank and Eva on a family picnic.

In rearing daughter Eva, Torres continually erred on the side of caution, consequently, she went dateless during high school. Even the bravest would-be swain quailed at delivering himself up to the coolly assessing eye of Torres. Still, Frank could be prevailed upon to make an exception under special circumstances. The most notable one of these was for Junior-Senior Prom. All the other girls had dates for this big event, but no boy had dared ask Eva. Crushed, Eva took her disappointment to Holy Trinity Church as advised by her mother, where she raised a fervent prayer to St. Anthony, patron saint of lost causes. On the way home a popular senior football player stopped her and asked if she would go to the prom with him. Eva flew ecstatically home to confide that blessed St. Anthony had heard, and two days later, with Frank's permission granted, floated joyfully off to the prom, oblivious to the fact that Crusita had bribed the young man to ask her. This did not mean Crusita believed, that St. Anthony could not use earthly resources to achieve heavenly ends.

Balancing his rejection of people who failed to meet his standards, Torres always spoke generously on the qualities of persons he admired, one of whom was Torres' neighbor, a Mr. Vercelli who still worked in the coal mines. Vercelli, Frank told his family, although of humble origin and circumstance, was admirable as a conscientious family man, a good churchman and an honest, hard working citizen. He held that of their own, position and wealth did not define the man and, in fact, sometimes camouflaged the true person.

Frank, who took small interest in money matters, conceded that what affluence the couple acquired came from Crusita's skilled management of his and her own earnings. Despite a lack of pretension he did enjoy living in tasteful comfort among furnishings and art that included his collection of Andy Andersen carved wooden figures of courtroom scenes. These outrageously caricatured figures of jury, witnesses, clients, lawyers and judges amused him as bits of satiric truth in the profession he followed. Beyond that, his only real personal extravagance was his books. The world of ideas and inspiration in books influenced thinking and freed one's mind, rather than tying it down as did material things.

In addition to his literary world of ideas, Torres did favor a good large car. In early days, he had driven his trusty Model A Ford all over Colorado, but as family and finances grew, he opted for large sedans which could hold more passengers on his outings, and had more cylinders to take him up and over the mountains without downshifting to find a gear equal to the grade. He admitted to keeping a heavy foot on the accelerator, thus shortening travel time, a large plus for an impatient, busy man. Although his children reported him as an irksomely careful driver, he exercised particular caution when he had youngsters in the car, but felt free to wheel along at a faster clip when alone.

Out on the road, Frank kept a wary eye on the map for the easiest routes across the jagged upthrusts of the Rocky Mountains that constituted his work space. Afflicted with acrophobia, he shunned heights and sheer precipices, one time getting out of a friend's car when the road climbed sharply above timberline, waving the driver on ahead as he sat by the roadside until the tension eased. Only then, carefully watching his feet rather then looking to the valley falling away at the edge of the road grade, he walked until it curved downward into timber before he climbed back into the car. He felt secure with trees standing on each side, seeming to shore up the roadway by screening out the hazy depths below. The phobia is common, but surprising in a man left unfazed by the real dangers of life.

Eva Marie, finishing at Holy Trinity in 1958, had enjoyed a wide variety of activities, including dance and cheerleading, but her protective father had not allowed her to learn to drive. Consequently, when cruising around town with friends one afternoon, the driver urged her to take the wheel, assuring her that he would tell her how drive. She accepted eagerly, got the car in motion down the street, only to drive it into a tree while turning the first corner. Eva and her instructor were unhurt, but the car fender was crumpled. Knowing what her father's reaction would be, the teenagers scrambled to get a story together. They agreed the boy would claim he had been the driver. Nevertheless, guilt assailed Eva when she heard Frank tell Crusita that having to pay for his carelessness served the boy right. Pragmatic Crusita quietly arranged driving lessons. Years later, when Eva confided the fraud to Frank, he showed no amusement nor was the evaluative yellow gaze softened as he replied, "You shame me." Not even a well-loved daughter received exemption from his standards.

After graduating from Trinity High School in 1958, and completing the course at Trinidad Junior College, Eva went off to Colorado State University to major in home economics. She enjoyed her first excursion out on her own. However, popularity and probably too many activities landed Eva in the hospital with a lung congestion later that year, badly frightening her father who remembered the damage to his health law school had inflicted on him. He drove to Ft. Collins and brought his daughter back to Trinidad for medical attention and home care. Although fully recovered by the next fall, she was not allowed to go back to Colorado State, but was enrolled at Adams State in Alamosa, a smaller, closer, less pressured campus. Deposited there, Eva made a new circle of friends, and completed her degree in home economics.

24

ON THE JUDGE'S BENCH

Successful and as well situated as he was in Trinidad, J. Frank Torres recognized a crossroads in his career. He could go on in private practice, making more money, avoiding conflict and working on limited goals, or he could enter the political arena and tackle broader objectives. Given his insistence that the law had to be used to address inequities in society, Frank long had recognized the power of a judgeship. A judge's scope of authority extended over a broad range of problems seeking remedy from the courts. Frank was bothered most of all by the lack of attention given young offenders. These were the future of the country, needing instruction and guidance into responsible citizenship or, failing that, facing a bleak future in a society itself short-changed by failure to prepare them properly. Other points of friction were a standard of justice that apparently favored those who had political power over those who did not, and a system where the Spanish still routinely received short shrift in the courts. The same Spanish cynically were courted for votes at election time, but afterward found the courthouse indifferent to their problems. Present deficiencies and their long memories of concerns ignored made a block of voters pin their hopes on electing Frank Torres as county judge. They could rely on him to be fair and honest and that was all they asked. Torres was tempted, but he had tried before and knew getting elected would be chancy. In earlier elections he had won a seat on city council by a tight thirty-seven votes and had been defeated when he made a first run for judge four years earlier. J. Frank Torres was the last person the party machine would support, long since having written him off as a radical troublemaker and a threat to its centralized hold on power. He recognized the odds facing him, but asked himself, "If not now, when?" and threw his hat in.

Predictably the party again rejected him as a candidate, but Torres had expected this and entered the Democratic primary as a write-in candidate against the party's choice, the incumbent. From this beginning, the 1960 campaign heated up rapidly with Torres dwelling on deficiencies at the court, and a clique of local politicians working to nullify the effectiveness of Frank's campaign. They knew that Torres could not be influenced or bought and that he would accept the party platform only so long as it did not conflict with his own standards and political philosophy. Additionally, as one not afraid to stand alone, he frequently did so. In answer to someone's offer to stand behind him in a hot political debate, Torres brushed him aside, saying, "I don't need anyone to stand behind me. I stand by myself!" His refusal to back away from confrontation earned support among the voters and, likewise, spurred the efforts of his opposition.

His stump speeches underlined that issues must be considered on merit, not political advantage, and wrong doing would be held up for public inspection and correction. He steered clear of any convenient deals and assured his listeners that his courtroom would be the one place where equal representation was upheld. He was particularly incensed by what he saw as political cronyism that operated behind the scenes in the Las Animas County legal system.

Before the primary, the political bosses intensified their campaign to discredit Frank. Since he remained unassailable on the specifics of qualification, character and performance, his opposition fell back on race, a proven technique since a receptive audience always conveniently lurked somewhere, delighted to feel superior over supposed inferiority. As a "Mexican," so the tales went, J. F. Torres did not represent and could not understand the American way of life, which rendered him unfit to represent true Americans. Frank had lived with this a long time, but still it rankled. In a talk before the Trinidad Chamber of Commerce, he defined his stand. "First," he said, "we are human beings, second Americans, and only thirdly are we Spanish, English, or any other designation." Referring to the racist barbs, Frank spoke with tightly controlled anger, "I do not care if they like me or not, but they WILL respect me!" This was unarguably true, both supporters and political enemies respected Frank

Torres because his integrity was non-negotiable, which fact formed both the core of his support and the basis for his opposition.

Frank, who did not suffer fools gladly, impatiently forced himself to endure the windy, no-substance rhetoric usual at political gatherings. When one speaker sat down after droning through a mis-mash of platitudes, clichés and vague promises, completely missing any pertinent point, Frank was heard to mutter, "I always knew you had no brains and now you have proved it." Also, those politicians who, lacking any association with a law school, insisted on spouting "the law," annoyed him intensely with their legal pretensions that routinely failed to apply to the issue at hand. A layman, he said, might know about gallstones, but that did not qualify this person to remove a gallbladder.

Torres stumped throughout the county stating his views and objectives, and listening to people. Rallies for Torres were held, ads run in the *Chronicle-News*, all countered by messages bearing the full weight of the party. The incumbent was not about to lose his position without a fight and felt that, with party backing, he could hang on even in the face of Torres' growing popularity. Frank stuck to the issues but on the other side, it was a down and dirty campaign all the way.

Primary election day came and voters flocked to the polls while each side, worried but hopeful, waited it out. The contest had been too close for comfort. Although the incumbent issued confident predictions of a win, no one was willing to forecast the count, leading to a round of bets among the sporting minded. After the polls closed, Torres passed a long evening while ballots were tallied. The next morning, September 10, 1960, the *Chronicle-News* carried as its lead story the fact that Attorney J. F. Torres had upset the incumbent county judge by a slim edge of 3,353 votes to 3,251 in one of the most bitterly fought county primary elections in memory.

Torres was gratified, his supporters jubilant, but the general election remained to be won. For his part, the incumbent decided not to accept defeat and resumed campaigning immediately, this time as the write-in candidate himself. Both men again visited all precincts of the county, making their speeches and shaking hands. Torres pushed his message for speedier disposal of cases, more help for juvenile offenders, and equal application of the law. His opponent stressed continuity on the bench and defended his record there. Torres scrimped by on limited funds given by a wide variety of supporters, and his opponent again received the backing and financial support of the political establishment. Torres' issues and policy approach drew appreciative crowds, while the opposition again made use of the race issue as a handy ploy to deflect a true exchange of ideas. When, rarely, he referred to the racial slurs, Torres observed that background should be immaterial, with qualification, record and program the only considerations in deciding who could serve the office best.

Frank continued hammering on the inadequacies of the courthouse operation and his opponent sounding the alarm of danger in change. Election day came around, including a presidential vote, in addition to the state and county positions to be filled. A record number of voters turned out. After the polls closed on that November evening, no final count was needed to determine the outcome. J. F. Torres won in a landslide. The Friday, November 11, 1960 edition of the *Kim County Record* headlined that Senator John F. Kennedy had won a tight presidential race over Richard Nixon and also gave bold space to the fact that lawyer J. F. Torres had won the position of county judge by an unofficial tally of 7,241 votes against 925 for his opponent. The people had given Torres a resounding vote of confidence.

Frank was joyous and Crusita was glad for him. He and his supporters also celebrated the victory of another broken barrier. He had achieved what no one had done before as he became the first elected Spanish judge in the State of Colorado. Settling his professional affairs was done quickly. He turned his law practice over to his partner, Gilbert Sanders, and gave up leading a troop, but kept his position on the regional boy scouts counsel. He resigned as head of Holy Trinity Credit Union, where the board promptly hired Crusita who knew the operations and policy as well as Frank. This arrangement insured a continuation of management. Frank, proud of Crusita, still could give advice and had no intention of relinquishing a finger in the operations of his hard won credit union.

To manage his new office, Frank recruited Rose Marie Wheeler away from another lawyer. She had campaigned for Frank and liked his rule of equality and respect for women. The new judge approved her professional manner and soon depended on her management skills. He took pains to make his staff aware of what was going on in the court by conducting daily meetings on schedules, problems, and procedures. His administration aimed to be out in the open, honest, and with no questions left unanswered.

Frank's duties as judge included seven departments: wills, trusts, domestic relations, mental health, juvenile delinquency, criminal cases and the county Motor Vehicles Department of Colorado. Added to his local work, he also would sit by designation on cases in other Colorado courts where, for whatever reason, a judge was not available. For those hearings, he had use of the state highway patrol for transportation to each assigned courtroom.

The wide spectrum of his court responsibilities pretty much covered the whole range of human experience and conflict, with their resulting broad issues of law. Individual attitudes and principles varied but the law was collective and uniform. Torres was wary of tinkering with the Constitution itself which underpinned the law, he said, believing the document allowed sufficient flexibility for interpretation and, if needed, corrective legislation. The challenge of the bench suited and invigorated Torres, offering a far broader approach to social improvement than had private practice. He carefully studied case records for a clear picture of what he faced.

Frank knew and loved the courthouse building. The structure, its cornerstone laid on September 12, 1912, replaced the old utilitarian Las Animas County Courthouse where countless outlaws had been brought to justice. Las Animas County, encompassing four thousand seven hundred ninety-eight square miles, and largest county in the state, had used ambitious design plans. Built of grey-white Bedford Indiana limestone, the structure was dedicated on June 3, 1916.

An entryway wall displays a handsome mural depicting the march of Conquistadores, Indians, the Army of the Frontier, and wagons on the Santa Fe Trail. Grey marble floors, mellow wood wainscoting and ornate brass banisters create an atmosphere of dignified elegance.

Throughout, the classic design holds enduring merit, with a quality of materials, space, and craftsmanship not generally found in present day public structures.

Human services departments took up the first floor, while offices of county officials used the second, and the third taken over by the judiciary; courtroom, judge's chambers, juvenile probation and support offices. Disguised by the elegant exterior, the south half of the building actually houses the county jail. In later years, multicolor vending machines were installed and stood gleaming garishly out of place in a street level hallway earned the judge's disapproval. Water could take care of thirst, and working up an appetite resulted in pleasure at mealtime, he said, while vending machines spoke of undisciplined habits and led to overweight people.

Newly elected Judge J. Frank Torres walked the familiar, marbled third floor halls of the courthouse with assurance. He knew his job and he intended to do it. The muted sounds of busy offices on the lower levels echoed up the stairwells. When the court was in session, attorneys and clients occupied the chairs and benches of the third floor halls, seeking last minute review of their cases and reassurances from each other. Frank viewed the scene fondly. He had come often to this place to conduct the business of law.

Now, on a brisk January morning, with a dusting of fresh snow on the ground, and white capped Fisher's Peak standing remote and dark against a pale blue winter sky, Frank Torres from Weston, with all the preparation and striving which had gone before, arrived at his ideal and goal, the courtroom of law and justice. The district attorney's office, just around the corner from the courtroom, promised heavy contribution to the load of his court. From a west window in his office, he could look up the Purgatoire valley, not that many miles away but a long road of hope, work, and determination that had brought him to this place. To the right, across the rooftops, the clean spire of Holy Trinity Church rose, an enduring symbol of the source of Torres' values and strength, a place that kept his optimism fueled and his idealism intact. His unshakable belief in the necessity of civil law impartially applied, his faith in moral law, and bolstered by the reliable equation of cause and effect in the human situation, would serve as foundation upon which to enforce safeguards for a just society.

The courtroom, contrasting with the white, blue and gold elegance of the rest of the building, featured beige and buff painted wall panels and ample spectator seats, with a low divider which separated the court from the rest of the room. The jury box and witness chair stood behind the divider, and a classic portrait of a dour George Washington, flanked by the United States and the Colorado flags, hung on the back wall, bringing focus to the judicial bench and judge's chair. It was not a cozy place, but exuded an uncompromising, somber dignity.

As Frank Torres put on the robe of office, he was challenged to do right by the needs of all the people brought before him. A kaleidoscope parade of varied humanity passed through his court, rough clad workmen from ranch, field, and industry, fashionably dressed secretaries conscious of the public eye, stiffly dressed up litigants, sharply suited lawyers. Rich and poor, young and old, parents and children, embittered losers, perpetual optimists, calculating gamblers, determined plaintiffs, outraged defendants, they all appeared, their comings and goings controlled by the dark robed judge who carefully applied the written law to each case, looking to the best resolution for all concerned.

Judge Torres knew the rhythms of the place and the people, listened to the pleas, the evidence, the arguments, and always, from what he learned, knew and believed, tried to improve those who came before him. As well as issuing rulings, he used the place as a classroom of instruction on how to live more successfully. This approach soon gained him public trust and respect by all but a handful of unrelenting political enemies, the type who, in Torres' opinion, threatened the integrity of the legal system. These same people would be watching and hatching plans to get him at the next election.

Torres' courtroom presented an unending chronicle of human misdoing, misunderstanding and misery, of broken dreams, broken promises, and broken lives, of divorces, evictions, foreclosures, battery, assault, auto crashes, spite, bad faith, and swindles. As such, the office did not provide an upbeat experience. In addition to hearing the ongoing, frequently pathetic stories of people caught in hard times, through the Torres court also passed thieves, the improvident poor, crooks, wronged husbands and wives, neglected children, con artists, deadbeats, drunks, young punks, brawlers, jealous lovers, defeated venturers and scoff-laws.

He took time to find out the circumstances and assess the motives of each who appeared before him. Most of these he respected as honest people living with some basic lack, be it education, comprehension, opportunity, health, or background. For these he worked tirelessly, trying to find a formula for discharging obligation through a structured system of reparation which, meeting the requirements of the law, would benefit both plaintiff and defendant. Additionally, mental health cases coming before him required Judge Torres to make a determination on requests by an officer or member of the family for the committal of a person to the State mental hospital. On these, he moved cautiously, listening to evidence, involving the district attorney in the process, and relying on the testimony of two doctors who had examined the person as to whether confinement was required to protect this person and, or, others. Such decisions were hard.

For deadbeats and repeat offenders, those who thought they could play the system, evade responsibility or cheat their fellow men with impunity, the new judge had no patience. The only way to improve someone who didn't want to be improved required getting that one's attention. Sometimes, handing out the stiffest sentence allowed was the only route to insure the person didn't appear again and again, moving further down the spiral of irresponsibility and law breaking each time if he was let off too easy. Frank believed in the permanency of amended lives as opposed to recidivism and repeated token punishments for those caught time and again in like infractions. Professional crooks always lived at the expense of others, in the cost of the crime to their victims and the tax money required to deal with them in court once caught. Ending the cycle early made civic good sense.

25
JUSTICE FOR ALL

Torres found many of the Spanish Americans intimidated when they came into court. They clearly anticipated from it the same second-class treatment they received in other "official" situations. He recognized such experiences frequently generated a "get back at society" attitude, leading to crime and appearance in his courtroom. Denial of equal opportunity for education and work to accomplish according to the person's ability crippled people and raised the cost of government accordingly. Frank had every confidence that the Spanish Americans, given equal, open, democratic opportunity, could compete and achieve equal success, and this he worked to make possible in any way he could. But even though he had a special feeling and connection with the Spanish Americans who came before him, they were given no preference. Something wrong when done by an Anglo American was equally wrong when done by a Spanish American. He cut no slack for anyone because the law did not recognize social or ethnic divisions.

He worked in court to show the Spanish Americans who came before him how to achieve through doing their best, admonishing them to look to their courageous and self-reliant forebears and be proud of themselves and where they came from. He was both saddened and angered by people who failed to use the benefits of democracy, particularly education and the vote, and equally, to gainfully use their minds, bodies, homes, health, and opportunities. They had to look, choose, and stick to their goals. Laziness, excuses, self-pity, and weak will were non-productive and to be guarded against, no matter what. It could be done, he had done just that, himself.

One particular area of concern occupied much of his time. Torres long had perceived the handling of youth cases as the county court's most pressing challenge. The patterns young people developed during their growing-up tended to stay with them the rest of their lives, and it was dismaying to find his court overloaded with roughly one third of the cases juvenile offenders, many up on repeat charges. This came from a number of causes. With the town's economic slump, there were few opportunities for youth entry-level jobs, the traditional family structure that provided motivation and support was breaking down, and racism and prejudice still poisoned lives. In the middle of this, the media painted visions of a society where privilege, license, possessions and fame awaited anyone bold enough to ignore rules and claim them. Responsibility, work, deprivation, and pain never entered the charmed lives that floated enticingly across the screen, where standards of behavior were discarded, and violence carried out with no negative consequences. Young people saw and accepted this version of "reality." It might be made to sound and look honest, but Frank knew better. In growing up, he had living heroes to admire and emulate, not one dimensional images on a screen, and his view of life had been formed by his own senses and intellect rather than from a camera and soundtrack.

To counter these regressive social influences, Torres' court made youth welfare and the shaping of healthy values a first priority, soon reaching beyond the bench to straighten out future offenders before they would appear before him. He saw the vital importance of young people being compelled to face their mistakes and amend the behavior that led to them. With customary zeal, he set out to implement his convictions and found solid help from within the courthouse in the person of John Hinton who, under Torres, oversaw the Las Animas County juvenile social work for the court. Acquaintance with Frank's no nonsense youth philosophy, simplified Hinton's job as he found the Torres court absolutely honest, innovative, and skillful. He noted with approval that Frank displayed pride in his Spanish heritage but was not hung up on it and it played no part in his interpretation of the law.

Frank assessed each youngster brought before him. First time boy offenders frequently were ordered by the court to join the nearest boy scout troop to benefit from the structured leadership, character building and the useable skills offered there. This involved accepting discipline, learning good citizenship and developing a sense of personal pride. Invariably the scouting program filled some need, made up for some neglect, and the junior trouble makers soon became devoted to the program, abandoning their mischief making. Girls were recommended into girl scouts, or if such were lacking, to church activities, placing them in a program under a caring woman who would be their mentor and friend.

Torres articulated a ten step process which he felt necessary for young people to grow up and succeed. Primarily aimed at his own Spanish people, but he believed any home with children could benefit from their guidance. "First, educators must supply the framework for success onto a solid foundation already built by parents. Second, education never ends for the open mind, there are always opportunities. Third, children must have good role models for them to establish high goals. Fourth, you are master of your own destiny, no one else can direct it. Fifth, don't let your present situation be seen as an obstacle or impediment to your success. Sixth, you are not limited by what you come from, so make the most of opportunities, using the good and discarding the bad. Seventh, honor your forefathers who accomplished much against great obstacles. Eight, do not complain of ill treatment or lack of a chance until you have made the most of your 'stuff' given you at birth, which the Creator gives to each of his children. Nine, gain confidence, pride and courage through combining your education with hard work. Ten, develop a strong faith in yourself, your country and your God to carry you through. Following these rules can make the difference between success and failure in your life."

Judge Torres also applied the wisdom of the Bible in his courtroom. The values and goals found there exemplified what he was trying to instill in the mis-directed young people who came before his bench. He might be old fashioned, he admitted, but he had not found anywhere a better set of guidelines for successful living. Whatever worked he used, and the Bible offered a time tested, versatile textbook for self-betterment, responsible citizenship and an orderly society, he believed.

The previous court had tended to put each youth who appeared there on probation, but with only token provision for supervision and follow-up. This resulted in the same young lawbreakers being brought up on charges again and again where, each time, they were sentenced to more probation. These courtroom regulars shortly had come to the justifiable conclusion that the law possessed no teeth or bite, and had acted accordingly.

The arrival of J. Frank Torres changed things dramatically as he immediately enforced the dignity of the court and demanded respectful behavior. Probation was essential in dealing with juveniles, but only if it functioned as a learning experience. The usual lolling around and joking from those brought up on charges ceased as the Judge briskly outlined their options. The defendants could either straighten up through a prescribed, supervised program, or the penalties stiffened with each new offense. They would stay in school, maintain passing grades, make regular reports to the probation officer with immediate follow up on failure to appear, they must not be found loitering in groups downtown, and they had to be at home by nine o'clock each night unless accompanied by a parent.

One of Torres' first actions on the bench rid the town of half a dozen young punks who had basked overlong in the leniency of the previous court. Shortly after he took office, this group was brought in on charges of malicious mischief for destroying someone's yard fence. Frank regarded them with no hint of friendliness, stated the charges, and how many previous times they had been there for the same general reasons. Expecting the usual probation, they eyed him with carefully blank faces, prepared to sit through a moral lecture from the new judge as part of the process. In their experience, an unwritten law granted underage offenders soft treatment. Torres, skipping the lecture, informed them they had been given ample opportunity to amend their ways and had not done so. They had failed their responsibilities to their families, their town and county, and the court was tired of seeing them. No community could put up with law breaking, property destruction and ignoring other's rights. This brought a muffled, smart suggestion from the ranks that Torres could save himself the bother and just turn them loose. Having seen and heard all he needed, Frank gave them their sentence, "No, gentlemen, you are going to the state boy's school in Golden for eighteen months, and if you come back and get into the same trouble again you will be a year and a half older, so there is the state penitentiary in Pueblo for you to think about while you are in Golden." Under his coldly assessing yellow gaze, it took a moment for the hard reality to register in their shocked consciousness. Judge Torres left the courtroom satisfied he had done what was necessary. Although well within the law, it was a tough sentence, but they would receive counseling, job training and, hopefully, a new direction in their lives.

Word of what had happened in the courtroom spread to the other youthful offenders of Trinidad, underlining that Torres meant business. Long harassed by offensive behavior and juvenile petty crime, the townspeople quietly cheered. But Frank knew that one sentence did not eliminate the problem and there would be more to come.

Generally, he preferred a flexible approach to accomplish the goals of his court. In one instance, he kept a careless young hunter from being railroaded into prison. A carload of Trinidad high school boys out riding around one evening had their guns with them, planning some night hunting by spotlighting game in the car's headlights. Catching the reflected gleam of a pair of eyes, one of them fired off a shot, only to discover that instead of the deer they had assumed, their game was a white face steer carrying the brand of a prominent rancher. Knowing they faced serious trouble, the boys made a visit to the rancher the next morning but he refused to talk to them, filing charges instead. Shortly before the hearing, a contingent of ranchers, determined to make an example of the youth who fired the gun, arrived at the courthouse to demand that Torres deliver a conviction and maximum prison sentence. Western law of the time laid out penalties for rustling or killing livestock which could draw a stiffer sentence than a human murder or kidnapping.

Torres investigation of the underage youth brought a good report from his school and a clean record with the court. With this in his file, Frank listened to the rancher's demands, then angrily showed them the door, informing them, "This is a court of law and I am the judge, not you. I will do what is best for this boy. I will use the law as it is meant to be used and you don't tell me what this court is to do." In talking to the defendant, Torres concluded that it had been a careless, if costly, mistake by boys out on a lark. He then lectured the group on the proper handling and responsible use of firearms and pointed out that no one else should be made to bear the cost for their foolishness. He ordered the defendant to work and pay for the steer out of his earnings with proof of this to the court, placing him on probation until the debt was discharged. By the time the rancher was repaid, the young man likely had acquired valuable insight into the consequences of heedless behavior. None of the group ever again showed up before Judge Torres.

Rice Junior High, located on the south edge of downtown, and across the street west from the courthouse, drew from the south and east areas of Trinidad. It mirrored the growing problems found in all schools, with truancy, dysfunctional families, broken homes, behavioral infractions, and petty law breaking. Torres made a point of getting acquainted with K. J. Shaddy, the principal of Rice, as well as the rest of the town's school principals. He formed a particularly solid relationship with Shaddy whom he came to see as an ally in turning young lives around. Frank credited Shaddy with the moral fiber, intelligence, and will of an exemplary educator. Added to this, he liked the school principal as a person. Shaddy returned the esteem, years later pronouncing Frank, "First, a statesman, second, a jurist, and third, a role model," and adding, "No matter the setbacks, Torres never quit or gave up because he was committed to people getting a fair shake, especially children." Shaddy credited Frank with extraordinary insight and in using his court to the fullest to help shape better habits. The two men worked together in an effort to reduce the number of Trinidad's problem youngsters. They set out to keep children from going astray, and if this failed, to make their first offense also their last one.

Shifting societal values in the popular culture conspired to make petty criminal behavior seem easy and attractive to impressionable young minds. Contemporary morality too often conveyed the idea that smart people grabbed what they wanted, semantics making thievery a "rip off" without suggesting it was in any way wrong. Just do it, spoke the messages. But to Torres, it was against the law with good reason. Rip-offs cost someone else work and money. Youth, allowed to express contempt for property and the rights of others, eventually would produce a society in which their own rights also would matter little.

However, sensitive cases frequently came up where small problems were less simple than petty law breaking, especially during the formative childhood years. One such unpleasant little situation on which the judge and Mr. Shaddy combined forces involved a Rice ninth grade girl who accused an eighth grade boy of molesting her. To Shaddy, it appeared that, although rude in his comments and actions toward her, the boy actually had not overstepped, but the girl, pretty and somewhat spoiled, held a grudge and had enlisted her parents who pressed charges.

Frank looked out from his third floor window at the courthouse, reviewing what Shaddy had said, idly observing a lowered, lumpy blanket of grey cloud draped across the western sky from south to north, obscuring the tree dotted hills he knew so well. Mid-autumn gave a soft, clean stillness to the air and a calm held in the scattered, yellowing masses of trees rising among the buildings across town. Directly opposite, the Rice playgrounds were quiet, but the tranquility registered by his eyes did not carry through to his mind. The boy was at the adolescent "hate girls" stage, while the girl, a year older, already looked to attract the opposite sex. Two young people were in danger of becoming trapped in a destructive, unending circle on the path of spite and revenge. How could he get through to the youngsters and parents that honesty and responsibility were needed to avoid stigmatizing a young life?

Judge Torres called Principal Shaddy, the boy, the girl, both sets of parents and Probation Officer Freddy Gómez into his office to try to resolve the conflict. It was apparent that neither set of parents was prepared to give an inch on the innocence of their child. Torres started the proceedings by asking Shaddy of his responsibility to his students; had he counseled them about proper behavior between boys and girls? After Shaddy explained school rules on respectful playground behavior, Frank turned to the parents of the boy and asked, "What is your responsibility to your son? Have you instructed him on proper behavior with girls?" After their attempted justification, Torres asked the girl's parents the same question; had they counseled her on appropriate behavior around boys, and received another flustered non-answer.

Then Torres, something of a baseball fan, used the game to set up an instructive analogy, observing, "Now we have the facts and we are on first base but," he went on, "apparently there is a problem. You," indicating parents and children, "did not fulfill your responsibilities. That leaves us to get to second base." He turned back to the boy asking if he had been responsible and respectful in his actions. The boy gave an embarrassed reply that he had teased the girl, but meant no harm. Torres nodded, "Good, that gets us on second base," and turned to the girl, asking if she had been responsible in her exchanges with the boy. She sat, looking at her shoes, mute. The judge waited a moment and announced smoothly, "That takes us to third base." Once more he looked squarely at the girl, saying, "Now we have to figure out how to get to home base." He pointed out her responsibility as a young lady to not indulge in provocative behavior that could get others in trouble, then asked what she felt he should do with the boy? By now, squirming with guilty conscience, she replied almost inaudibly, "Whatever my parents decide."

At this, Torres excused both sets of parents to go out in the hall and confer on what they could agree to. It took only a few minutes for them to return and announce they had decided the complaint should be dropped. Frank smiled approval. "Excellent. Now you can continue to live as good neighbors, and we have scored the home run." The hearing ended with sobered parents and children abandoning accusation in favor of common sense.

In another case where Principal Shaddy assisted the Court, a Spanish Rice student had been caught shoplifting. After explaining to the boy the charges, possible penalties, and consequence of such behavior, Frank asked, "Will you pay for what you took?" The boy replied that his parents would see to it. For this wrong answer, and in keeping with his policy of acquainting Spanish youngsters with their heritage, Torres gave the young man a concise history of the Spanish and their contributions to culture and progress in the Southwest. "You," he challenged the boy, "why are you in Trinidad?" and went on to answer his own query. "Because your great, great, great grandfathers had guts and self reliance. They came in with horses and what they could carry to be able to stay the winter, and beyond that, to stay permanently. They respected their neighbors and did not steal from them. They were faithful to their church, and worked hard. If they lacked something, they either made it themselves, earned it or did without. And you, young man, are a disgrace to them in taking what belonged to someone else. Now, I want you to explain how you, not your parents, intend to repay what you took."

Avoiding looking at the judge, the boy confessed, "I did it and I will try to make it right." With this answer, Torres worked out a schedule with the store owner where the boy would repay by working the cost off cleaning and doing odd jobs at the store after school and on Saturdays. Additionally, he ordered the boy to apologize to his principle, "because Mr. Shaddy trusted you and believed in you." The case settled, the family left the courtroom with Mr. Shaddy. The boy kept silent until they reached the street side door, then blurted out in profound puzzlement, "How did Judge Torres know me before I was born?" Amused when Shaddy repeated the words, Torres hoped this exercise in taking responsibility would remain with the young man.

Trinidad unwillingly gave space to small time gang members whose thievery, fights and vandalism Torres found entirely contrary to his concept of municipal well-being. One particular group of town trouble makers, the Pachucos, copied gang behavior and aped the Pachuco style then popular on the West Coast. Frank determined to eliminate their attraction for impressionable town youth and rid the community of the problems they caused. He and his probation officer, Freddy Gómez, worked closely together, making an amusing pair, one short, sociable and jolly, the other tall, lean and serious. Freddy, attuned to his town, instinctively sensed where Pachuco trouble was apt to break out. Members, with their duck tailed haircuts, ballooning black pants and overlong "zoot" jackets, swaggered around town together, trying for an image of toughness, causing trouble in school and out, as petty criminals who set their own rules in defiance of the social order. To improve the town, Frank set about getting rid of their visible presence by eradicating the physical badges of their affiliation.

He ordered officer Gómez to round up any Pachuco found hanging out around town and, courtesy of the court, usher them into the nearest barber shop for the crew cut then generally worn by young men.

At the same time, Gómez strongly recommended to them they abandon zoot outfits and return to standard clothing. Torres reasoned that shearing the hair which proclaimed Pachuco membership and changing their attire, would eliminate their ability to set themselves apart. If he spotted one of them on the street, Frank did not hesitate to haul him off to court on the spot. Then he called in the parents, pointing out their responsibilities to the town they lived in, and delivering the message that he and they were going to stop the problem. Further, they, themselves, would be charged if the delinquency continued. It worked. The prospect of being hauled into court and fined convinced the parents of their duties, and the ex-Pachucos, deprived of their identity, blended anonymously into the scene. In recounting this, the Judge ruefully observed that in the present day he would be inhibited in his actions by civil rights challenges, no matter how much community problems might multiply as a result of failure to act.

Using variations of this technique, Torres successfully stopped almost all gang activity during his tenure When the Judge advised, "Unless you abandon this behavior at once, I will see you in my chambers if I have to send the sheriff to bring you in," culprits and parents hastened to comply, knowing that Torres kept his word.

26
Everyday People and Problems

Frank Torres devoted endless time beyond the responsibilities of his court in helping Las Animas County's young people understand that they could turn their lives around, whether the problem was of their own making, originated in the home, or came from the pressures of society. In most cases, he found more than one of these acting as contributing factors. Torres felt society's future lay in the young and anything that improved one child, indirectly improved all. He preached, scolded, reasoned, ordered and enforced, keeping faith in democracy as the best social system with law the only tool able to make it work at all levels.

As he dealt with cases of petty thievery, bankruptcy, Saturday night fights, motor vehicle violations, and personal and property disputes among adults, Judge Torres continued to focus on the best long term interests of any youngster brought up on charges. Usually there was a penalty aimed at making the offender think on what he or she really wanted out of life rather than allowing them to drift.

Frank recollected one "smart young fellow" who had taken up swaggering around town with a whip in hand, lashing it back and forth threateningly. People complained, yet, although the action was hostile, it did not constitute a misdemeanor unless he actually struck someone. Torres learned indirectly that the whip had been used on another teenager, but when he ran down the victim, the youth hedged, apparently afraid to speak out of fear. Knowing that without a witness or physical evidence there was no case, Frank awaited an opportunity to nab the whipster and turn him from the trouble he was headed into. His own boldness brought the teenager and his whip within reach. Frank spied him one evening parading up and down the sidewalk outside the Torres home, giving vicious whacks to trees, bushes and the gatepost.

At this deliberate provocation, the judge marched out, blocking the culprit's way, demanding just what he thought he was doing. The injudicious reply of "what's it to you?" brought a summons to the county court. When the young man and his whip appeared the next day, he received a dressing down for making himself a public nuisance, and pointed information on where his anti-social behavior would lead. The fact that the youth was bored and resentful of his life was no excuse. Then came positive reinforcement. Where did he want to be in five years? How would he get there? He was of an age where he should be working instead of aimlessly roaming the streets making a nuisance of himself. Indeed, he should find something useful to do. At the conclusion of the session, the youth dropped his whip on a courtroom chair and left, to disappear from the town scene.

Torres scarcely thought of the incident until two years later the same young man showed up on the Torres' doorstep on Christmas Eve to report that he had joined the Navy, liked it and had earned his first promotion in rank. He thanked Frank for opening his eyes and pointing him in a positive direction. The Judge was pleased but not surprised. If a person could be made to see that his own actions would determine his success or failure, nearly all would choose the path of greatest personal reward, he thought.

Torres' instincts served well in another case involving a teenage black girl who had been brought to juvenile court several times earlier on charges of petty thievery, chronic truancy, running away from home, property destruction and fighting, She was labeled as incorrigible by her teachers. Frank recognized a very troubled girl at war with society around her and with herself. She came from a broken home of a single, welfare mother who drank, entertained men, and exercised no supervision over her daughter. He talked at length to the girl, probing her anger, and coming to recognize that she had the intelligence for superior achievement if set on the right track. At the end of her recital of unhappiness at home, he dug further, asking, "What other things bother you?" to which she answered, "Everyone makes fun of me 'cause I'm black." "What color am I?" parried the judge. "You're white." "No, I'm not. I am a Caucasian, but my color is not Anglo white, it is Spanish tan. You call yourself black, but you are not black like my black shoes. No two people are really the exact shade, so color becomes a varied thing of little meaning." She dismissed his explanation with youthful contempt, "Don't make no difference, they still make fun of me."

The judge was sympathetic. "People have made fun of me, too." Disbelief showed on her face. Prominent people like the judge existed on a level far above such indignity. Frank gave her a smile. "I know it's hard for you, but just remember, inferior people always try to feel superior by putting themselves above someone else. You are not what someone says you are, you are what you yourself decide to be. That you are black is part of who you were born to be. This does not make you any better or any worse that anyone else. Everyone is born different, but everyone is born to be treated equally. Those who cause you trouble don't believe that because their parents don't either, so the injustice goes on. Why don't we stop it with you? You have the mind and ability to prove them wrong."

"Ain't gonna make no difference 'cause they're still white and I'm black."

Torres reached into his briefcase and drew out a magazine with a colorful landscape scene on the cover, holding it out for her to see. "Look at this painting," he urged. "It's beautiful, isn't it? But notice all the colors. Each is necessary. Look how much black there is in the clouds, the trunks of trees, in rocks on the hillside, and the fresh plowed field. The blacks are strong, solid and necessary, balancing all the other colors to make the picture complete. How beautiful would an all white painting be? It would have no interest, would it? Society is like that painting, it needs all colors. Not everyone sees this, but it is true. So remember, you have a place no one else can fill. Be proud of who you are, be proud of your people, and use who you are to be the best you can be."

Something in the girl's face told him she had glimpsed what he meant. Still, he knew she should not stay in Trinidad. The harassment would not stop, and she would be back, fighting on all fronts, once again in court and getting nowhere. The one place where she would be treated as an equal and given the schooling and training she needed was the

Colorado Girl's School in Denver where he sent her for two years.

At the end of that time she came back, assured, self-confident and ambitious. He had been right, she said, she was as good as anybody else at school. Her record there, forwarded to Torres by the school, indicated she was popular among the other girls, presented no discipline problems and led her class in grades. Frank kept up with her progress in the years following as she worked her way through college, majoring in education, and went on to become recognized as one of the outstanding elementary school teachers in Denver. Perhaps, he mused, she showed her students a landscape painting once in a while.

Seeking more ways to reach out to the youth of Trinidad, Torres made himself available at schools to counsel students with problems, to emphasize the importance of an education, and to make sure teachers carried out their responsibilities. Having taught school, Torres understood classroom dynamics and the recurring problems there. At one of the town schools someone had stolen a radio and a boy was blamed for the theft. Investigation proved that this child had not taken the radio but he remained crushed by the accusation, isolating himself from others and his grades dropping. Hearing of it, Torres sat down and talked with the boy, explaining that regrettably mistakes happened and it hurt badly to be falsely accused but still, it was better to be wrongly blamed than actually to be guilty. The person he was mattered in the long run, not what people said about him. This attention given by the judge did much for the boy, who felt he now had an important friend who understood and supported him. However, Frank had more ears to address. At a staff meeting held with the teachers and principal, he pointed out their responsibilities to ascertain all facts before making an even-handed judgment, and to remember that they were there to help students, not to demean them. As a reinforcement, he reminded them that the law controlled public education. It had been years, but Torres remained a teacher.

In court or out, Frank always took time to talk with children, discussing their heritage, whatever the origin, and how it was an asset in their lives. With them, he explored how they had gotten into difficulty and tried to give them higher expectations. Without fail, parents or guardians were brought in as responsible for the child's best interests. He accomplished significant progress with the non-criminal, delinquent youth, despite what the court's juvenile case worker, John Hinton, termed, "lazy, beer parlor parents who resented any order to appear in court or to watch out for their kids." In dealing with parents, Torres made sure that parental anger against him was not vented on their own offspring. For the slackers, Frank had no patience. If their children were in trouble, a good share of the blame fell on them as the child's earliest example and teachers, and he grew heartily sick of the progression through his courtroom of indifferent and irresponsible parents.

Sometimes Frank resorted to sleuthing in seeing to the welfare of children, one time going with Hinton, the case worker, to catch a neglectful welfare mother who had been avoiding the school nurse and the case worker rather than answer for her dirty, underfed children who skipped school regularly. They arrived at the slatternly home deliberately after office hours one day where Torres hauled a blazingly angry mother out of hiding in the bathroom, and gave her a choice of cleaning up her home, using her welfare money and commodities to provide for her sons and get them to school regularly or face a court hearing on her actions. When she spit back at him that what did he know about housekeeping, the impertinence promptly earned her a three day jail sentence to show her that the court meant business. While she thought about it in her cell, Frank had the welfare department stay with the children, clean the house and cook meals. At the mother's release, he laid down the rules: "Being poor does not keep you from providing the decent home your sons need. Your county assistance check enables you and your sons to have a roof over your heads and nourishing food on the table. You are to stay out of the bars you have been hanging around, and if you don't get yourself, the children, and the house cleaned up, make proper meals and see the boys are in school, I will see you in court two weeks from today and remove the children from your custody as an unfit mother." She left jail with a new attitude for despite her neglect, she loved her children, and confronted with the judge's uncompromising orders, she went home to carry them out. Regular follow ups revealed a clean house, well fed boys and perfect school attendance. As final evidence of the judge's success story, the woman went on to get a job and join the PTA (Parent Teacher Association).

In a similar case remembered by Trinidad social worker, Phyllis Maniot, Torres took more unusual action. A couple were found to be keeping their two children penned in a filthy chicken coop, too lazy and too given to drink to be bothered with them. Torres placed the children under permanent custody of the court and found a suitable foster home for them. After charges had been filed against the couple, Torres recognized that limited intelligence and long time drinking had rendered them incapable of comprehending responsibility. But to underline the court's view of such behavior, Torres sentenced them to spend a day locked in the same chicken coop, with an officer of the court standing by to make sure they did so.

As the court commonly placed abandoned, badly neglected or abused children in foster homes until a better future could be devised for them, the judge personally checked up on all foster parents to be sure the children were well treated and the county money these people received for expense and effort was used in the direct interest of the child. He quickly weeded out those who used foster parenting as a way to augment income by skimping on the child's needs. However, Frank believed the birth home the best place for children, and made every effort to awaken responsibility in the parents and, when possible, return the child to them under court supervision. If the parents showed substantial improvement the child went home, failing this, some did not. The child had to come first, and the court worked endlessly on the problem. The judge was equally careful with adoptions, investigating the home, life style, and circumstances of the adoptive couple prior to placing a child in the new parent's care. Further, he always returned, post adoption, to be sure the child was happy and well parented.

Although Torres controlled his volatile temper, gratuitous wrongs made him deeply angry. His reading of the law, both moral and civil, gave no allowances for anyone who deliberately harmed or took advantage of an innocent as happened once when, for safe keeping, he temporarily assigned to jail an early teenaged girl from an abusive home. Since there were no other relations to whom she could go, the jail provided a safe shelter, meals, and care while the judge worked out a solution to her problems. While he had ordered county welfare workers to check on her twice a day to be certain she was comfortable and secure, a male on the jail staff sexually molested her. The terrified girl reported this to the county worker who immediately relayed the information on to Torres.

Outraged at this betrayal of one who was under court protection, Frank ordered the head jailer into court. The resentful functionary saw nothing too bad about what had happened, explained that men sometimes got carried away with natural urges and besides, the girl had been willing. Having none of that excuse, Torres directed him to fire the staff member, sending along a deputy to bring in the offender for a hearing and maximum jail sentence. After this, he hauled the jailer back in for a blistering dressing down, ordering him to get out of the office from which he stirred too infrequently and clean up his department permanently or face a return to the courtroom to answer charges himself. Thereafter, Torres added the jail to his list of places needing his regular oversight.

Torres maintained objectivity although much of his work dealt with humans variously caught up in hurt, anger, despair, revenge, or the struggle to survive with dignity. Some of these conflicts saddened him and tried his faith. Those in the court at times wondered why the judge recessed a hearing and where he went during the time out. The answer, he withdrew to Holy Trinity Church to pray for guidance and there found strength and renewal by addressing his patron saint, Sir Thomas More, trusting that in the stillness and peace of the church, the answer would come.

He related intellectually and emotionally to More, believing that as lawyers, he and the martyred English churchman of the 1500s shared much in common. King Henry VIII named More Chancellor to the Crown as judge in the royal court in 1529, about which an observer wrote, "The meaner the suppliant was, the more affably More would speak to him and the more speedily he would dispatch the case." More dispensed justice as the law was written, once even ruling against his son-in-law who expected special treatment. Torres shared this approach to law and, in dealing out balanced justice, was closely akin to his patron saint in that both were men of courage, character, and questing intellect, and both were opposed and rejected because of these same qualities. Sir Thomas More was put to death by Henry VII, but beatified in 1886 and canonized in 1935 by the Church. Frank Torres court undoubtedly benefited, indirectly but positively, from his talks with the sainted Sir Thomas More.

Frank's first priority remained juvenile court although he neglected no other area of law. In his chambers, he talked over puzzling youth cases with probation officer, Freddy Gómez, who often played the devil's advocate on what would or would not work. In contrast, dealing with adults generally was a matter of sorting out motive and damage. These people already were set in their ways. With them, the court determined who was right, who was wrong, and what could be done about it with least damage to the persons involved. If lessons had been learned, it was a bonus. But children just starting out with their whole lives ahead of them required more.

Many of the children brought before Judge Torres came from dirt poor homes with parents unable to pay fines or make restitution for their youngster's infractions. Knowing this, Torres adjusted penalties to fit each situation, determining the controlling factors in settling a case to be the cost of providing a just outcome, the seriousness of the infraction itself, and the circumstances, age, and health of the parents. Where actual momentary damage to person or property had been done, he invariably required the debt be worked off knowing this onerous experience would make a young law breaker stop and consider before again putting himself in that position. Usually the crime was petty with Torres putting the culprit on probation, but unlike his predecessors, holding the parent, grandparent, or guardian responsible to see the terms of the sentence carried out, and requiring regular reports from the probation office to the court. If adult or child failed to show up in court, Torres sent the sheriff to bring them in to explain their lapse. As time went on few had to be sent for. It was easier to meet the order of the court than have to justify themselves before it. Torres believed that the law must be respected completely or, in time, no one would pay any attention to it, creating social disorder as a result.

His fairness combined with a stern but compassionate understanding of human foibles, and his own strictly lived, personal high standards, gained Torres the respect and almost awed regard of his fellow citizens. Parents confronted with intractable children frequently brought them around to have the judge give them a talking to. He never refused, always taking time to question the child. What did he want out of life, how did she think she would get it, were their present actions such that they worked toward those goals? Responsibility was taking charge of one's life and, step by step, working at it, first by using the opportunity for an education, and second, by not expecting anyone else to do the work for them. He made clear to each that, while individualism was normal and expected, under the law disrespectful and destructive behavior could bring curbs on the very freedom they valued. His little talks usually served their purpose.

Torres ran his court solidly convinced that education could resolve most problems in society. On the bench, off the bench, in the office, at home, at meetings, traveling and working. he educated, trying to get people to reason for themselves. Proper teaching likewise should impart usable knowledge and sustaining values, not simply partisan attitudes, which he saw as happening all too frequently in educational institutions. He also held that people treated with fairness and respect could be motivated to improve themselves and his court functioned on the belief that all parties should leave there better off than when they came in.

In Frank's courtroom, cases proceeded on time, reasonable and impartial justice was handed out, the humblest were heard. There were no pay-offs, no favors, no lines drawn between important people who would be given favorable attention and lesser ones who could be ignored. It was a court for all people, regardless of circumstance or origin, and people instinctively recognized this as assuring equal justice for all.

Torres' former WPA secretary, Sarah Cunningham, had reason to appreciate his principled approach to justice when she landed in his court as a defendant through a soured deal her brother had made with a member of one of Trinidad's prominent families. Unable or unwilling to settle the matter, the man sued Sarah to pay what he claimed her brother owed. Torres heard the arguments from both sides, examined the slim evidence and then ruled that no law on the books held one adult responsible for the debt of another because of family relationship unless the second person gained from the transaction or unless custodianship was involved. The standing of the plaintiff had no bearing on the case, and Sarah, even though an old friend, benefitted only under what the law said to the situation.

Trinidad suffered another blow to its faltering economy in 1961, when the last of the large coal mines, the Valdés, closed, leaving only the Allen mine that employed just three hundred men. As jobs were eliminated, welfare applications increased, and hard times enlarged the court case load. That same year the federal government's abortive Bay of Pigs invasion of Cuba failed in bringing down Communist dictator Fidel Castro, leaving a hostile Communist presence close to United States borders.

In 1962, Frank's brother Manuel died on December 28 in Denver. His funeral brought the remaining family back together for the final rites and burial. That same year, President Kennedy won a cold war victory in a showdown that forced Russia's Nikita Kruschev to remove nuclear missiles shipped earlier to Cuba. In Vietnam, divided into North and South by the French who had been ousted in 1954, the Communist North pushed into non-Communist South Korea using guerrilla warfare. U.S Troops had been sent there and increased military operations required reliance on the draft for more manpower. Other issues, too, occupied the President. Blacks, long forced to live under "Jim Crow" laws, were uniting under the leadership of the Rev. Dr. Martin Luther King to demand equal rights in voting, accommodation and opportunity, with pressure focused in the South. Protests and confrontations followed. Frank Torres, who unequivocally opposed discrimination in any form, supported the new political cause. Citizens must work together to promote needed reform and convince a majority to approve change through the ballot box. A democracy could operate no other way. Given time, this method worked and nondiscrimination became the law of the land.

The judge, a strict constitutionalist and upholder of democratic principles had no patience with deliberate law breaking, particularly by those who justified their lawless behavior as "acting on their principles or conscience." He needed to know where those principles or consciences came from, what formed them, and how they benefited people in general, he said. Acting lawfully on principle produced the most beneficial action, but not from falsely using such claim as a mask for personal ambition and agenda.

27

PROBLEMS AND PRINCIPLES

As he sat the bench, Torres came to dislike what he saw as the long term results of politically based social engineering. Welfare, he believed, provided an example of this, necessary in crisis cases, but not as a way of life from generation to generation where it provided unbroken cradle to grave subsidy for perpetually failed families. Used too long, welfare became a crutch for the very people it was designed to benefit. Welfare exempted and discouraged intelligent, capable people from fulfilling a deep, unconscious human need to be independent and to make a contribution to life around them. Society had a responsibility to care for the young, the aged, and the handicapped but for the able-bodied, long term support corroded pride and warped the recipient's view until, eventually, they saw assistance as one of the basic rights in life.

To break this cycle of failure, Torres prescribed education, to be initiated by careful parents, proceeding through primary and secondary schools, finishing with either trade schools or college as fit the aspirations and ability of the person, preparing these to lead independent, successful lives. From such a background, young people would be shaped to honor, honesty, citizenship and pride of vocation. Self motivation and self reliance would replace dependence, passivity, and non-achievement. If people had it too easy, they never grew strong, he felt.

In attending political meetings, Frank spoke against too much reliance on social welfare as ultimately detrimental to those it served, creating a victim mentality that had no requirement for personal responsibility. The judge's stance earned little support, due to the fact that such programs invariably appealed to politicians and fuzzy reformers where both found long term purpose and power by organizing programs for those who lived in life-long disadvantage. These dependants, encouraged to see themselves as victims of society, learned to pressure authority to enlarge their dependencies, thereby eliminating any serious effort on their part to stand on their own.

Nor did Frank approve of quota systems for preferential treatment to rectify whatever might have been wrong in the past. This method, he argued, established governing groups who selected participants and directed outcomes where immediate good too often was overbalanced by long range thwarting of individualism and personal ambition. Encouraging individual effort, by contrast, paid off in pride, better lives and a more cohesive, progressive society.

Torres found confirmation of his views among his own Spanish people. The honor and pride, self-reliance, courage to venture, and strong family, church and community ties which had long characterized the traditional culture no longer held true for many. Social change, political tinkering, and a certain resulting apathetic dependence weakened or eliminated these vital strengths. And the same result readily could be observed in other groups. Weakened people could not maintain a strong nation.

Such ideas were exchanged between Judge Torres and Rice School Principal Shaddy, where a liking and an appreciation for each other grew as they worked with wayward school children. Shaddy found Frank's philosophical ideas challenging and Torres acquired new views from the plain spoken educator. Where the general public found Frank too intellectual and remote for easy association, the school principal developed a casual rapport with him. Shaddy acknowledged Torres' foresight on problems of the future. During a discussion of student discipline, Frank predicted a wide range of juvenile problems escalating in the 1980s and 1990s, which government would be unprepared to meet, he believed. The reigning permissiveness would have disastrous results down the road with students believing that achievement was a right that could be gained by token effort only, and disregarding the importance of an education for its own sake. Frank felt it imperative that citizens and government develop a comprehensive plan to deal with the societal problems resulting from this. The judge went on to say, "In our democracy, where citizens are required to support schools with their taxes, they should be vitally interested in the results produced." Unless respect and discipline were restored, the formal learning process would largely vanish giving place to the wish to make the young feel good about themselves regardless of merit. Frank maintained that a decline in achievement would adversely affect the whole nation. Present-day schools where academic standards are lowered to prevent failures, where truancy and vandalism are common, make it apparent that Judge Torres had sized up the issue correctly as leading to a failed educational system.

Following his dedication to improving society through improving the people in it, J. F. Torres made time to work with the law abiding young people of Trinidad, never missing a chance to instruct and encourage them in the ways of good citizenship. A newspaper clipping of the day related one such instance in 1962 where Torres introduced Law Day, USA, into the school system and continued it thereafter. He set up and presided over a mock trial staged by the students in which the superintendent of schools was brought to trial on a charge of violating the speed limit. The student lawyers argued their case and cross examined witnesses, others gave testimony, while a student jury listened. After deliberation, the jury found the educator guilty as charged. Judge Torres then issued a suspended sentence and stern warning that the superintendent err no more or he would face prosecution to the limit of the law. The students learned by seeing and doing, enjoying the exercise as much as did Torres.

The judge also held an instructive court proceeding in 1962 for the Trinidad Elk's Boy Scout Troop No. 181 that presented him with a Colorado state flag for his courtroom. Although no longer leading a troop but still a faithful member of the regional scouts board, Torres was delighted at the opportunity to educate. Following strict court procedure and reading from a formal document, Frank led the troop through a ceremony in which the scouts presented the flag to the court, followed by the judge's commendation to the boys and a rousing pep talk on the good citizenship and affirmation of scouting's values which they displayed, before he pronounced the final, "The Court stands adjourned." A text of the ceremony reveals the law school orator speaking from his heart on the good citizenship he deeply believed essential to a fulfilled life and strong society. This particular vision came through whenever and wherever he took the podium.

One privilege of the court, conducting weddings, remained unexercised by Judge Torres. Couples frequently asked for this service, but he always declined. Marriage, he conceded, was certainly a legal affair but more than that, it was a personal commitment, freely given. The state had a legitimate interest in property rights, fair and equal treatment of those signing the marriage contract or born under it, but a true marriage was greater in its scope. With smitten couples in haste to marry and a soaring divorce rate, Torres felt marriages stood a greater chance of lasting if given the benefit of moral values and counseling by the church. For those with no church, or unwilling to submit to religious instruction and discipline, there were plenty of other people, who gladly would oversee the exchange of vows for a fee.

The years from 1960 to 1970 were a decade of hard times in Trinidad. National economic slump, loss of population and a corresponding decline in real estate prices, lack of jobs, and business failures all contributed to the problem. These hardships showed up regularly in Frank's court. He found the adults who appeared there fell into two loose categories, financial or personal and the two frequently were linked. Cases of unpaid bills, defaulted loans, delinquent rent, appeared again and again as the downturn pinched tightest on those at the economic bottom. The well-off had property, savings and investments as a cushion but, despite Crusita and Frank's best efforts to give help at the credit union, most of the poor never got far enough ahead to acquire security. In court, Torres applied the same "work it out with them" technique used by the credit union. By and large, the people were not dishonest, and to punish them for failing merely intensified the problem. However, the person to whom they were indebted also had rights, which challenged Frank to find the most fair and beneficial solution for both parties. Sometimes delayed repayment worked, sometimes the debtor had to take bankruptcy as a best option for another chance.

At the courthouse, Judge Torres' records chronicle an endless progression of civil matters that passed before him, the settlements signed with his graceful script. Domestic and criminal cases were held confidential by the court, but the bulk of his entries, open or closed, chronicled the lives of those dearest to his heart, the common people from every walk of life. Lack of money aggravated personal problems, but usually did not act as the base cause. These conflicts resulted from overheated disputes that lead to divorce or criminal complaint, beatings, or denial of individual rights. Many emotionally volatile situations came from adults who retained child-like attitudes toward life, including possessiveness, jealousy, desire for instant gratification, dominance, short attention span--all conspired to create problems which ended up in court. As in youth cases Frank believed education the only real solution. Education brought logic and reasoning, instilled moral values, and provided skills for both work and personal relations. Realistically, he knew that for some, it was too late, but adult education could set many on the right path, helping balance the scales toward society rising rather than slipping downward.

The world around Judge Torres increased in complexity. After President Kennedy's assassination, Vice-President Lyndon B. Johnson succeeded to a presidency troubled by social unrest. Involvement in Vietnam was violently opposed by a large and vocal segment of society. Many of the intelligencia still regarded Communism as the superior and inevitable government of the future and worked diligently to spread the philosophy of this brand of totalitarianism. Young people, idealistically convinced in the wrongness of intervention half way around the world or simply unwilling to serve, continued to oppose the military draft. If change were to come, it should be from working within the law, otherwise social conflict would result, Torres believed.

As a break from his discouraging Las Animas County court load, weighed down with the economic woes of people he knew, Judge Torres enjoyed his sitting by designation on out of town cases. A state highway patrol car would collect Frank and transport him to wherever he was directed to preside. At one time or another, many Colorado courts heard his gavel. These assignments became a sort of holiday without, in any way, diminishing the seriousness of the cases he heard. New people, new settings, unusual situations, however, broke the depressing sameness of his own court where the dismal causes for legal action repeated themselves endlessly between the occasional case involving more complex legal issues.

Torres took particular pride in his ruling on ENSOR VS. KEY, May 12, 1961, the first case on which he sat as judge by designation. This litigation involved a dispute over water rights for a condominium complex being constructed in the Rocky Mountains above Denver and was tried in Adams County court. Water rights and water distribution are critical issues in the dry Western states where, frequently, there is not enough available to satisfy all claims. Although the monetary stakes were not high, the issues involved clearly presented the water questions raised by new development. Land owners along the river sued to block a new condominiums' use of water until proper adjudication had been made. Opposing attorneys spent days arguing the complex case. Lengthy testimony, documents, old water law, and current water consumption were presented before the case went to judgment. The defendant owners of the new development, Torres recalled, relentlessly argued their right to water for the development on the land into which they had invested their money. The plaintiffs held firm for the first rights of established water users and asked for compensation for the court expenses incurred. At the end of the trial, Judge Torres reviewed the evidence and the provisions of water law that did not support the defendants, and decided in favor of the plaintiffs. He denied any further water claims by the defendants beyond those attached to their land holding until they could show legal right to additional water above that amount. He assessed payment of costs to the plaintiff by the defendants and closed the hearing. The angry defendants blasted Torres for bias as he gave them twenty days in which to file an appeal. Despite their complaints, time ran out with the defendants failing to appeal and, at the order of the court, they paid up the damages. The money was minimal, but in the water-scarce west, putting established user's rights ahead of new development demands created a significant precedent for future cases in water litigation. Torres put his correspondence with the Adams County court in his file as a good omen of things to come. Perhaps the most significant achievement of Judge Torres' legal career was that during his time on the bench not one of the cases he ruled on ever was overturned on appeal. This is a record not often matched.

Frank's acquaintances in Trinidad were many and varied, from political detractors who opposed him to the working people who saw him as honest, fair and a friend. One candid assessment of his time on the bench came from Gertrude Brunelli, an old friend and a no nonsense nurse who had spent fifty-one years in nursing, supervising, and teaching health care. Frank came under her direction when his old hernia acted up in the 1960s, sending him to Mt. San Rafael hospital under Gertrude's care. When he fumed and fussed about the waste of time, the unsympathetic Gertrude reminded him, "You are the boss in the courtroom but I am the boss here." She cleared up the symptoms by manipulating the tissue back into place and a truss to support and keep it in and the doctor released him in a few days. Despite his being a difficult patient, she held him in highest esteem, she said, considering him a remarkable judge of people, honest and uncompromising in his dedication to giving everyone a fair hearing. She admiringly recalled him as "tall, straight, and looking as if he had just stepped out of a bandbox." She also knew Crusita whom she described as a gracious, refined and quite beautiful Spanish lady. She also endorsed the Spanish people in her work finding them "remarkably kind and gentle," and reported the Spanish students in her nursing classes as bright and doing excellent work. This paralleled Frank's own view of his people.

On another topic, they differed in their perceptions. Mt. San Rafael hospital was the site of operations by one Dr. Biber who earned Trinidad the title of "Sex change capitol of the world." Personally, Torres liked and respected the doctor who had saved Eva's life a few years earlier when he removed a ruptured appendix, but found the sex change operations a "questionable and unnatural accommodation to people who were unsettled in all areas of their lives." He also felt the media attention given to these outsiders who came for Dr. Biber's services detracted attention from those who formed the character of the town and kept it going. Gertrude impartially observed that to her they were simply patients and nursing them was her job. Some of them were nice, others crude, but they all needed her care.

While Frank occupied the bench, the rest of the family pursued their own lives. Crucita headed the credit union, and Frank, Jr., reassigned to duty at Westover Air Force Base, Massachusetts, bid farewell to Europe and brought his family back to the United States. Putting Korea behind him, Lawrence had graduated from Denver University and with the assistance of his father's old friend, J. Edgar Chenowith, acquired a job at Martin Marietta in Denver. Without the legislator's help, most likely Lawrence would not have received a position there because prejudice against Spanish still remained a factor in hirings. He married Ann Houck in 1961 in Denver, and their wedding picture shows a beaming, dark haired bridegroom beside a proper, faintly smiling blonde bride. The marriage between two dissimilar people did not build into an enduring relationship. After three years at Martin Marietta, Lawrence accepted a better job as production manager for a truck equipment company in Streator, Illinois, a small town located roughly a hundred miles southwest of Chicago, where his marriage ended in divorce a couple of years later.

By the early 1960s, Eva Marie, newly graduated from college, took a job on the Apache Indian reservation in White River, Arizona, teaching creative writing and coaching the first cheerleaders in the school's history. She enjoyed the experience, pleased that under her tutelage, the shy Apache girls soon were wearing uniforms, bouncing, twirling, and leading partisan chants for the home team. Frank and Crusita visited her there several times where Frank was uniquely honored when he received an invitation to participate in a tribal dance. Usually these ceremonies were restricted to members of the tribe only. But one of the influential matrons of the tribe had come to like him and ordered him there. At the early morning affair, the judge was partnered by four girls, one the great-great-granddaughter of Chief Alchasy, the Apache ruler who reconciled his people to live peacefully as neighbors with the English and Spanish. Eva, young and adventuresome, in a short while found other horizons beckoning and moved on, going to Chicago where she would be closer to her favorite brother, Larry, and experience life in a big city.

A snapshot from the early 1960s shows Frank and Crusita by the family Buick LeSabre, and includes their big German shepherd, Kaiser.

Crusita looks to the camera with her invariable gracious smile, but, as in nearly all photographs of him, Frank stands, gazing challengingly into the lens, making no concession to posing. Using one of his phrases, he obviously had "no patience" with having his picture taken. In like manner, he found the party scene perpetually boring, taking him from more interesting occupations, and resented what he saw as enforced socializing, devoid of any uplifting purpose. Forced to go to mandatory affairs by his socially adept wife, he attended with a stiff impatience, usually positioning himself somewhat apart, his cat-eyed gaze assessing the foibles and foolishness around him. If the occasion demanded it, he knew exactly how to act, graciously extending courtly charm, although always escaping as swiftly as possible. Among party goers, he was viewed privately as a social dud.

Although he could project unapproachable aloofness, and displayed a limited sense of humor except for the foibles and follies of humans, he nevertheless valued his social contacts with fellow judges at their regular meetings and conferences. At one party ending a meeting at the historic Stanley Hotel in Estes Park, his non-participation provoked a protest. Amid a happily noisy crowd enjoying their drinks and conversation, Frank, the tee-totaler, as usual stood back against the wall observing, his intense yellow gaze following the ebb and flow of people. His cohort and friend, Judge Jacobucci of Denver finally sought intervention. "Crusita," he pleaded, "can't you pry Frank loose from that wall? He's dampening everybody's fun." Crusita, accustomed to this situation, glided through clusters of people to speak in his ear, "Frank, cut it out! You're just standing there looking disapproving and making people uncomfortable," then smiling sweetly, she marched him out to mingle gamely with the rest. He and Crusita had been over this ground before and he honestly had no wish to be off-putting, always allowing her to set the social pace, appreciating her ease and grace that he himself lacked. But he still drew the line at drinking which, he had seen too often became a health threat and a detriment to family finances Having once experienced the threat of death himself, he would never knowingly and gratuitously jeopardize his own well being, and that was that.

28
Challenges

Life as judge brought a variety of experiences, including threats on Frank's life. One such incident was defused by the Torres' German shepherd, Kaiser, a trained guard dog, whose loyalty and attentiveness eased his owner through a tight spot. Since Frank's court load included cases of sociopaths and the mentally ill who might need commitment to a care facility for their own and others' safety, he occasionally received threats of physical retaliation or death when he pronounced disposition in custodial cases or sentence in the case of convicted criminals. Some were simply blowing off hostility, some nursed actual intent. In this particular case, Frank, at home alone, answered the doorbell one afternoon to be confronted by an unkempt, visibly distraught young man who shoved past him into the living room. Frank recognized a deranged and unstable person whom he had committed to the state hospital in Pueblo for the man's own safety, and for his family's protection, and who had vowed to "get that damned judge" for it.

With a hand held meaningfully in his pocked, the man informed Torres that he had come to settle the score. Coolly, Frank invited him to sit down and discuss the matter, motioning him into an easy chair. Reading his master, Kaiser stretched out at the feet of the man who seized the opportunity to vent his grievances. The escapee poured out a rambling tale of unfair treatment, and unknown forces out to get him, and of slipping out an unlocked door at the institution. He spewed out an angry tirade against the hospital, his family, acquaintances, and Torres as part of a conspiracy to pen him up. He momentarily forgot his grudge against Frank as he disjointedly catalogued the wrongs dealt him, allowing Torres to motion Kaiser to "stay." Politely excusing himself, he slipped into the next room and made a call. Las Animas County Sheriff, Felix García, appeared a short half hour later and took the man into custody without incident. Loading him into the back seat of the car, the sheriff returned him to the institution where he obviously belonged.

When Crusita heard of it from Frank, her appalled "You could have been killed," was answered by Frank's smiling, "But I wasn't." She gave him a look and dished up the best meal of Kaiser's life. Soon after, the patient's family came by to thank Frank for treating their relation with understanding and, even though Torres life had been threatened, not pressing criminal charges. For his part, Torres was unruffled. Better to live confidently and free of fear than to become crippled anticipating the worst in every event, he said, giving Crusita the old quote: "the coward dies a thousand deaths, the brave man dies but once."

Another day a different type of drop-in visitor, a garrulous and dull townsman showed up bent on passing the afternoon basking in the company of the town's judge. Frank, deep into a new book when Crusita came up to his study and reported a guest below, met the news with a firm, "Send him away. I do not wish to be bothered with him!" "But that would be rude," protested Crusita. "I don't care, this is my home and I won't waste my time with him. He is stupid and has nothing to say but gossip." Crusita's jaw firmed. "Frank, stop complaining and go down there. Propriety demands you come." Frank, recognizing the key word, propriety, bowed to the inevitable and greeted his guest while Crusita escaped to her kitchen. Ruefully Frank recognized once again that a harmonious home required compromise.

In 1964, Torres ran for another term as county judge, this time on the Democratic ticket with luke-warm endorsement from the party which, while not liking him any better than previously, would not again risk the embarrassment of having a write-in candidate on the ballot win over the man of their choice. Predictably there were anonymous potshots and attempts to derail Frank by this unyielding clique who opposed everything Torres stood for. At one hot and partisan political caucus, the usual jibe about his being Spanish and therefore incapable was voiced again. That did not sit well with a big fellow who had been sitting quietly toward the back. With the denigration barely out of the detractor's mouth, Frank's longtime friend and upriver neighbor, Bob Parsons, president of the Colorado Cattlemen's Association, rose to bellow angrily,

"The only white man in the courthouse is Frank Torres." This observation brought a scattering of cheers and some defensive mumbling as the meeting settled down to civility. Rugged rancher Parsons was not a man to cross and Frank valued his gesture of support, appreciatively recalling it years later. "Oh, it was a fierce meeting, they were really out to get me," he remembered. Despite all efforts to disparage him, the popular incumbent judge breezed through the elections and the court continued on course. The frustrated opposition party bosses settled back to await a better opportunity.

Frank's new term witnessed more conflicts in society. The launching of the anti-male National Organization of Women (NOW) initiated a campaign against what it depicted as a biased, power holding, patriarchal society, lobbing verbal shots at any defense of the male position and exhorting women to throw off their bondage. Frank heard the rhetoric through a skeptical ear, telling Crusita he could not endorse that agenda. Putting someone down in order to gain advantage advanced nothing, and people too focused on power, personal wishes and total freedom would leave negative side effects. In this case, he believed that the worst results would fall on children and, ultimately, confuse women's position. Not that Frank lacked respect for women or considered them unequal. But men and women were not interchangeable. Down through the years, the women in his family had worked alongside their men to build community, manage property, deal with life and death, all without being slaves of men. As the judge saw it, both sexes working cooperatively together gave the best balance to society. Granted the Industrial Revolution, the right to vote, and universal education had changed how work was done, and in the process had shifted the working roles of both women and men. Still, Torres remained convinced that for the good of society all, men and women alike, must be given equal respect, opportunity, pay and advancement for the same work, as individual performance justified it, with both committed to maintaining stable homes and family life, but the sexes were not interchangeable.

While Frank issued judgments and sentences in the courtroom, Crusita skillfully ran the credit union, keeping him informed, but operating independently. She was the calm, reasoned, unflappable stabilizer who successfully balanced the volatile, obsessively active, and continually battling champion of justice and equality who was her husband. In truth, Crusita had needed the challenges Frank offered, where she either grew to meet them or risked being sidelined by the multiplicity of his interests and demands. Crusita managed it all. She understood her man completely, supported him or, when deemed necessary, opposed him, following her own mind and making her own decisions. Holy Trinity credit union quadrupled its assets during the time it was managed by the two Torres, gaining under Crusita no less than under Frank.

However, Crusita operated the credit union in an opposite manner from her husband. James Passerelli, a credit union associate and friend of both, observed that although Frank operated the business from his head, Crusita ran it from her heart. Frank, a stickler for rules, had investigated each application impartially and carefully, his first commitment was to the stability of the institution. Soft hearted Crusita differed, responded sympathetically to each applicant's need, helped them to the limit of the credit union's by-laws. An excellent judge of people, she maintained a skilled and friendly staff who dealt well with the public, and her management style won Crusita the admiration of customers and workers alike, plus solid support from the board. When she gave up her position there, she asked John Passerelli to take over and, although well qualified, Passerelli, occupied with other business interests, declined and the job went to someone else. This ushered in an era where ill-advised management cost the credit union three quarters of its assets before the course was righted and it began gradual regrowth, relieving each Torres of the guilty feeling for what more they could have done.

Although fully as independent as her husband, people Crusita met, both in business and socially, tended to see only the charming woman and assumed her to be a sweetly submissive wife. Such was not the case. Holding her own in her marriage mattered to Crusita. Once, rather than stir an argument by telling him of her intention ahead of time, she simply left him a note and took off on a bus to collect two of her grandsons for a visit, leaving Frank to fume about her contrariness until she arrived back home with the boys where he still lamented that she should have asked him to plan it for her.

As his time on the bench lengthened and practical, even-handed justice became the norm in Las Animas County, Frank kept his eyes and ears open for any wrong doing in his areas of responsibility, knowing that shady deals had slipped by some previous occupants of his position.

One such abuse came under his investigation on a tip from two nurses at a local nursing home. They reported that opportunistic help there were "assisting" the aged and mentally unclear patients to make out their wills with bequests to benefit those doing the assisting. Frank immediately called up all the questionable documents. What he saw confirmed the nurses' story. Written in new ink and of recent date were wills designating the caretakers as beneficiaries of money, personal property, and land. Torres summoned the nursing home employees into court where he delivered a sizzling denunciation on manipulation of defenseless people for illegal personal gain. He then ordered those who had participated in the scam to destroy the bogus wills they had written and witnessed and abandon the practice permanently, or he would refer the matter and staff involved to the district attorney for prosecution. Resentment and self-justification met the edict, but everyone complied. Frank refused to countenance taking advantage of vulnerable people.

On the national scene, President Lyndon Johnson had launched his "great society" introducing new welfare programs and enlarging existing ones. The approach, in many instances, countered Torres' belief in the need for personal responsibility. However, he did approve of the launching of Medicare, Medicaid and the food stamp program. Legally enacted, they provided health care and adequate food for countless people who formerly had to do without one or both. Politically the bitterly opposed conflict in Vietnam, the anti-war demonstrations and opposition in his own party, prompted Johnson to quit the upcoming presidential election.

In Trinidad, the landmark Coronado hotel burned and the Sisters of Charity closed Mt. San Rafael Hospital, which property then was turned into a regional medical center and the historic structure replaced with a modern facility. Trinidad Junior College was incorporated into the Colorado State College system, expanding its scope.

East of town a new community sprang up. This counter culture center, named Drop City, flourished in the late 1960s to mid 1970s. Many of the hippies living there were college educated or came from affluent families, and took a perverse pleasure in offending the regular residents. Wearing dirty, patched clothing, they refused to work and drove around in rattling, psychedelic painted old cars. At fall registration, they brought their children to school nude, but having made that gesture, stopped short of actually having them attend. Frank took a dim view of it. He firmly believed that education was a first priority, and such material goods as one owned deserved care and respect. Real thrift made good sense and he faulted the hippie movement for its disregard of this essential. While many of the young people involved sought a better world, and there was merit in their objecting to the increasing commercialism in society and finding war morally wrong, the counter culture's call to arms by dropping out under the banner of "drugs, sex and rock" offered no blueprint for improvement, Frank thought. Showing scant respect for the property of others, they squatted on unoccupied private land and carelessly trashed forest campsites. Torres found repugnant their lack of personal cleanliness, likewise the music exalting offensive behavior, and the use of drugs posed dangers to mind and body.

Playing at being poor by people who were not became a slap in the face to the truly poor and no society could be improved by those who scorned and turned their backs on it. Torres found this social phenomenon anti-democratic. Hard work and sacrifice by generations before them had secured the freedoms the Hippies frequently misused. Frank was not surprised to see the movement itself gradually fade out, destroyed by its own careless excesses.

But society had been altered in the process. Encouragement to break any law that did not suit immediate ends showed up in many ways, including as the theme of clever movies featuring popular stars. Accepted values were reversed. The traditional "good guy" became the actual bad guy and the usual bad guy became a figure of admiration. Established institutions which controlled society; the military, police, schools and church became venial or stupid, existing only to be ridiculed. Marriage became a trap with wives cold and conniving, and prostitutes the honest, loving women. The literate world with its values came under assault, the target of a post-literate, existential groundlessness. A new set of stereotypes took over. Torres believed that a large segment of society living outside the boundaries of long-accepted behavior posed questions for the future of a democracy. A society bogged down in self-indulgence and disregard for law faced the danger that consequent social problems and crime would increase to overwhelm government and the courts.

The succeeding years produced further complication in Torres' efforts to instill respect and responsibility in the young people who appeared before him. One was the seductive new trend toward individual "self fulfillment" which became the primary objective, with other's rights secondary. Frank found this markedly different from self-reliance. Self-fulfillment rather easily fell into self-indulgence, leaving duty and responsibility as outmoded concepts. This trend included changed attitudes toward sex and sexual controls, the results of which Torres foresaw as an impending social, financial and emotional disaster for children neglected or pushed aside in favor of parental self-preoccupation. In the long haul, society could not countenance neglecting the rights of one group for the preferences of another without suffering deep dislocation, he said.

These concerns influenced Frank's work with juveniles during his years on the bench, and seen from the present, his court serves as a model for what progressive courts are focusing on today. Although firm and fair in his attempts to help young people set their lives in order, he was not afraid to impose fitting penalties to assist in the recognition of cause and effect in human behavior. He worked to give children an honest sense of importance and self-identity, gained from what they learned and achieved. This was especially true among the young Spanish who too often were dismissed in school as unimportant unachievers, ignored and brushed aside. He wanted no child forced by others to experience demeaning which could fester and infect for a lifetime.

Respect and equal rights for all placed the judge on the side of the Civil Rights movement that was gathering momentum during the mid 1960s. The black people were equal citizens by virtue of their birth, and as such, were entitled to the same opportunity, freedom of movement, and the privileges and responsibilities of everyone else in the nation.

Less than this was contrary to the Constitution and the Bill of Rights and could not be tolerated. As in his law practice and Credit Union work, Judge J. Frank Torres felt that people must live by the rules, appreciate their privileges, accept their responsibilities and work for their own benefit. But he also exhibited a rare understanding of the hopes, dreams, foibles and frustrations of human life, dealing kindly and gently with the old, the uncomprehending, the innocent and the needy. Society was accountable to help them live in dignity and security, and he was firm in meeting this need. He laughingly told of once listening to a sermon on "The Meek Shall Inherit The Earth," and thinking no such thing ever occurred in everyday living where, instead, the arrogant and powerful usually grabbed it first.

TO THE VOTERS OF LAS ANIMAS AND HUERFANO COUNTIES

As you already know I am a Write-In Candidate For District Judge

I have chosen the Write-In Method of Voting and in so doing I am within my legal rights under the law. For your information and guidance here is a brief explanation of the 1965 Law passed by the Colorado State Legislature and approved by the Governor May 27, 1965:

On Ballots for General Election: At the end of the list of candidates for each different office there shall be as many blank spaces as there are persons to be elected to such office, in which the voter may write the name of any eligible person not printed in the ballot for whom he desires to vote as a candidate for such office. NO CROSS (X) Shall Be Required TO THE RIGHT OF THE NAME OF ANY CANDIDATE WRITTEN IN BY THE VOTER.

Whenever the judges of election discover in counting the votes that the name of any candidate voted for be misspelled, or the initial letters of his name be transposed or omitted in part or altogether on the ballot, the vote for such candidate shall be counted for for him if the INTENTION of the elector to vote for him BE APPARENT.

Again, I want to make my position clear, the time has arrived for the voters of Las Animas and Huerfano Counties to take the Courts out of the influence of the tremendous political power concentrated around the image of the incumbent District Judge which appears to have been built gradually since 1933 to the present state of affairs. Now, when he is about to retire from office as District Judge he sets the stage to have his son succeed him as District Judge without any opposition.

No right-thinking American citizen will tolerate this state of affairs. This is a challenge to our precious fundamental rights. And when we are thus confronted, whether it be from over-life-size political figures who impose themselves on their communities, or anybody else with concentrated political power, money ambition and consuming dreams, there is only one answer: Meet the challenge in full faith that right makes might. It is every citizen's duty to do so.

Respectfully yours,
J. Frank Torres

Campaign announcement.

29
LIFE MOVES ON

Judge Torres recounted events that made the years 1967-1968 a turning point for himself and Crusita. The position of judge fit him like a second skin and he saw he was making real progress in using his office for the betterment of his community and people. His comfortable reelection had served to show that the voters approved of his court, and agreed with his methods, seeing that the law worked for them if they upheld it themselves.

In his private life, each one of the Torres family held challenging jobs. Under Crusita's efficient management, the credit union operated smoothly. Frank, Jr., still was in the Air Force and Lawrence managed production of hydraulic equipment in a small town not far from Chicago. Eva had left the Apache reservation and, putting her home economics degree to use, took on the position of planning special events for the restaurant division of Marshall Field's department store in Chicago.

Despite all the positives, however, a long term negative intensified. Successful Judge Frank Torres accumulated more animosity from vested political interests. He was a maverick, whose independence, compulsion to follow the highest path, and immunity to toadying rendered him useless in their established world of politics. The faction Frank earlier defeated redoubled its efforts to find a workable scheme to reduce his influence and ultimately defeat him.

His popularity as county judge made Frank virtually unbeatable at the polls in that position, they knew. But bent on having control of key offices, the group found new ways to get at him. With help from those already in office, they succeeded in gerrymandering away some of the county court's most important responsibilities. An agreeable district court took over certain jurisdictions, thereby removing programs and their funds from the Torres court. This was accomplished under the guise of consolidating work for greater efficiency and economy and, in the process, effectively reduced Torres' scope of authority. Echoing what had happened to him in Tucson when the AHA management turned against Frank for not accommodating their self-serving schemes, this maneuver left him in an untenable position. The local party exerted its muscle to deprive Frank of further success by forcing him out through taking away the heart of his court. He was effectively blocked because he would not be accommodating at the price of abandoning his principles in order to hang on to a position. The juvenile division, closest to his heart, was removed from his jurisdiction. This was doubly disastrous that, in getting Frank, the best interests of the community youth also were gotten. Torres' court had significantly cut local crime and recidivism, so that the people of Trinidad commonly referred to Frank as "the only honest judge we ever had." Unfortunately, this rectitude and fairness got in the way of personal agendas, so that which others most admired in him remained his greatest drawback in political circles.

Torres had worked to influence and form legislation and law that advanced the guarantees of the Bill of Rights, adhering to the guidelines of the Constitution. But in the 1968 election, Frank faced a bold set-up against him. In addition to meddling in his court, the opposition was pushing to elect a man as district court judge whom Torres saw as far too limited in experience and qualification for the position. The systematic undermining of his jurisdiction had canceled out an effective county court, leaving him prepared to listen when a group of local supporters urged he run against the party's choice for district judge. Torres recognized that office as less vulnerable to outside manipulation than the county one and with comparably greater influence. In a piece of blatant nepotism, the current judge had laid the groundwork for his own son, unopposed on the ticket, to take over the district judgeship at the end of the father's term. When Frank attempted to get on the ballot for the primary election, he was denied at the nominating convention. Left to consider his options after the primary, principle and strong pressure for him to run anyway pushed his decision to go forward, to try to defeat this manipulation of the election process. Winning against the odds would be the run of Frank's life, but he felt it essential if an impartial court system was to prevail.

Long unwelcome in the cozy political circles of Las Animas County that had their candidate already in place, Frank's only chance lay in running once again as a write-in candidate. He had won earlier by this route and he felt that his record would speak positively for him, although this time the territory was much larger and he lacked substantial campaign funds and any real name recognition beyond the county lines. Nevertheless, he believed it could be done.

Ever astute, Crusita analyzed the political climate and read a negative message. Frank would lack party endorsement, and was anathema to the politicians out to get him. His support came almost entirely from the working middle class and poor people who had seen and received the benefits of his court, and voters beyond the Trinidad area would know little of him and therefore be most apt to vote the party line. Realistically, she knew her high strung, seventy year old husband's health would be endangered in such a contest. She saw the deck as stacked against him from the start and voiced adamant opposition. Frank was too intense, too tightly wound up, and the opposition too well organized. The clash would be brutal. Crusita told him flatly that he no longer was a young man, that he would destroy himself in the campaign, and begged him not to consider it. In her concern, she even threatened to divorce him if he ran, an unthinkable act for a devout Catholic, but indicating the depth of her opposition.

Frank was not prepared to listen. He had been blocked from running the county court as the law and justice required, and with district court in the hands of political enemies, the whittling away of his own court's authority would continue. Running for district judge was the only realistic hope for effectiveness and reform, putting him back in a solid position to continue his work of upholding the law to which he had dedicated his life. Crusita, however, saw correctly. It was to be ugly.

Frank launched his candidacy by inserting a plain speaking announcement in the local paper. True to the man, this reasoned piece laid the election situation on the line, stating: "To The Voters Of Las Animas County. Fellow Citizens, I hereby announce my candidacy for election as a write-in candidate for District Judge in the Third Judicial District of Colorado, composed of Las Animas and Huerfano Counties at the coming General Election, November 18th. In due course, I propose to address myself in this particular to the voters of Hurefano County, also.

"A due regard to the expressed wishes and continued insistence of many of the voters in the district brings me to this decision upon which I have arrived after careful deliberation and even, a great measure of reluctance, but in strict obedience to what I consider my clear civic duty under the circumstances.

"First, I wish to point out that in 1965, the Colorado General Assembly passed a law then designated as House Bill No. 1092, which was approved by the Governor on May 27, 1965. This is a fine and much needed law. It enhances the right of the voter to exercise his right of choice of candidate for any particular office even in the case when only one candidate's printed name appears on the ballot, as it will on Election Day for the Office of District Judge. The voters have the absolute right, if they see fit, to pass up that printed name and in the blank space immediately below, provided on the ballot, there write in the name of the candidate of their choice. In fairness to all concerned, I now wish to state that I am deeply grateful to all the voters who saw fit to honor me with their votes and support for the office of County Judge in the General Election of 1960 and again in 1964 when you reelected me for a term of four years.

"However, in this county, it has become clearly apparent that there is now a very definite pattern of concentration of political power in and around the person of the present District Judge of this Judicial District who I am informed will retire at the end of his present term this coming January. All this power is oriented towards electing without any opposition whatever as District Judge the present District attorney, the son of the District Judge, who only two years ago was elected for the first time to the office he now holds. He ran unopposed in the Third Judicial Assembly last summer and he ran unopposed in the Primary Election last month. The election of your District Judge should be based strictly on merit.

"Under the political planning, in one broad sweep, the Nominating Convention became a farce, the Primary Election was merely an empty and expensive gesture and the two-party system of government which assures good government to the American citizen, through proper checks and balances, is rendered almost completely impotent.

"Any government thus brought about is, in the long run, essentially weak and undemocratic. It does not make friends, does not inspire confidence and is brought with a train of evils. I, for one, as an American citizen, am unable to reconcile myself to such a state of affairs and with such a situation as now revealed, I am entirely out of sympathy.

"As to my record, training, experience and qualification as a Judge and my way of life as a citizen, I am confident that you know them and all I wish to state here is that if elected to the office of District Judge, I propose to follow the same pattern of service and dedication to duty as always. I trust my candidacy for District Judge merits your most favorable consideration and support during the campaign and your write-in vote on November 8.

    Respectfully yours
    J. Frank Torres."

So he ran and had everything thrown against him. The opposition knew that Torres had to be defeated if they were to retain power. Each and every politician and political hanger-on in Las Animas County long since had recognized that Frank Torres never would accommodate their methods and values over his own standard of justice, fairness and right. They also expected patronage from the incumbent's son if they got him elected. Beyond a doubt, Torres would cut no corners, make no deals, would support what was right and oppose what was wrong. In marked contrast to most successful politicians, Frank never dealt in shades of grey.

His opposition talked against Torres wherever they found a credulous ear, criticizing his style, his background, his methods, using whatever way they could to place a burr of doubt under the blanket of his acceptance. As in such campaigns, they succeeded to some extent, creating an element of discord and uncertainty. Frank ignored it and continued dispensing reasoned opinions and fair sentences in his court, maintaining the highest standard of judicial balance and interpretation of the law. He spent no time advertising his virtues and successes as judge, but let his actions and record speak for him. The idealist in him remained convinced that right must triumph in the end. But an idealist has a harder time making converts than a pragmatist. The idealist is handicapped in that he only can articulate and detail the steps needed to accomplish beneficial goals. He cannot compete with appeals couched in rosy promises, made in plausible phrases that speak to the listener's self interest and immediate gratification. And unfortunately, the ranks of politicians are infested with a certain percentage who only want to deal in people's usefulness to their own agendas which are then presented as a "mandate of the people." The idealist is fixed on the long haul to remake how people deal together for their own good.

Crusita watched uneasily as the tension built. Frank maintained his court calendar, worked hard on his campaign, slept less, ate irregularly and was constantly in motion. Her apprehension grew as the bitterness of the contest intensified. Frank's hands sometimes shook when, late in the evening and grey with fatigue, he sat in the kitchen to drink a cup of coffee and eat what she had kept warm for him. The run was no longer political, it had been transformed into mortal combat.

Only the determination to retain power fueled the ugliness against Torres. None honestly objected to Torres because he was Spanish, even though this was employed strongly against him. There were Spanish who fit comfortably into the reigning political fold. At base level, the power structure opposed Torres because they feared him and the destruction he surely would inflict on their well-ordered system. He would institute reform, open up the political process to all and make the court truly democratic.

Torres put his whole heart into the fight. The everyday people of Trinidad and the valley strongly supported him and were not swayed by insinuations and slurs. He was their honest judge. But further away, out of the county in the district, voters relied on what they heard, and what came to their ears was what a well-financed opposition wanted them to hear. Frank criss-crossed the two counties, speaking out on issues and challenging the opposition. The points raised by Torres, reform and rehabilitation for juveniles, judgments which best served both the individual and society, a uniform standard of court operations, and equal access to justice, remained unanswered while the other side drummed out its theme: "Elect one of our own. Keep things they way they are. Don't rock the boat. Vote the straight party ticket." Torres was represented as soft on dangerous young offenders, that he had gotten too big for his own people, that he was radical and disruptive, that he was . . . A MEXICAN!

The opposition avoided discussing Torres credentials, which they knew were unassailable, in favor of using the old, well-worn race card. And it made a difference. Prejudice, aside from a suspicion generated by differences, is an easy route to self-esteem of a sort. Because of what his race is, one is somehow better than someone else because of that person's race. A warped logic, but it worked for little minds and defensive personalities.

So they hammered out their message. Frank was a Mexican, this despite the fact that the Torres lineage on the Spanish northern frontier long predated the brief interval of Mexican rule over the territory, and despite the fact that the Torres family had been American citizens since 1846. Nevertheless, a man who was, in background, intellect and education, superior to his detractors, found himself again presented, one dimensionally, as a Mexican, culturally different, unable to be a "true American" and incapable of representing real Americans. Ironically, many first or second generation immigrants to the area could listen to the dishonest smear without even recognizing that their own speech markedly differed in intonation and idiom from text-book Anglo-Saxon usage, the standard used, apparently, to measure only Torres. The treasury of the opposition fattened as money came in from threatened interests, and their candidate gained as the Democratic Party strongly endorsed him, which weighed heavily with unquestioning, straight party line voters. Frank's supporters, the everyday people, could not match the dollars, although they campaigned for him wherever they could.

He stubbornly stuck to the issues as the campaign progressed and the denigration continued. Politicians' children and their friends were slyly encouraged by adults to mock the judge's Spanish accent. Frank ignored it, but it cut. He had thought, with all he had worked for and done in his community and on the bench, that this old charge would be considered irrelevant. Also his command of the English language, both verbally and in writing, surpassed that of his critics. Torres was easily, fluently, bi-lingual, a qualification not shared by his detractors, some of whom were, by and large, inadequate in one and illiterate in the other.

In the final weeks leading up to the general election, Torres fought the battle with his whole heart and strength. He did not indulge in self-pity or complaint. Such would waste his time, deflect him from his purpose, and ultimately render him ineffective. But the stress got to him. Although he brushed off her concerns, Crusita fretted that he was not eating or sleeping well, and that it was taking a toll on his well being.

The bitter campaign to get rid of Frank Torres once and for all, ground down to its nasty end. Crusita never totally forgave the insult afforded her husband and the dishonesty of tactics employed against him, the sheer hypocrisy in action, for she knew his political opposition, in their own minds, gave no real credence to their own tales. At base level, they knew Frank to be a truly honest and competent judge who would stick by his principles, come what may. Stumping for votes, Torres offered a favorite quotation from Theodore Roosevelt. "This country will not be a good place for any of us to live in unless we make it a good place for all of us to live in," which he saw as an enduring truth.

Election day dawned with uncertain weather and an uncertain vote. Frank and Crusita voted early, walking under a cloudy sky to the polls where voting was brisk. Frank greeted acquaintances cheerfully, Crusita nodded politely, but a knot of fear kept her mute. After the polls closed, Frank sat through one of the longest nights he ever endured. By early morning, the ballots had been counted and the returns were in. Torres was defeated by a slim margin, but it was enough. His idealistic belief that if you were in the right you would win against the odds, for the first time, completely failed him. He took the news with his usual calm, but Crusita knew the inward pain he felt.

30

IN SICKNESS AND IN HEALTH

The next day found Frank back in the courthouse, impeccably dressed as always, and with no outward sign of distress as he dealt with the varied problems of justice. He stayed at his desk all morning even though feeling a little off physically, which he attributed to missing sleep the night before. As he took the elevator down at noon, he was hit by a funny weakness, he said, and had to be helped off the elevator by three lawyers who rode down with him. Waving off their concern, and promising to check with his physician after he wound up court business for the day, he took off down the street to see a man, and then go home for lunch.

He didn't make it. An acquaintance, alarmed to find him wandering, dazed and disoriented, in the middle of the street, guided him into a nearby doctor's office and stood by while he was given a cursory examination by a nurse who concluded that it was just an overreaction to the election or, perhaps, Frank's imagination. Crusita, who had been called, arrived minutes later and saw at a glance that her husband was in serious trouble. Martin Mendine, Frank's court clerk came to drive him and Crusita over Raton Pass to the office of Dr. Visconti, a Torres friend who after quickly checking Frank's eyes and vital signs, bluntly pronounced it a major stroke and checked him into Miner's Hospital. Torres stayed in intensive care, bedfast and immobilized, for six anxious days before he was pronounced out of danger.

After his release and his recovery was assured, Dr. Visconti hauled him back in to surgically repair Frank's old hernia and then ordered painful personal change in Frank's life. Although his heart was damaged, Frank could live out a normal life if he took care of himself, otherwise the outlook was not good. He could not go back to the courtroom, much less run for another term. He would have to resign from the court and never practice law again. In probably the most painful decision he ever made, Torres complied and Las Animas County lost its most respected and revered "only honest judge we ever had." What his political enemies started, the stroke obligingly finished.

If Frank Torres' health had not failed him at this crucial point to end his professional career, undoubtedly he would have mustered his forces and tried again. He was not a quitter and, given his qualifications, judicial record, unimpeachable reputation and the respect of friends in positions of power, he also would have been a candidate for higher court appointment. Ironically, election on the party ticket had been stacked against him for exactly the same reasons that he should have moved up in the court system.

The changed circumstances fell heavily on Crusita who was thrust into the role of caretaker and head of the house while Frank regained strength and mobility. On a slightly diminished basis, this remained the case for the rest of their lives. She quit at the credit union, but held a deep bitterness against the careless medical office that misdiagnosed the case and endangered Frank's life, and never really forgave the dirty attacks during the campaign that prompted it. She cared deeply for her husband, but one part of her resented both the loss of her own freedom and the curtailment of Frank's. She had warned him but he had refused to listen. She had known both that he deserved to win on his own merits and that he would not.

Following his lifelong custom, Frank sat back to think through his situation. Crusita and the children were the focus of his existence, he had friends, interests, with much still to live for, and he determined to avoid complaining and resentment and make the most out of his remaining years. He would have to exchange perfectionism for acceptance, and become more observer, less participant. Never given to self-pity or looking backward, he pledged himself to be happy. But in reality, the limitations of forced retirement were difficult for the old fighter to bear.

Not long after Dr. Visconti released Frank to complete his home recovery, the judge and Crusita received a happy announcement. Eva, who had taken a leave from Marshall Field's to help her parents after Frank's stroke and now back on her job, called from Chicago to inform them of her engagement to Carl Aschenbrener, a rising young engineer with Westinghouse and, happily, also a Catholic. The couple came to Trinidad for Carl to meet his future in-laws and to receive the judge's blessing. Frank appreciated what he termed Carl's "brilliant mind" and Crusita liked his well-bred good manners. Eva had broken the long tradition of arranged marriages, becoming the first in her line to freely choose her bridegroom without prior approval by parents.

Judge Torres walks Eva up the aisle.

Frank and Crusita caught the Super Chief east to Chicago for the formal wedding on November 4, 1968, at St. Clement's Catholic Church, an even year after Frank's stroke. A radiantly beautiful Eva and a soberly handsome Carl made their vows, cut the cake, and when the music struck up, the dancers included Frank and Crusita. In their Pullman for the trip home, Frank savored the complete rightness of the match, and the bonus of new friends in Carl's Wisconsin based banker father and teacher mother.

Back in Trinidad it seemed that the successful trip east had freed Frank and Crusita from the spell of illness, shown them that life was less restricted than they had thought. Frank determined to reach out to people, one way or another, exercising the knowledge and insights seventy years of living, studying and working had given him. Money would not be a worry as Crusita had made astute investments from their income through the years. And, most importantly, they still had each other to face the future together.

In a footnote to Torres' legal career there, Trinidad was subjected to a grand jury investigation by the state of Colorado some time after his resignation as Judge. This centered on the same illegal and unethical situations in the courts and local government that Frank had worked and campaigned against so vigorously. A news story of the findings appeared in the February 1, 1976 issue of the *Denver Post*, which revealed graft and mismanagement in Trinidad's government offices, featuring misdemeanors, fraud, misuse of Federal funds, and inaccurate bookkeeping. The grand jury produced indictments and prompted a recall election. None of the indictments touched the Torres' court. Frank felt a reassuring justification with the findings. The clean-up was long overdue.

The late 1960s and early 1970s brought more change. President Nixon ended the Vietnam war. Frank said he found it ironic that meeting the highest priority of the liberal left by ending the war in no way diminished their detestation of Nixon. He, himself, found Nixon adept in international affairs but bogged down at home with a deficient staff whose maneuvering forced his resignation from the presidency. Frank also anticipated the mid-East would face a long term struggle, with Yasser Arafat and his Palestine Liberation Organization (PLO) fighters making hit and run attacks against Israel, displaying only a small portion of the long held hatreds in that area of the world. As a lover of wide open spaces and wilderness, Frank was disappointed that closer to home, Fisher's Peak had been considered, then dropped as a possible new national park by a tightened Federal budget. This left Trinidad's landmark geographical feature in the hands of the Colorado Fuel & Iron instead of it being held as open space, immune to commercial development. Trinidad itself, with no industrial or commercial development, was economically stalled and losing population.

Sticking to his regimen of diet and exercise, Frank put concern for his health behind him even if Crusita did not. Together, they retained their interest in the political and social scene. The garbled innovations of the hippie era gradually evolved into acceptance of some and transformation of the rest into enduring political battlegrounds. The issue of women's liberation occupied editorial columns, university courses and whole editions of women's magazines. Torres believed in women as equals, but he did not approve of dividing the sexes into warring camps. He preferred cooperative equality, he said. As for the environmental movement, he agreed and disagreed with it on various points. The colonial Spanish had lived on the land for some four hundred years without appreciable damage to the land, air or water. But recent development was not so benevolent. Where humans despoiled the land, as with the coal mines around Trinidad, there was a need to restore it, but he also feared that sometimes the enthusiasts who would put the land above human use entirely failed to factor into the equation the needs of an increasing population. Proper care of the land would take balance, not conflict.

As the couple adopted new approaches, Crusita privately looked back to the challenges of the credit union, and Frank deeply missed his lost place in the world of law. Nevertheless, neither accepted a rocking chair existence. Both were doers, and it became a question of how and where they could make the best life. Coincidentally, at this time, their three children each were in the process of life and career changes.

Frank, Jr., a major, retired from the Air Force and with his wife, Patricia, and four sons, Bruce, Mark, Matthew and Brett, looked for a place to settle down. Lawrence, tired of the pressures in the manufacturing world and disillusioned from his failed marriage, cut free of corporate rules to find a way to be his own boss. Additionally, Eva and Carl and their new baby daughter, Tara, born on February 23, 1972 in Omaha and baptized at the Boy's Town Chapel there, deserted Chicago's big city demands for Santa Fe, New Mexico.

Trinidad, while holding memories on every block, offered limited opportunity so that a new location seemed in order. For this, the younger family members chose historic old Santa Fe. Frank and Crusita, who knew and liked the town, raised no objection. The nation's oldest capitol, with spectacular scenery in a vast and changing mountain and mesa landscape, offered cosmopolitan interests, a varied mix of people, and opportunity to explore new directions. Therefore, in a reverse of grandfather Antonio Domingo Torres' trek from northern New Mexico to southern Colorado a hundred years earlier, grandson José Francisco Torres made his own trek back from Colorado to northern New Mexico in 1973. It was a move never regretted, although Frank Torres' heart stayed permanently anchored in Trinidad.

Once in Santa Fe, Frank and Crusita placed their investments in real estate and other holdings, living comfortably on the returns. By mid-1973, the couple and bachelor son, Lawrence, were living in a spacious pueblo style home in southside Santa Fe. Lawrence and Crusita acquired and operated the Quivera Indian Arts shop across from La Fonda and Lawrence found a couple of downtown buildings which were bought by the family as an investment. Frank, Jr., although inexperienced, moved into real estate development. Eva put her artistic and organizational skills to homemaking, raising baby Tara, volunteer work and involving her parents in congenial activities. Carl, a private person, shunned public attention and settled into the world of finance avoiding what the judge termed the "peanut politics" of the town.

Judge Torres met and mingled with people downtown and around the state capitol, enjoying the varied humanity and keenly observing the local scene. In the tri-cultural town, he found the attitudes less concerned about ethnic origin and more attentive to the individual. Once, in talking with friends, Frank articulated his own stand on race relations: "We have to accept, appreciate and understand each other as we are, or else we are in a perpetual stalemate of contesting forces." However, in his living out this belief, the reward frequently had been attack from both sides of the question.

Although he missed Trinidad and his legal work, Frank closed out regrets and busied himself with renewing old acquaintances, making new ones, investigating what went on around him, and, as always, reading. As a Catholic, the old judge differed with the landmark *Roe vs. Wade* decision which affirmed a woman's right to abortion and triggered a protracted values fight and single issue political campaigning. Life, he believed, was meant to be lived not to be cut short because someone found a child inconvenient to accommodate. But, he observed, the branches of government could never satisfy a majority of voters when it set out to legislate conflicting moral issues, detracting from action on unmet social needs, particularly in the area of improving education and health care upon which all society could agree.

All in all, the new situation was highly agreeable. Crusita saw to her husband's well being, enjoyed her work in the shop, and delighted in having a world of ideas, fashion and social events to share with Eva. Both grandparents found joy in having baby Tara to coddle and spoil.

Lawrence became the mainstay of his elderly parent's life, shielding them from problems, shouldering work around the home, keeping shop with Crusita, whipping up one of his Italian specialties in the kitchen, in the process cheering and animating their days. Torres once remarked that he saw Lawrence as a combination of General Patton and an un-broke bronco, with a heedless, go-ahead zest for life. Settled in Santa Fe, home loving, family oriented Larry married a second time and again it soon ended in divorce. Neither of his brides, apparently, had shared his desire for children and a solid home. But Larry had weathered these disappointments, the judge explained, remaining a generous, giving and loving person, only more guarded and private in expressing these qualities. The one person he openly adored was his little niece and goddaughter, Tara.

31
MORE CHANGES

Life moved on. 1974 elevated Gerald Ford to the presidency in the aftermath of Nixon's Watergate resignation. A boycott by Arab oil producers created an energy crisis and high gasoline prices that prompted new alternative energy research at New Mexico's Los Alamos National Laboratory. None of these events disrupted the tenor of life in Santa Fe. Frank Jr.'s and Eva's families each took a turn in sharing the spacious home of their parents while their own were being built. These times reminded the judge of the happy extended family life of his youth up the Purgatoire, and he proudly called the group his little United Nations because of their mix of backgrounds, Spanish, Anglo, British and German. To Frank, living together represented the ideal for both the individual and the whole human family, with acceptance, equality, support, fairness, and goodwill, adding up to how a family should live, and likewise, the basis for all successful societies. While everyone else worked at their jobs, Frank frequently made himself useful at home. From this he created a small joke with a bit of culinary history. They would be having company, he announced one night, and the guests would be a fat, empty headed blonde and a hot headed chap named respectively "La Dona Sopapilla" whose background was Arabic and who usually was sweet and "Don Juan Chile" who traced his ancestry to Velarde and Chimayo.

Ever the jurist and teacher, Frank mediated family spats, dispensed advice, gave information and listened to complaints and ideas. In all, he respected the right of choice, never attempting to force his personal faith and beliefs on others, although always ready to advocate high moral positions. Frank and Crusita actively missed each family when they moved on to their own homes. If a family member disappointed him, Torres always spoke to the person in private, but beyond that, he never revealed anything but approval and pride in those with whom he shared a family tie. To speak ill of one member would be to bring shame to all. If nothing good could be said, he said nothing.

Doting Grandpa with baby Tara.

Exercise, ingrained into him from the farm chores of his youth, and his self-directed recovery from tuberculosis kept Frank lean and fit even as old age gradually asserted itself. Mind and body worked together, explained the old philosopher, the proper function of one dependent on the other, immaterial which was engaged first. Regularly walking the dirt streets near his home, relishing the weather in sun or shade, wind or snow, he greeted people, exchanging ideas, sharing insights, even advising an aggressively "cool" teenage neighbor to be more respectful of his parents, settle down, concentrate on getting his education and raise his goals. Questioned on how he saw the younger generation, Torres stated, "They do not aim high enough, their dreams are limited!" explaining, "Dreaming gives goals to work for. Without dreams and work, people live their lives by the chance of the day."

Frank viewed with disapproval the effect of what he saw as changing and eroding moral values in all levels of society, but especially among the young. History proved that if you set out to change a society, you started with the youth. Society's elite of the 1970s and 1980s ridiculed and ignored established standards. Respect for others and for one's self disappeared as in-your-face-role models dominated the media world. Youth became increasingly rude and unruly, focused on gratifying immediate appetites and urges. Educational standards were lowered to allow laggards to make it through school. The concept of cause and effect ceased to be a factor in reasoning, as things were seen as happening randomly. The need to be "tolerant" made everything acceptable. As the end result, Torres foresaw a society confused, without common standards and values to hold it together, and drifting out of control. Tolerance was needed for the harmless foibles of people living in a varied society, he knew, but never simply applied as cheap elastic to stretch ethical values.

Torres scrutinized social trends, global political conflicts, contemporary fads, all in the light of the law and democracy. He observed that with abandonment of colonial rule and setting up of new nations in Africa, the people there, too long forced to obey others' law, would have trouble developing and gaining obedience to a just set of laws authored and enforced by themselves. In a few generations, they had leaped from subsistence living tribalism to foreign rule, and then to control of their own destiny in a complex technological world. With no experience in national self-determination, trouble would result from the necessity of curbing total individual freedom while new nations learned that just law was, ultimately, in their own best interest.

As he became known around Santa Fe, J. Frank Torres received significant recognition for his values and accomplishments. The high intelligence, the creative ideas, the simple goodness and idealism of the man impressed those who met him. He accepted the admiration and attention with grace and good humor, but remained solidly himself, philosophical, fascinated by life and people, and nobody's fool. Famed flamenco dancer, María Benitez frequently took the Judge to lunch, then governor Jerry Apodaca developed a genuine liking for him and included Frank and Crusita in functions at the executive mansion. Torres also mingled with writers, painters, primos, assorted locals, and tourists on the Plaza. Ernestine Evans, then secretary of state, officially made him an Hidalgo in 1975, enabling him rightfully to use the title of "Don." He and Anita Gonzales Thomas shared a commitment to preserving Spanish history and culture. Orlando Romero, the strongly opinionated head of the Museum of New Mexico Historical Library and social critic, exchanged with him views on past discrimination and current lingering racism. Frank became acquainted with writer Marc Simmons whom he admired, particularly for Simmons' meticulous research and balanced books on the early Spanish people in the southwest. Myra Ellen Jenkins, crusty director of the state archives engaged him in lively discussions. E. Boyd, an authority on Spanish Colonial arts, and Fray Angelico Chavez, priest, author and researcher into the genealogy of Spanish families, shared his quest for making clear the unique value of the Spanish cultural history. It all was deeply satisfying.

Although he was no less Spanish than he always had been, Santa Fe accepted him without the pin pricks of discrimination. He and Crusita were invited to parties in elegant homes, met interesting people, and appreciated their inclusion. But the egalitarian Frank was not always impressed, remarking after one such affair that he wondered what most of the guests there had done with their lives except live up to their position and money. Social acceptance never dulled the edge of his social conscience.

Judge Torres received one particularly cherished honor when he and Crusita were among a limited number of guests invited to a reception for the King and Queen of Spain on their official visit to Santa Fe in 1987. At the reception, Frank had a private audience with King Juan Carlos who, speaking in Spanish, told him, "Judge, we are Spaniards in essence and in spirit, Spanish in different locations, but Spanish united in culture and heritage. We both are guardians of the Spanish culture, you in New Mexico and I in Spain" This unique meeting merged past and present together in a fulfilling reconfirmation of identity.

In retirement, Torres retained, undiminished, his trademark feistiness and proclivity for speaking his mind regardless of who might be offended by the lack of sugar coating. The lifelong proponent of a democratic social order believed it must be based on truth, adhere to the same, or eventually crash in disarray. To some listeners this could be disconcerting and verge on heresy in an age tilting toward political correctness and celebrating diversity over unity.

His adherence to principle never was more clearly illustrated than when he spoke at a Hispanic Chamber of Commerce luncheon meeting. The members sought to recognize him as one of their own, but were not well acquainted with the man and his convictions. On the day appointed, Judge Torres greeted members and visited his way through the meal. Afterward the members sat back in anticipation of a reassuring perspective on life from a fellow Spaniard.

They failed to get what they expected. After the introduction and applause, Frank launched into his talk. Cities prospered, he told them, through the cooperative efforts of all citizens, working together for common goals, and this applied to diverse groups as well. Civic organizations were a strong support of society which best served its people by inclusion, not by separation. As he warmed to his subject, his next words fell on appalled ears. "Gentlemen, if you asked me to join your organization here today, I would refuse! Your organization, setting you apart from the rest of the town, does not belong in our United States. In a democracy, there is room for only one Chamber of Commerce in a town, representing everyone equally. Your organization does not do that. Two separated, competing groups, no matter how politely their operations are carried on, are detrimental to long range community harmony. There should be only one group where common values, aims and efforts are pursued and where differences and inequalities can be addressed. Gentlemen, I would respectfully suggest that you should disband and take up membership and work in the existing chamber." The members met this with stunned silence, but Frank only spoke vintage Torres, unwilling to compromise his principles for acceptance or approval from anyone. He never received another invitation, which bothered him not in the slightest because he had spoken only the truth. How the members received it was their problem, not his, he thought.

32

VINDICATION AND VALUES

During this time an unexpected vindication came, belatedly fulfilling the defiant prediction Frank made when he was refused entry at the University of Denver Law School half a century earlier. An invitation from the University of Denver, couched in great courtesy and professions of pleasure at "sharing in his achievement," invited him to a reunion of the 1925 law school graduates there, at which he would receive his Juris Doctor. Denver University had absorbed Westminister School of Law into its operations and now claimed him as its own graduate. Although denied entrance fifty-three years earlier, the university apparently had been prodded by social stirrings and a need to make amends for a distasteful chapter in its history.

Crusita and the judge went to Denver for the ceremony where Frank stood, gowned and stoled, among his peers to accept the new degree. Having the last word was vastly satisfying even if the long-ago Dean was not there to hear it. But amid the spirit of *bon homme* and commendation, one pure, unadulterated Torres stand on principle interrupted the smoothly orchestrated harmony of the festivities. The day before the final banquet at a socially prestigious Denver country club, he found out that the place barred Jews from membership or events there. This predictably raised Torres' hackles and he voiced his opinion at an afternoon meeting. "Gentlemen, we were taught better than this. We have studied the law, we have practiced it, and we have sworn to uphold it, and you would allow this? Of all people, we should be aware this is unacceptable, an affront to our national Constitution, and if our banquet is to remain at that place, I, for one, will have no part in it. We should meet them in court rather than sit down at their table!" The discomfited reunion committee quickly changed the dinner to another country club that drew no such lines.

Judge Torres receives a Juris Doctor fifty years late.

Did this long delayed recognition make up for the treatment accorded Torres in the past? Did Denver University's law school "share in" his achievement? Certainly not, but the temper of the times had caught up with what Torres believed; that equal rights should mean just that. Frank was pleased but not overwhelmed by the gesture since Westminister remained his true Alma Mater. It had enrolled him as an equal, and graduated him in the same manner, and it remained first in his affections.

Another occasion spotlighted Torres' impatience with generalities and his distaste for pomposity. He accepted an invitation to attend a New Mexico credit union convention held in Santa Fe. The speaker, a well-known politician, clearly enjoyed being the center of attention. Prefacing his talk with jokes, he confidently spoke in polished platitudes, giving scant information on the purpose, operations and benefits of credit unions, and nothing on their history. The speaker's not doing justice to an important public service institution irked Torres, who had attended the founding of the national movement and worked in it with a religious zeal. As he listened, it became obvious the speaker, woefully deficient in knowledge, presumed to speak as a gazetted authority on the subject. He gave no indication that this process of making savings and loans available to all was a significant gain against historic discrimination.

Frank, who never tolerated inaccuracies, rose during the discussion period to set the facts straight, quoting Filene on the whys and wherefores of credit union development, adding details from his years of involvement in Colorado. Bristling, the speaker attempted to squelch Torres, remarking that no one cared about Colorado. Judge Torres nodded benignly, "You show your ignorance," he observed and sat back down to listen. The speaker attempted to retaliate later during a coffee break, when he intimated Frank was an out-of-touch old man. This was too much, and Torres, his yellow eyes narrowing, replied with icy contempt, "You, sir, are everything I despise in my own race." But in the grip of annoyance, Frank was overly specific. In truth, the same attitude from anyone would have gotten its own rebuke, regardless of ethnicity.

The United States, celebrating its bicentennial, was calm and busy in 1976. It signed a treaty with Russia limiting underground nuclear tests. North and South Vietnam had been united under Communist control. Blacks in South Africa battled government troops as rioting and violence marked rebellion against apartheid and demands came for self-government. Jimmy Carter was elected president over the incumbent, Gerald Ford.

Frank still viewed the proliferation of social welfare programs skeptically, where decisions that shaped people's lives were made without the individual's participation, and he also found imbalance in some programs. A democratic society could not grant particular rights to one citizen and not another, and rights had to be balanced with corresponding responsibilities. He gave the example of government responsibility for a needy child, to assist that child in growing into a useful citizen, or, if neglected, setting it up as a lifelong drain on society. The mother also had a responsibility not to produce more dependent children and increase her burden on taxpayers. He observed that many rights groups failed to address personal responsibility, which in time, through these programs, created a parasite mentality of expectations. Years earlier, he had cautioned his political party that, "By the welfare process, you keep people dependant." The message remained unheeded.

Another development that met with Torres' disapproval was the increase in frivolous lawsuits filed in expectation of gaining money by the simple expedient of making a claim in court. Faced with paying high court costs, many large corporations simply settled for a lesser sum before court action occurred which was an automatic payoff for the defendant. Honest cases would be given less attention in the courtroom as opportunistic pleadings filled the judges' dockets. Torres maintained the law was to protect against injustice, not to compensate for personal stupidity or cupidity.

As satisfying and interesting as his life had become, Judge Torres was nagged by a lingering homesickness for Trinidad and the Purgatoire Valley and he journeyed back as often as he could wheedle family or friends into taking him including the author of this book. Happily on the road north, each place prompted remembrance of people, incidents and the life he had lived. Watrous recalled visits to his grandfather, Antonio Domingo. Raton brought back his stay in Miner's Hospital after his stroke. And winding north down Raton Pass around the canyons and rocky lower reaches of Fisher's Peak, Torres recounted improving the pass road as one of his WPA projects where the dynamiting had been done by the talented and profane Manuel C. de Baca of Las Vegas who earlier had blasted out the channel for the Panama Canal.

The road down Raton Pass prompted a history of the slag heap remnants of coal mining days with its abandoned houses crumbling on hillsides overlooked by a roofless adobe church. Starkville, with sturdy rock homes built by the earliest Italian immigrants, was fondly remembered as people he liked and a solid block of votes for Frank when he ran for office.

A highway turnoff gave access to a graveled road leading westward up the winding Purgatoire River. The verdant valley basked in late summer sunshine and tranquility, rendered fragrant with clean air, evergreens, ripening grasses and warm earth. A dam impounded water for municipal use, irrigation and flood control, had beneath its waters the foundations of the old town of Sopris, a vital mining center in the days of Torres' youth. Standing on the dam itself, the slim and aristocratic white haired old man gazing toward the land of his growing up, saw again in his mind how it all had been, trial and triumph, betrayal and defeat, courage and overcoming, the panorama of his life.

Westward revealed abandoned tan, grey-black and red slag heaps, and a bank of decaying coke ovens at Reilly Canyon, below the tidy town of Cokedale. The abandoned Madrid school where a young José Francisco once taught now stood empty and neglected, but fondly remembered as his first step out of the valley. The old life, still functioning amid a few acceptances of modern convenience showed up in Valdés, Segundo and Weston, presently only wide spots in the road but of great significance in the judge's eye.

There still were people he valued. At a gas station, Mary Jane Chavez, granddaughter of Torres' Uncle Juan, came out to greet him with real delight, a scene repeated at every stop with family and cherished friends eager to reconnect. On west past the historic Parsons ranch, modest homes, colonial era churches, a couple of modern mining operations, and scattered adobe structures slowly eroding, blending back into the earth from which they were formed, gave glimpses of the bountiful and sheltering land that Antonio Domingo Torres first saw.

Stonewalls' battlement, dominating the valley, provided access through a notch in the upthrust rock for the river and road, and gave opening to the high mountains. Behind this, lay Monument Lake, its stone, skyward-reaching monolith reflected in the clear blue waters, and recreation facilities Torres and his WPA crews built stood near the south shore.

Back down valley, Sus and Eva Torres' modest grey clapboard home in Cokedale where Frank had healed himself from tuberculosis now housed strangers. But a solid core of residents remained whose roots went back to homesteading days. Here he was joyfully welcomed at every stop. However, fifty years had transformed the bustling company town into a neighborly Trinidad suburb for retirees and working people.

Supper at a popular truck stop just south of Trinidad produced another rush of greetings as awareness of Torres' presence spread through the dining room. People reaffirmed him as "the only honest judge we ever had," with a pretty waitress explaining, "He cared for us." Later that evening a visit to surviving brother, Pete, brought talk of old times, family, and concerns about Pete's failing health. Sentimentally, the now seedy Columbian Hotel, a tarnished, ornate relic of an earlier more opulent time, provided rooms for the night. The place was a victim of change. Famous people now fly over Trinidad to east and west coast destinations where in times past they broke their journey at the elegant Columbian. Instead of stopping, the transcontinental trains now roll right on through Trinidad with the briefest of pauses and the interstate highway skirts the outer fringes of downtown, offering standardized conveniences to drivers who arrive and depart, unaware of the grand old hotel or the historic town itself.

Breakfast in the morning at eighty-five year old Onesimo Vigil's Savoy Cafe produced a lawyer and client reunion as the two old men clapped each other on the back, happily retelling cherished old jokes. The railroad car layout of the eatery placed booths on one side, counter and stools on the other with kitchen in the rear, and turned out large plates of solid food to local ranchers, laborers, civil servants, and merchants, all old friends. These included Frank's cousin, Tony Maes, a former Madison Square Garden National Rodeo Champion, retired by the inevitable broken bones and smashes in the arena, and now a local rancher. The ex-bronc rider talked with a soft western drawl and modest, self-deprecating humor, spoken in the understated, short hand language of the range. Torres was inordinately proud of "that boy."

The working people of Trinidad, old friends and associates, clearly held their Judge in highest regard and affection. Barron Córdova, a long time friend saw Frank as a defender of his Spanish culture, serving as an example of positive achievement. But, Córdova made clear, Torres did not cut any slack for his own people, recollecting that Frank had explained that he felt more highly of his fellow Spanish as intelligent, capable and upright as to match anyone else, not needing preferential treatment, only equal rights. A distant relation, white haired Elias Torres, observed that Frank improved the situation for all Spanish because he stood up impartially for everyone.

A stop at the Las Animas County courthouse brought forth well-wishers crowding around their judge. Only one chilly acknowledgment stood out, it from a man whom Torres had roundly defeated in an earlier election. For his part, Frank's dislike of the man showed in a slightly distanced reserve and precise formality of greeting. But the courthouse itself remained the fond focus of his years in law, the place where he had been able to work toward his vision for a better, less prejudiced, world and use the law to help bring it about in his own small corner.

Although showing a depressed economy, Trinidad stayed an unhurried, friendly place, its history visible in red-bricked streets and the venerable buildings a refreshing contrast to the numbing sameness of much modern business structures. Probably there remained, as everywhere, tensions over difference in background and position, yet it was a long way from the days of Torres' "We don't want your kind here," reception at law school, and he had played his part in the change.

At home in Santa Fe, Frank and Crusita's easy give and take, ability to laugh with each other and shift from spirited clash of opinion to comfortable amity continued into their last years. Their days revolved around family, church, friends and local events, regularly broken by trips, and by visits from out of town relatives and friends.

33

THE WHEEL TURNS

The years flew by too fast. President Carter signed a new Panama Canal treaty, giving the waterway over to Panamanian ownership. China and the United States established diplomatic relations, and the Shah of Iran was driven from the Peacock Throne by the Muslim cleric, Ayatollah Khomeini. A Camp David meeting, called by President Carter, hammered out a peace treaty between Anwar Sadat of Egypt and Menachem Begin of Israel.

Frank and Crusita watched their grandchildren finish high school and go off to college with Torres typically urging them to work harder and aim higher. The old couple read widely to keep up on politics and decide how to vote. They believed you could not measure a man by his appearance on the TV screen where the candidate invariably presented a friendly, but carefully serious image, proclaiming his will to "fight for" the people, as he made good use of the advantage of lighting, make-up, camera angle, and a people pleasing script. The message usually was short on specifics and long on generalities. Such empty rhetoric, once installed in office, could be expected to fail the voter's trust as the elected politician advanced his personal agenda, negating his promises, whether by overt action or failure to act at all. This brought forth Frank's searing scorn. Public office was serving the public good, not one's own. No accountability was tied to the undefined, feel-good generalities and promises issued in campaigns. Both Torreses voted for Ronald Reagan in 1980, Frank said, because they found him a strong man of reason and good sense who avoided extremes and called out the best in people around him.

Frank and Crusita studied new trends in society, including the gay rights movement that was gaining momentum. Torres was wary.

All had a right to be themselves, he believed, as long as this did not take precedence over the rights of others and the rights of an orderly society.

Running a business in Santa Fe, with the town's particular blend of quirks, characters and attitudes, lost its attraction for Crusita and Lawrence. Although the shop prospered, pilfering, soaring prices, noisy cruisers heckling sidewalk pedestrians, and endlessly torn up streets added to the work and overhead. Crusita felt her age in weariness at the end of a work day, and Larry grew tired of coping with city functionaries over trivialities and with rude or bargain hunting customers, so mother and son closed the shop. Crusita spent her days with Frank and the family, while Larry launched forth as an independent Indian trader, searching the pueblos and reservation for the art which fascinated him. He gained the respect with those who dealt with him, and was honored by being selected as a judge for the annual Indian Market in Santa Fe.

Crusita and Lawrence in their Indian art shop.

The halcyon period did not endure, and a light went out in Frank and Crusita's life at Christmas in 1983 when on December 24th, Lawrence suffered an aneurism. Taken to St. Vincent hospital, doctors held out no hope for recovery and the stunned family abandoning holiday preparations took turns at his bedside, Crusita holding his hand as the final silent night closed in forever on her son. After the funeral mass at St. Francis Cathedral, Lawrence was buried in late afternoon on a bitter end of December day, in the depth and bleakness of winter. The air, edged with a cutting wind, numbed the bones of those gathered at the open grave. With Crusita huddled in a warm coat at his side, Judge Torres stood, terribly alone, hat in hand, white hair bared to the icy wind, tall, pale and frail, lost in a grief too deep to assuage or share, beyond pain, to a loss that excluded all else save the darkness and ultimate vacancy which opened in front of him. After the familiar words, given by a black robed priest and the sharp gunfire crack of the military salute, the old couple, exhausted and silent, were helped into a waiting grey limousine's padded plush seats and borne away to confront the task of bearing the unbearable.

As winter yielded to spring, and spring turned to summer, life moved on. Since Frank and Crusita had experienced death regularly, there was no part of their hearts that had not absorbed that pain but this loss was hardest to bear. As he had so often before, Judge Torres shut the door on past hopes and concentrated on the now, committed to living as long as he breathed. Yet without Lawrence, advancing old age and retreating strength intensified the task. For Crusita, a space in her heart that Lawrence had occupied remained forever empty. Nevertheless, she knew life offered no second chances and what good would come in the life she and Frank had left was mostly up to her.

Without Lawrence, Frank and Crusita could no longer keep up their large southside home, and reluctantly sold it, recognizing the implications of the change as they moved into a smaller, downtown apartment. Crusita relied more on Eva who came frequently to help, and to take her parents out, bringing Tara with her. Now university bound, Tara had developed into a dazzling, dark haired young beauty, very like her father, slim, elegant and reserved, but with her grandmother Crusita's glowing brown velvet eyes. Young, vital, spontaneous, Tara lighted up her grandparents' days, and the mother-daughter closeness Crusita had shared with Esther extended through Eva on to Tara. Custom might shift slightly with each new generation, but its essence strengthened those who shared the common bond of family. As Crusita advised Tara, "You are lucky to have good parents, and you can keep your loved ones' finest qualities by living them in your own life."

Frank took advantage of the fact that he still could walk to La Fonda and its busy lobby just a couple of blocks away through the Plaza, and he made it a nearly daily destination, greeting friends on the way, and making acquaintances among tourists resting on iron benches under the stately trees. He also found his own niche at La Fonda Hotel on the southeast corner of the Plaza. This historic "inn at the end of the Trail" had served the noted and the notorious for some one hundred fifty years. Built in rambling pueblo style, with softly rounded walls, grilled windows, massive hand carved doors, and an interior featuring wooden vigas, tiled floors, brightly painted glass panels, with well padded leather chairs and sofas scattered about the lobby, the multi-level hotel had been skillfully refurbished by owner Sam Ballen to project comfortable southwestern ambience. Here the judge enjoyed conversing with the varied people who checked in and out. Many were new to the Southwest and he took the opportunity to educate them on the history and culture of the area, believing as always that if people really knew each other they would accept and respect the differences encountered among new groups. Most were fascinated with his chronicles of the past and its people, and appreciated his conviction and depth of knowledge.

In the process, Torres became a sort of unofficial ambassador for La Fonda and developed a friendship with Ballen, another multi-talented man. The two shared a particular interest in little-known Whiskey Pass in the Southern Colorado Rockies where Torres had built roads with his WPA crew and where Ballen held land. From his lobby hang-out, Torres earned recognition as a Santa Fe "character," as had summer visitor composer Igor Stravinsky, Horace Aiken, B.B. Dunne and a handful of other colorful individuals. To honor the judge, Ballen placed his snake cane, his picture, and a *New Mexican* feature story of his life on display in a shadow box just off La Fonda's lobby.

The Catholic Church also recognized Frank's many years of service and contributions, making him a Fourth Degree Grand Knight of Columbus, one of the church's highest honors, and Archbishop Sanchez received him into the order at a special service in Albuquerque. Torres had not worked for honors, only for the value of the work itself, but appreciation capped the satisfaction of a full life.

Judge Torres, Crusita, Eva, Carl and Tara when the judge was made a Grand Knight of Columbus.

Carl, Eva and Tara took Crusita and Frank on trips, back to Arizona and old Tucson haunts from the Alianza Hispano Americana days and on an auto excursion deep into Old Mexico. On the road in Mexico, the old couple, bickering amiably over precise translation on signs, relayed billboard and road marker information to Carl, the driver. Despite a family history handed down from the earliest days of the Spanish in

America, Judge Torres felt no close kinship with Mexican life. Here was rampant discrimination of another sort. The unbridged gulf between rich and poor, the lack of education and opportunity for those living in poverty, put him off. Where crowded shacks squatted on land only blocks from walled and guarded mansions of palatial magnificence, his democratic instincts rebelled. Give him the U.S.A., where, if he tried, every man had a chance, could make a difference.

Visitors flowed in and out of the Torres' downtown apartment, but Frank's strength was failing and Crusita could not keep up with caring for her husband and home. Again they recognized, however reluctantly, that another change had to be made. With no better alternative, they took the step of relinquishing their independence when Frank, Jr., and Pat offered their adjacent guest house to Frank and Crusita in which they would have a place of their own but still have help immediately available. It was the usual ungraceful accommodation between wish and necessity that brings no real happiness. Care of their needs was a burden to them and to their care givers. Everyone tried, but it was a period of trial and frustration.

Frank, now in his nineties and ailing, would not reach the hundred years he had set for himself. His body no longer responded to his will as he fought against encroaching weakness. Long independent and used to ordering her own world, Crusita, too, shared his frustrations, finding it hard to accommodate herself to relying on others. On a day in late June 1992, Judge Torres took a particularly nasty fall which left him helpless and in great pain. Taken to the hospital, he was moved immediately from emergency to a private room where he lapsed into a coma, his hands fretting the sheet that covered him. Nurses hooked him up to a variety of machines, the doctor applied his stethoscope, frowned, folded it into his pocket and shook his head.

With the family gathered in the sterile room, Crusita took up watch at the bedside as her husband's life inched agonizingly to its close. Finally, drained and unable to bear Frank's suffering, she took his hand and spoke to him. "Frank, it is time to go. You have given me the heights of life and years of joy. You earlier faced death and won, but now, now is the time. I release you to go in peace." Still holding his hand, the hand that had held hers through the marriage sacrament, through childbirth, joy and sorrow, through all the years of working together, the strong, graceful hand that had clinched in anger, applauded achievement, waved in triumph, had consoled and blessed, she willed him to perfect peace. Gradually the agitated movements lessened, breathing grew shallower, the body stilled, and with Crusita yet holding the beloved hand, life ceased altogether. It was June 27, 1992, ninety-five years and one hundred twenty-nine days from when he had opened his eyes and squalled his way into the world "up the river" on the Purgatoire

Replete with accolades and tributes, the large and stately funeral was held at St. Francis Cathedral, where, in a part that Frank would have approved, Sam Ballen, a temple Jew, gave the eulogy in that hallowed bastion of Catholic faith. Afterward, Crusita sat alone winding up the details of a lifetime in the small guest house which had been not a home, but rather, a way station. At eighty-two, her years would not be many, she knew, and she accepted Eva and Carl's invitation to come and live with them. This decision gave an interval of acceptance and caring, free from demands, and providing comfortable security. As throughout her life, prayer lifted her through the low spots and gave her serenity in each day of living.

A series of small strokes sapped Crusita's energy but, remarkably, did not confuse her mind, her doctor reported, while privately informing Eva that a large one probably would end her mother's life. And so it was. One summer morning when Eva came into the room to see how Crusita had slept, she found her mother gone. On July 3, 1994, a massive stroke had taken her, quickly and silently, as the doctor had foreseen. Two years after Frank's interment there, she was buried beside her husband at Rosario Cemetery in Santa Fe, following her husband into that realm where all are equal and the only law is unfailingly just and good.

34

SUMMING UP

What then can be made of Judge J. Frank Torres and his impact upon the world in which he lived? Was he truly great? Was he a failed reformer? Was he an unrealistic idealist? How does he fit in?

There can be greatness in all areas of life: in sports, in public service, in the arts, in faith, in business, the list is endless. These lead to the acceptance of ethical codes from which come the standards and laws that produce change. These directly shape how people live and interact with each other. Frank Torres combined both civil law and moral law in his unrelenting fight for equality and non-discrimination. How much was his crusade worth? Was it an exercise in foolishness?

A version of this question is set forth in Torres' favorite book, *Don Quixote de la Mancha*, the classic tale of a "mad" Spanish Don. This character produced much turmoil as he tried to combat what he saw as wrong in a futile effort to make his world better. The judge's worn copy of this masterpiece, in the original Spanish, as he believed the work lost nuances of meaning and subtly changed when translated into English, testified to repeated reading.

An interesting comparison can be made between Judge Torres himself and Cervantes' Don Quixote. Both were great readers, immersing themselves in ennobling works of literature and philosophy, both were idealists, both were fired by a vision of truth and justice, both set forth to right the wrongs of the world. The character and excursions of Don Quixote and the life and actions of Judge Torres present a view of ideals and a possible better world if the values of the two men, fictional and real, could be brought to pass. As knights committed to highest goals, each man remained true to his vision through every trial and mischance.

The reader finds in Don Quixote insights on two types of wisdom; the first, to see things only as they ought to be, exemplified by Don Quixote, and the second, to see things solely as they are, as shown by Sancho Panza who followed him on his adventures. Although Don Quixote and Sancho Panza have two entirely different attitudes on life, each is needed by the other. Out on quest together, Don Quixote and Sancho Panza become, in essence, two parts of one whole, extensions of each other, and interdependent on each other, so that one without the other is incomplete.

In making a comparison between the man, Torres, and his literary hero, certain strong resemblances present themselves. Torres was the dedicated, knightly visionary, true to a higher calling, frequently impractical for his own personal interests, always entering the battle against negative forces of evil, never allowing defeat or setbacks to deter him from his goals. Largely above things material, he drove himself endlessly, seeking what was good for those around him and the world he lived in.

Applying the analogy to Torres' life, who would be the sturdy, donkey mounted Sancho Panza riding behind the Don, faithful, undismayed, and practical through all the challenges? Who but Crusita? She was the down to earth, accepting, and loyal influence who supported and calmed her feisty companion. As the years passed, they, too, became extensions of one another, neither complete without the other. Frank kept his illusions and Crusita, while recognizing his vision and sharing his concerns, remained solidly grounded and a realist in all things. Frank may have fought the battles with all the courage of his convictions, but his companion, Crusita, was a master of practical tactics.

Who then is Dulcinea, the idealized love of the Don's life in the Torres version of Don Quixote if not Crusita? A good argument can be made that she is the Lady of Liberty who, in the United States Constitution and Bill of Rights, shines forth in beauty and goodness with justice and equality for all. Dulcinea is the symbol that prompts seeking the highest good. She is the vision of goodness and justice, who inspires men to work and sometimes die in her service. Without her, there is no force to send the knight forth to uphold good against evil. She inspires him to strive for the ideals she represents, and this commitment occupied Torres as he selflessly served her cause his whole life long.

Finally, what of Rosinante, the other main character of the book, the spavined nag ridden by the Don on his adventures? Who carried Torres over the ground to engage in his battles? Surely Rosinante was Torres' deep Catholic Faith that upheld him through every trial. In the eyes of the present world, this Faith might appear an inadequate steed, many seeing it as crippled by modern "reason" and too slow to meet contemporary demands for gratification. But faith carried Torres strongly and surely into his battles, never stumbling or unseating him, but bringing him safely through each confrontation and test. At the end, this same Rosinante carried him through the door of life on a flawed earth to the faith-ruled eternity beyond.

Ultimately, with Torres as with this masterpiece of literature, *Don Quixote*, the question remains: does only a madman go out and battle wrong in order to make a better world? Present day attitudes seem to answer the question affirmatively. There is too much wrong, only a fool would pit himself against it. Many engage in smaller skirmishes but shun commitment to over-all good as hopeless and unprofitable. Or they prefer defining the nature and character of true good and true evil to the exclusion of actually trying to do anything about either. Another current thought trend finds good and bad as not absolutes, but merely situational and relative. Torres never harbored such reasoning, but boldly took action against each recognized wrong. He battled the actual problems which loomed as monsters over the lives of those who tilled the fields of life. No knight of old ever fought a better fight against the enemies of human dignity and made less of the wounds he received along the way. The answer as to whether Torres was a true latter day Don Quixote is both yes and no. Was he a true Don out to right the wrongs of the world? Yes. Sometimes his efforts were dismissed by those around him, but was he a madman fooled by illusions? Never.

Perhaps the vote on human greatness rests on one's view of what attributes produce it. What are these essentials for greatness? The indispensable qualities which stand out are integrity, courage, steadfastness and vision. Torres possessed them all. However, relaxed modern

Judge Torres in the courtyard of the Palace of the Governors in Santa Fe.

society seems frequently to equate greatness with celebrity, relying on how well known is the face and the name rather than the quality of the person. Although such people, who lack the qualities of greatness but upon whom attention is focused, may stir up interest and admiration, society generally gains little or nothing from them, their influence failing to endure beyond their hour in the limelight. Great persons leave a traceable record of good in the lives of others that are made better by their efforts.

As he challenged the negatives in his world, Torres retained honor and pride without arrogance of conceit. Yet he was resoundingly human in curiosity, temper, impatience, and a wish to be respected. He never avoided a challenge but fought his battles with logic and eloquence, disregarding the sneak attacks of bigotry and racism that never ceased to be an element in his running war against discrimination. Amazingly, he never threw in the sponge. In the conflict between right and wrong, he chose right and never yielded.

J. Frank Torres saw democracy as offering the greatest opportunity for individual fulfillment, and its laws providing the best framework for a fair, equitable and inclusive society. To advance this premise he dedicated his whole life. Early on he recognized that for the benefit of all races, colors, and creeds, the obvious way to make the system work was to impartially enforce the laws which had been set up to govern the democracy. In doing this he served as way shower, leader, untiring teacher, and advocate for the necessity of never giving up.

It is hard to explain Torres without making him sound a "goody-goody" which he most certainly was not. "Goody-goodies" seek approval above all, and applause was not high on Torres' priorities list. Nor was he "nice" in the sentimental concept of the word. He could be as tough as any situation required. In the thick of controversy, he never shrank from fighting for what he believed necessary and his idealism kept him convinced that right must prevail. In the end much did.

Bound by the oldest verities, but far ahead of his time in ideas, Frank avoided occupying a remote, moral peak where the messy confrontations and endless decision making of every day life could be avoided. No setback stopped him, no opposition daunted his purpose.

He believed and bet his life's work on an unwavering conviction that people had a right to live free to make their own choices, unimpeded by bias, hatred, crime, lack of education, poverty, or whatever in the outside world served as a limiting circumstance. However, he insisted that making the right and sometimes difficult choices to claim this freedom also required the individual exert himself. Obstacles were to be overcome, and a person was given body, mind, and spirit to accomplish the task. None should expect anyone else to do it for them. Torres' vision was so complete, so compelling, and so enduring that no temporary negative could destroy it.

It seems obvious that people get into trouble when they do wrong, work against the best interests of those around them, or live at the expense of other's efforts. Rare should be the person who runs into opposition for being helpful and positive. Yet curiously these same qualities can produce strong opposition in others who then exert intense effort to get rid of such a person as was proven true in Judge Torres' life.

All records attest to the fact that J. Frank Torres was a thoroughly good man and by all standards, possessed a brilliant mind, was creative and intellectually curious. He acted with scrupulous honesty, labored endlessly to help anyone in need, and worked at practical goals for a better society. Certainly there was nothing wrong with that? And yet, he stirred up conflict wherever he went, putting him frequently at odds with the existing status quo.

Unfortunately, Torres' most worthy virtues brought out the strongest negatives against him. In the struggle of good versus evil, right versus wrong, some warp of discontent or grievance propels a drive to have done with the very people who work only for the best. Some of the backlash is caused by inconvenience; a Torres interferes, rebukes, preaches, scolds, and holds accountable. No one cares to be wrong and there is a tendency to resist changing of attitudes and habits. A type of this evasion can even be seen in modern theology which carefully avoids that which might prompt the prickings of conscience in favor of focusing on the goal of one perpetually feeling good about one's self.

Given that Torres spent nearly all his life in a settled rural community working among people with a common ancestral history of survival against all odds, never occupied a highest office, never received nation-wide acclaim, gained no imposing wealth, did not have his name and face on national TV, is not credited with producing any single significant change on the national scene, can he be classified as a great man? The answer still is yes. He worked where he was for necessary change and achievable goals, never losing sight of what was immediate and possible. He put public good above all else in his efforts.

Judge J. Frank Torres was a leader to whom people responded. Those he worked to help acted. They took part in the political process, they demanded an equal chance for education, for jobs, for financial security. Countless people who came in contact with him became more hopeful and determined to gain equal representation and treatment in political and social life. They ran for office, they supported what they saw as right. While one person alone could not bring a complete transformation, if pushed by many, the political system yields to the demands and acts. Frank's conviction that applied democracy worked was proven over and over in the winning of civil rights struggles and enactment of laws to enforce those rights.

The working people of the Trinidad community, friends and associates, unanimously held their judge in highest regard and affection. He cared for them and they loved him for it. They regarded him as a defender of his Spanish culture, serving as an example of positive achievement they could follow. He truly was "The only honest judge we ever had." They also respected and took a certain pride in Torres' well known position; that he would make no special allowances for his own people, somehow heartened that he refused to give them preferential treatment, holding them to be as intelligent, capable, and upright as anyone, anywhere. Although the feeling was not universal, many also came to appreciate the fact that the Judge's inclusive view of justice, that where the non-Spanish held equal, but not superior, rights with everyone was no more and no less than essential for a harmonious society.

Torres' positives were recognized among the non-Spanish, too. People up the Purgatoire, Spanish and Anglo alike, viewed Frank as practical, weighing each situation and then acting with intelligence and common sense, a man you could depend on and "as fair a man as ever walked." They noted that his opponents were afraid of Torres because he could be counted on to oppose and expose any compromise or action that went against his rigid standards of honesty and fairness. Torres used the law and influenced people for the better wherever he met them. In answer to a question, one rancher replied, "Flaws? No, he had none whatsoever."

What then qualifies J. Frank Torres to be seen as standing significantly above the crowd? Several things. He never once abandoned his principles and goals. Far ahead of the times, he was a crusader for civil rights from the nineteen twenties onward. This same cause belatedly surfaced as a national issue in the 1960s. His was among the earliest voices to be publicly raised against discrimination. Generations in varied places and situations throughout the world had been prevented from realizing the full extent of their abilities and controlling their own lives because of discrimination. But nowhere was this negative factor more relentlessly opposed and condemned as a violation of human rights and moral and civil law than was done in Colorado by this man.

Similarly, he promoted the importance of education and adequate institutions of learning as necessary to the individual's progress. And with rare perception, he perceived trouble ahead in the educational system long before it surfaced in its present day inadequacies and failures, and tried to convince those involved of the need for remedial action.

He had a rare and uncomplicated patriotism: he lived in the best country, under the best government, with the best people on earth. This was his country therefore he must work in it, defend it and strive to make it a better place and he had no patience with people who slacked on these duties.

Did Frank Torres make a difference? The record he left behind solidly supports the assumption. In addition to his personal involvement in advancing major causes and progressive movements, Torres emerges as an untiring teacher, an advocate and guide. He recognized lacks and failures in society and formulated remedies for them, actively involving himself in the process. He gave his all to many and varied outward problems, prompted to act by his inward vision and will.

J. Frank Torres lived and led through a major turning point for the Spanish in the American Southwest and from this improved society as a whole. He early recognized the gap between what the United States promised and what too many of its citizens received, beginning his crusade to secure their rights as soon as he was able to equip himself to do so. Law school supplied the needed tools.

With passion and persistence, Judge J. Frank Torres demanded fair government for all, challenged the denied rights of many, especially in the right to vote and emphasized a citizen's responsibility to exercise this right. He demanded and worked for the establishment of equal access in financial institutions and set up credit unions to help supply the need. He guided young workers and the elderly to avail themselves of social security, enforced equal justice and protection under the law in his court, enlisted in the struggle for equal education including the establishment of Trinidad Junior College, and provided equal employment opportunity under the WPA work programs. He demanded equal access and equal respect for each person in public places, regardless of background. And he insisted that government and its representatives uphold an inclusive and unequivocal moral standard in dealing with the people it represented and served. One goal inevitably tied into another; equal education was a requirement for equal employment, equal access to financial institutions was necessary for home ownership. Each gain raised the level of equality and fairness another rung. With it all, he unwaveringly supported his country and its highest purposes. Did this influence stop with him, or did his strivings to improve society continue outward and onward? The latter is demonstrably the case, where progress once started, propels itself onward until it gains enough force to bring acceptance.

So what really makes J. Frank Torres a man to remember? In the first place, because his number is so few; second, because he never gave less than his best; and third, because time and events have proven him right. His complex character included idealist, radical, reformer, and trouble maker. All were employed to benefit those around him. To remedy social problems, the process must start with individuals, he believed, who shared responsibility for their own destiny, having an obligation to follow their dreams by educating themselves, setting goals, exerting persistent hard work and honest dealing. This would lead to fulfillment of the promise America offers through its laws: equality, opportunity, and justice. There were no shortcuts to attaining this vision, nor would it fail when all freely pulled together to claim it. This is what he lived for, what he fought for, what he insisted on, and his own life provides the enduring truth of his methods.

    Not all Torres' goals were immediately met and neither are they in the years after him, yet the start was made, the idea planted and from it reform grew. His ideal society still eludes us, but his own Spanish and all other marginalized people within this country have made significant gains. They have learned to reject bigotry and prejudice and to demand their own rightful place in society. There still is injustice, discrimination and need existing in countless places around the globe but this Don Quixote held to his course against it in his own place, in his own time. Cervantes' character, written of long ago, still remains a fascinating figure that occupies a unique position in the great literature of the world. For a lifetime of leading the battle to outlaw wrong, Frank Torres occupies a similar position that is validated by the gains in his American Southwest. He set a barriers-breaking precedent when he was elected as the first Spanish judge in Colorado opening new doors in the political scene there, he opened them in many other areas as well. He stirred action wherever he went. Judge J. Frank Torres stands as one man who made a difference.

www.ingramcontent.com/pod-product-compliance
Lightning Source LLC
Chambersburg PA
CBHW030136170426
43199CB00008B/87